DATE DUE			

THE HOLOCAUST AND THE
LITERARY IMAGINATION

THE HOLOCAUST AND THE LITERARY IMAGINATION

LAWRENCE L. LANGER

NEW HAVEN AND LONDON, YALE UNIVERSITY PRESS, 1975

Published with assistance from the Louis Stern Memorial Fund.

Designed by Sally Sullivan
and set in Laurel type.
Printed in the United States of America by
The Colonial Press Inc., Clinton, Mass.

Published in Great Britain, Europe, and Africa by
Yale University Press, Ltd., London.
Distributed in Latin America by Kaiman & Polon,
Inc., New York City; in India by UBS Publishers' Distributors Pvt.,
Ltd., Delhi; in Japan by John Weatherhill, Inc., Tokyo.

Acknowledgment is made to the following publishers for permission to quote:
Atheneum Publishers, New York, for excerpts from *Herod's Children*, by Ilse Aichinger.
Translated from the German by Cornelia Schaeffer. Copyright © 1963 by Atheneum House,
Inc. Originally published in German under the title *Die Groessere Hoffnung* © 1960 by
Fischer Bucherei. Copyright 1948 by Bermann Fischer Verlag.
Atheneum Publishers, New York, and Oxford University Press, London, for "More Light!
More Light!" from *The Hard Hours*, by Anthony Hecht. Copyright © 1961 by Anthony E.
Hecht. Originally published in *The Nation*.
Farrar, Straus & Giroux, Inc., New York, and Jonathan Cape, Ltd., London, for "What
Secret Cravings of the Blood" and "Chorus of the Rescued," from *O The Chimneys*, by Nelly
Sachs. Copyright © 1967 by Farrar, Straus & Giroux, Inc., and copyright © 1968 by Jonathan
Cape, Ltd.
Christopher Middleton has granted permission to quote his translation of Paul Celan's
"Fugue of Death," originally published in *Modern German Poetry, 1910–1960: An Anthology
with Verse Translations*, ed. Christopher Middleton and Michael Hamburger (Grove Press,
1962).

For Sandy

Art, in a sense, is a revolt against everything
fleeting and unfinished in the world.
Consequently, its only aim is to give another
form to a reality that it is nevertheless forced
to preserve as the source of its emotion. In this
regard we are all realistic, and no one is.

Albert Camus

CONTENTS

PREFACE

The genesis of *The Holocaust and the Literary Imagination* provides the clearest commentary on the book's guiding literary idea. On a warm spring day in May 1964, I first visited the Auschwitz concentration camp. I still recall my astonishment upon seeing Polish children playing beneath bright sunshine in sandboxes no more than twenty yards from the entrance to the camp. They lived in neat brick buildings adjoining the site of the former camp, SS barracks that had been converted into apartments after the war and whose windows looked out on the barbed wire that still surrounded the area. The disparity between expectation and reality which that image inspired lay like a constant weight on my consciousness for several weeks, until it suddenly resurfaced later that summer as I sat in a courtroom in Munich at the war-crimes trial of Karl Wolff, Heinrich Himmler's adjutant and liaison officer to Hitler during part of World War II.

By 1964 Wolff was a mild-mannered businessman with silvery hair and a vague memory; he was unable to remember having visited the Warsaw Ghetto prior to its destruction, although the prosecutor had documentary evidence of his presence there at that time. Again I was unable to connect the appearance of the man with the crimes he was accused of, as if some vital link joining normalcy with horror had dissolved, leaving the two ideas suspended in solitary and separate chambers in a void. The dilemma achieved a more concrete focus a few days later, as I stood before a painting in the Neue Pinakotek art museum in Munich and once more experienced that uncanny sensation of discontinuity, of a fact inaccessible to the imagination in any coherent or familiar form. The painting itself was undistinguished, an early landscape by an obscure artist—there were some cows, a grove of trees in the distance, a few peasants working in a field. But the title struck my eye and produced an instantaneous shock and finally a moment of perception that eventually led to the writing of this book.

The title of the painting was "Dachau." The disjunction between that tranquil village of an earlier era and the site of the notorious concentration camp in our own age, just a few kilometers from Munich, was so enormous that I was unable to reconcile it by a simple act of the imagination. It was then that I wondered for the first time whether the artistic vision of the literary intelligence could ever devise a technique and form adequate to convey what the concentration camp experience implied for the contemporary mind. For Dachau, like Auschwitz and in a related sense like Hiroshima, is no longer merely a place-name with grim historical associations for those who care to pursue them. All three have been absorbed into the collective memory of the human community as independent symbols of a quality of experience more subtle, complex, and elusive than the names themselves can possibly convey. The existence of Dachau and Auschwitz as historical phenomena has altered not only our conception of reality, but its very nature.

The challenge to the literary imagination is to find a way of making this fundamental truth accessible to the mind and emotions of the reader. The uniqueness of the experience of the Holocaust may be arguable, but beyond dispute is the fact that many writers *perceived it* as unique, and began with the premise that they were working with raw materials unprecedented in the literature of history and the history of literature. The result is a body of writing that forms the subject of this study, what I call the literature of atrocity. Although only a generation has passed since the events of the Holocaust, it is not too soon to begin assessing what this literature has achieved, and especially to call to the attention of readers the significance of the achievement. At a time when technology threatens more and more to silence the rich resources of language, it seems singularly appropriate, and perhaps even urgent, to explore ways in which the writer has devised an idiom and a style for the unspeakable, and particularly the unspeakable horrors at the heart of the Holocaust experience.

This book represents a consciously limited attempt to impose some critical order on a selected number of imaginative works which grew out of that experience. Although inclusion of a work for discussion suggests a favorable judgment of its artistic worth, exclusion does not necessarily imply the opposite. I have organized my study around a number of recurrent themes that illustrate the aesthetic problem of reconciling normalcy with horror: the displacement of the consciousness of life by the imminence and pervasiveness of death; the violation of the coherence of childhood; the assault on physical reality; the disintegration of the rational intelligence; and the disruption of chronological time. I have chosen works which seem to me to illuminate these themes. Moreover, since I believe that a main purpose of criticism is to lead readers back to the literature under discussion, I have confined my analysis of major works to titles that have already been translated into English. All this means is that many readers will certainly have their own candidates for themes and authors worthy of inclusion, and that numerous opportunities remain for students of this literature who wish to explore the subject further. Among the works of unusual distinction which I have omitted with regret are Piotr Rawicz's *Blood from the Sky* and Charlotte Delbo's *None of Us Will Return*. In addition, my passing mention of Tadeusz Borowski's *This Way for the Gas, Ladies and Gentlemen* does not begin to do justice to its impact and stature as an example of the literature of atrocity.

Acknowledgments are few. An essay by A. Alvarez on the literature of the Holocaust, which first appeared in *Commentary* and was later reprinted in *Beyond All This Fiddle*, turned my attention to certain novels in the tradition. In addition, some of the issues raised by Robert Jay Lifton in *Death in Life: Survivors of Hiroshima* inspired me to ask some of my own questions about the effect of the Holocaust on the literary imagination. But I owe my greatest debt of gratitude to the students in my seminar on the Literature of Atrocity; their persistence in pursuing with me a subject that could not have brought them joy in learning in the usual sense did much to confirm my own belief in the human significance of the theme.

I am also grateful to the Simmons College Fund for Research for grants to defray the costs of travel, duplicating material, and typing of the manuscript.

Finally, my wife, busy with her own work, was not involved in the writing of this book or in the preparation of the manuscript. But while I was immersed in the bleak subject of the Holocaust her humanity and equanimity of spirit helped me to preserve my own, and enabled me to come through inured, if not totally immune.

1: IN THE BEGINNING WAS THE SILENCE

Speech is a desecration of silence.
                              Samuel Beckett

The dialogue—or the duel, if you
like—between man and his God doesn't
end in nothingness. Man may not have
the last word, but he has the last cry.
That moment marks the birth of art.
                              Elie Wiesel

If the famous proposition expressed some years ago by the late T. W. Adorno—to write poetry after Auschwitz is barbaric—were to be taken literally, it might undermine the validity of many of the ensuing pages of this study. But Adorno never intended it to be taken literally, as his own elaborations of the principle demonstrate; it does, however, represent an irritant to the aesthetic and moral sensibilities of the student of literature, especially what I call the literature of atrocity, that one cannot afford to ignore. Adorno quotes the question of a character in Sartre's *Mort sans sépulture*— "Does it still make sense to go on living, while there are people who beat others till the bones in their bodies are broken?"—and then applies the question to art in the post-Nazi, post-Holocaust era. How should art—how *can* art?—represent the inexpressibly inhuman suffering of the victims, without doing an injustice to that suffering? If art, as Adorno concedes, is perhaps the last remaining sanctuary where that suffering can be paid honest homage, enshrining it permanently in the imagination of the living as the essential horror that it was, the danger also exists of this noble intention sliding into the abyss of its opposite.

There is something disagreeable, almost dishonorable, in the conversion of the suffering of the victims into works of art, which are then, to use Adorno's pungent metaphor, thrown as fodder to the world ("der Welt zum Frass vorgeworfen") that murdered them. "The so-called artistic representation of naked bodily pain," he adds, "of victims felled by rifle butts, contains, however remote, the potentiality of wringing pleasure from it." Adorno appeals here not to latent sadistic impulses, but to the pleasures inherent in artistic response; citing as an example the prayer of the chorus in Schönberg's brief composition, "The Survivors of Warsaw," he suggests that through the "principle of aesthetic stylization," the inconceivable fate of the victims appears to have had some sense after all, that a transfiguration occurs, that some of the horror of the event is removed. The prospect of art denying what it seeks to affirm (the hideous chaos of dehumanization during the Holocaust) raises a spectre of paradox for the critic, the reader, and the artist himself, that is not easily circumvented.[1]

Adorno provides a partial response when he quotes the reply of another prominent German poet and critic, Hans Magnus Enzensberger, to the charge that poetry after Auschwitz would be barbaric: surrender to silence would be a surrender to cynicism, and thus by implication a concession to the very forces that had created Auschwitz in the first place. But the validity of Adorno's apprehension that art's transfiguration of moral chaos into aesthetic form might in the end misrepresent that chaos and create a sense of meaning and purpose in the experience of the Holocaust (and hence, paradoxically, a justification of it in aesthetic terms) depends very much on how the artist exploits his material (neither Schönberg nor the medium of music is the best example here), and on the methods he employs to involve the sensibilities of his audience in the world of his imagination. Adorno, of course, recognizes this but prejudges the results perhaps too dogmatically. He tells the story of a German officer in occupied France who visited Picasso's studio and, seeing the *Guernica*, asked the painter "Did you make that?"—to which Picasso is said to have replied: "No—you did." Adorno uses this anecdote to argue that the autonomy of a work of art like the *Guernica* negates the empircal reality on which it was based, destroys its destructive nature, as it were ("zerstören die zerstörende"), and thus repeats the guilt implicit in that reality ad infinitum.[2]

But an essential characteristic of Picasso's painting, as of almost all the literature discussed in these pages, is not the transfiguration of empirical reality (a term perhaps appropriate for "The Survivors

1. T. W. Adorno, "Engagement," in *Noten zur Literatur III* (Frankfurt am Main: Suhrkamp Verlag, 1965), pp. 125–26, 127. Translation mine.
2. Ibid., pp. 127, 128.

of Warsaw"), but its *dis*figuration, the conscious and deliberate alienation of the reader's sensibilities from the world of the usual and familiar, with an accompanying infiltration into the work of the grotesque, the senseless, and the unimaginable, to such a degree that the possibility of aesthetic pleasure as Adorno conceives of it is intrinsically eliminated—such a sense of disfiguration has always governed my response to Picasso's *Guernica*. By a process of carefully contrived disorientation, these artists first "lose" the attention of their readers—sometimes gradually, as the unreal and fantastic encroach slowly on the world of the normal, sometimes almost instantaneously, as in the works of Jakov Lind, where an atmosphere of illogic and lunacy prevails from the beginning—then "regain" that attention, its premises having been thoroughly altered. The will of the reader is drawn into the autonomous milieu of the work of art and is subtly transformed—disfigured in the sense just outlined—until it is compelled to recognize, to "see" imaginatively both the relationship between the empirical reality of the Holocaust and its artistic representation in the work of literature, *and* the fundamental distinction between both of these worlds and the nonvictim orientation of this will. The reader is temporarily an insider and permanently an outsider, and the very tension resulting from this paradox precludes the possibility of the kind of "pleasure" Adorno mentions, while the uncertain nature of the experience recorded, combined with the reader's feeling of puzzled involvement in it, prohibits Adorno's fear that the reader may discern in the inconceivable fate of the victims "some sense after all." As we shall see, the principle of aesthetic stylization itself prohibits it.

A simple concrete illustration may clarify some of the implications of the premise that the literature of atrocity is concerned with an order of reality which the human mind had never confronted before, and whose essential quality the language of fact was simply insufficient to convey. The title of Anthony Hecht's poem "More Light! More Light!" represents the words Goethe is reputed to have spoken on his death-bed; outside of Weimar, his city, the Third Reich constructed Buchenwald concentration camp.

> Composed in the Tower before his execution
> These moving verses, and being brought at that time
> Painfully to the stake, submitted, declaring thus:
> "I implore my God to witness that I have made no crime."

Nor was he forsaken of courage, but the death was horrible,
The sack of gunpowder failing to ignite.
His legs were blistered sticks on which the black sap
Bubbled and burst as he howled for the Kindly Light.

And that was but one, and by no means one of the worst;
Permitted at least his pitiful dignity;
And such as were by made prayers in the name of Christ,
That shall judge all men, for his soul's tranquillity.

We move now to outside a German wood.
Three men are there commanded to dig a hole
In which the two Jews are ordered to lie down
And be buried alive by the third, who is a Pole.

Not light from the shrine at Weimar beyond the hill
Nor light from heaven appeared. But he did refuse.
A Lüger settled back deeply in its glove.
He was ordered to change places with the Jews.

Much casual death had drained away their souls.
The thick dirt mounted toward the quivering chin.
When only the head was exposed the order came
To dig him out again and to get back in.

No light, no light in the blue Polish eye.
When he finished a riding boot packed down the earth.
The Lüger hovered lightly in its glove.
He was shot in the belly and in three hours bled to death.

No prayers or incense rose up in those hours
Which grew to be years, and every day came mute
Ghosts from the ovens, sifting through crisp air,
And settled upon his eyes in a black soot.[3]

History provides the material for both episodes in this poem: the fate of the Jews and the Pole has been documented by eye-witnesses, and death by burning was the punishment of countless

3. In Anthony Hecht, *The Hard Hours* (New York: Atheneum, 1967), pp. 64–65. Hecht is the only native American author discussed in this study, and hence only indirectly connected with the Holocaust experience. But he dedicates "More Light! More Light!" to Heinrich Bluecher and his wife Hannah Arendt, both political émigrés from Nazi Germany. Hecht received his undergraduate degree from Bard College, where Bluecher was a professor of philosophy. Hannah Arendt is, of course, the author of *Eichmann in Jerusalem: A Report on the Banality of Evil*, which first appeared in 1963, and in a revised version in 1965, two years before Hecht's *The Hard Hours*.

political and religious martyrs in sixteenth-century England. To be sure, such death, whether a consequence of the whim or malice of the ruling power, or of a calculated policy of genocide, is always horrible; extreme cruelty is not an invention of the modern mind, nor is extraordinary and unmerited suffering, which raises fundamental questions about the purpose of existence, any less paradoxical today than it was in the time of Job. Yet in juxtaposing these two experiences Hecht implies that a distinct and substantive difference does exist between them, and bases the emotional and intellectual tensions of the poem upon it.

Three qualities distinguish the Christian martyr: his religion, his sense of self, and the attitude of his audience toward him. The brutal effect of the charged imagery in the lines "His legs were blistered sticks on which the black sap / Bubbled and burst as he howled" is qualified (if not minimized) by the succeeding words, "for the Kindly Light"; despite the possible irony of tone, immediate pain, however intense, always appears more tolerable sub specie aeternitatis. For the victim—if not for the reader—God, soul, and innocence represent concrete values, and "Christ, / That shall judge all men," stands at the center of his and his audience's religious universe. Against his persecutors he may call his God to witness, while the very fact that he speaks testifies to his humanity. He inhabits two worlds, a physical and a spiritual one, and the presence of the latter, his recognition of it (its acknowledgment of him is an unquestioned assumption of the victim) contributes above all to his dignity as a man—however pitiful. The spiritual context of his life mitigates the physical horror of his impending death; what man may do to man is no measure of the divine dimension of his existence, which remains unsullied—or so it seems, *from the point of view* of the participants in the first twelve lines of the poem.

The victims in the second section of the poem, who are totally anonymous and eventually, in a macabre way, even interchangeable, become agents in their own destruction, for reasons that are withheld from them and from us. Justly or not, the prisoner in the Tower has been condemned, otherwise he would not be in the Tower. The failure of the gunpowder to ignite—which would have brought instant and "merciful" death—is accidental, not deliberate; but death by suffocation in a "hole" (not a grave) seems the deliberate whim of a depersonalized and fragmented figure, a force

appearing only as a Lüger in a glove, or a riding boot. The link
between the two parts of the poem is the initial, courageous refusal
of the Pole to be an executioner; but his willingness to accept
martyrdom shares none of the dignity, albeit pitiful, of the victim in
the Tower, since in the desolate setting of a German wood,
unilluminated by the humanistic faith of Goethe or the grace of
heavenly love, it seems a vain gesture, merely substituting one
meaningless death for another.

Perhaps the grimmest bequest of the Holocaust experience was
that men were driven to choose survival at the expense of their
humanity, creating a kind of solipsistic animality as the supreme
value. The heroism of the Pole begets only indifference in the Jews
he would help; and this, in turn, extinguishes the spiritual light in
his eyes. The surfeit of "casual death" has turned the Jews of the
poem into soulless creatures, but the Pole at first refuses to believe
that others are capable of an act that he himself shrinks from;
nothing shatters the moral personality more quickly, however, than
the revelation of what other men are capable of doing in extreme
situations when their own lives are at stake, and *when they are not
permitted the "dignity" of known martyrdom.* The Pole's initial
error was to behave as if he were being taken from the Tower to a
public execution in a traditional atmosphere of spiritual reality;
"casual death" had taught the Jews the futility of such an
expectation. Recognizing his "error," the Pole has no recourse but
to abandon his "soul" too, as a commodity worthless in the context
of his immediate experience—for without the possibility of honor,
death loses its meaning.

Thus, unlike the opening stanzas of the poem, the closing ones
confirm that what man may do to man *is* the measure of all things,
and under these circumstances the participants in *this* episode are
offered no framework for evaluating their fate. The horror and
tragedy of the first part, which stretches to the snapping point but
finally leaves intact the bond linking man's spiritual aspirations to
his physical destiny, withers in the second part to the abrupt,
understated violence of "He was shot in the belly and in three hours
bled to death," and to the fine specks of mute black ash, sole tribute
to the "blind," anonymous corpse who shares with these unre-
corded victims the death of God, the death of vision, the death of

meaning—and the silence of the spiritual universe. Nothing survives—except the poem, except the vitality and tension of art.

It would be presumptuous to argue that only art can convey the fullest meanings of the Holocaust experience; but there is abundant evidence that the artist is determined to add his voice to those of historians, psychologists, sociologists, and memoirists who during the past quarter of a century have filled shelf after shelf in libraries with records and analyses of "the way it was." As the event recedes in time, however, and the testimony about it mounts, questions have arisen concerning the most effective way to convey what Günter Grass, in a related context, has called "the substantial reality that throws a shadow"; one of the narrators of *Dog Years*, shortly after the war, defines for a friend the challenge facing the writer:

> "Believe me, Matern, with your help we will work out a valid technique for getting at the truth. Not only for you, but for every one of our fellow men, this is a matter of vital necessity: we must break through between master and dog, design a window that will give us back our perspective; for even I—you can tell by my modest literary efforts—lack the vital grip, the quivering flesh of reality; the technique is there but not the substance. I've been unable to capture the this-is-how-it-was, the substantial reality that throws a shadow." [4]

Perhaps no one will ever clarify satisfactorily or portray completely the "quivering flesh of the reality" of the Holocaust; it remains the unconquered Everest of our time, its dark mysteries summoning the intrepid literary spirit to mount its unassailable summit. The uniqueness of the experience has been a major source of difficulty and confusion, since the temptation is to view the event merely or chiefly as the result of historical and psychological antecedents: Hecht's poem offers us this possibility, though I believe its ultimate strategy is to force us to repudiate it. For example, one might conclude that the modern martyrdom is simply an extreme form of the earlier one; but the urgency of the title—"More Light! More Light!"—in one of its implications, would seem to point in another direction. "I implore my God to witness that I have made no crime" falls comprehensibly from the lips of the earlier victim; but what meaning would it have for the helpless

4. Günter Grass, *Dog Years*, trans. Ralph Manheim (New York: Harcourt, Brace & World, 1965), p. 471.

and abandoned Pole or Jews? The "meaning" of their fate is shrouded in darkness, only "more light" might clarify it—but such light is not forthcoming: the poem ends in a sifting veil of black soot. The sequence in the poem, its very structure, *forces* us to search for a more adequate basis for apprehending the human suffering (and the inhuman fate) recorded in the latter half, while leaving us simultaneously aware of the *in*adequacy of the old "answers," emotionally enacted in the first part of the poem. The poem itself as a whole leaves us only mystery and silence, the paradox of *in*comprehension (despite the "logic" of the language and structure); and our experience of them, our sense of their presence, of their unaccountability, *becomes* our experience of the poem.

Perhaps we can say that there are two forces at work in this poem, as there are in most of what I have designated the literature of atrocity: historical fact and imaginative truth. The literature of atrocity is never wholly invented; the memory of the literal Holocaust seethes endlessly in its subterranean depths. But such literature is never wholly factual either, it perpetually designs windows, to follow Grass's image, "that will give us back our perspective," it is no mere docile dog on the leash of history. Without the Holocaust, such literature would not have been possible; with it, by a curious inversion, literature has taken as its task *making* such reality "possible" for the imagination. Richard Gilman, trying to create sense out of the critical confusion that erupted following the appearance of William Styron's *Confessions of Nat Turner*, offers us some valuable assistance here: he argues that imaginative writing does not wrest secrets and intimate meanings from history, but "inoculates history with a serum of invented insights which actually immunize the reader against mere factual truths and force him into a more painful confrontation with the implications about himself and his world that this serum sends coursing through his emotional and intellectual bloodstream."

For example, given the "mere factual truth" that one man is capable of ordering another to bury two Jews alive for no apparent reason, or, to use a more familiar example, given the "mere factual truth" that the same individual is capable of loving Mozart and murdering children without recognizing any contradiction in his personality or being affected by it—given these instances of actual human behavior, how is one to respond? How is one to interpret? How is one to understand a reality that includes such phenomena? History provides the details—then abruptly stops. Literature seeks ways of exploring the implications and making them imaginatively available; or, as Gilman concludes, "If anything, literature, like all art, is the account of what history has failed to produce on its own, so that men have to step in to make good the deficiency." [5]

One who has stepped in is Paul Celan, a Rumanian-born poet (in legendary Czernowitz) who writes in German but spent the war years in a camp in his native land. His "Fugue of Death" ("Todesfuge") is perhaps the most celebrated poem on the subject of the Holocaust in Western Europe. During his years of alienation (and, presumably, incarceration), only one thing, Celan reports, remained attainable in the midst of the other casualties of war: language. His observations, offered in an address some years after he wrote the poem, cast some significant light on a central paradox considered in this chapter. Language, Celan suggests,

> in spite of everything, remained available. But it had to find sustenance in its own inability to explain, to go on living through a dreadful imposed silence, survive through a thousand nights of death-dealing speech. It went on living and gave birth to no words to describe what had happened; but it survived these events. Survived and came to light again, "enriched" by it all.

During those years and the ones following, Celan continues, he sought to write poems using that language, seeking direction and orientation, "in order to design for myself a reality." A living language lacking a vocabulary to describe what it has "seen," a poetic voice echoing silence as well as speech—these are two of the paradoxes that constitute the ingredients of Celan's poem, and much of the literature that succeeded it. The "Fugue of Death" seeks to create a reality *about* another reality in which speech proved lethal and silence laden with terror while the victim trembled helplessly between the two; the poet, drawing his inspiration from this dilemma, is simultaneously attracted and repelled by it, in Celan's lucid formulation, "chafed by and seeking reality" but steering relentlessly toward the goal of making it available to the reader. Celan regards the poem as a species of

5. Richard Gilman, "Nat Turner Revisited," *New Republic*, 27 April 1968, p. 24.

conversation, and thus essentially of the nature of dialogue—a message in a bottle, to follow his metaphor, that sometime and somewhere may wash up on land, perhaps the land of the heart.[6]

The unusual pattern of "Fugue of Death," with its repudiation of normal punctuation and grammar, its fragmentary phraseology, its insistent return to a few dark metaphors and somber themes which submerge and resurface in differing contexts with an incantatory persistence, finally absorbs the reader in a nightmare of syntactical illogic which incites disbelief even as it overwhelms with an excess of emotional conviction. Perhaps one of the limitations of the Hecht poem is that it compartmentalizes too neatly the two kinds of suffering, martyrdom and atrocity; Celan avoids this danger by superimposing the tensions of his poem (different, of course, than Hecht's) on each other, creating a kind of palimpsest of images which importune the consciousness to retain their contradictions in the imagination *simultaneously* (thus approaching the condition of music—hence "*Fugue* of Death").

The result is an exact reversal of Wagner's *Liebestod*, which in its celebration of the ecstasy of love triumphs even over death; in Celan's poem, love and the romantic imagination appear almost as obscene stains on the landscape of funereal and pitiless grief which devours the victims of the Holocaust. Just as in Hecht's lines the anonymous decease of Pole and Jews calls into question the very conception of a civilization in which martyrdom was once possible, so in "Fugue of Death" the consoling alliance of love and death disintegrates, and the value, the very meaning, of love is cynically subverted by the brutal conditions of life and the looming horror of death in a concentration camp:

> Black milk of daybreak we drink it at nightfall
> we drink it at noon in the morning we drink it at night
> drink it and drink it
> we are digging a grave in the sky it is ample to lie there
> A man in the house he plays with the serpents he writes
> he writes when the night falls to Germany your golden hair Margarete
> he writes it and walks from the house the stars glitter he whistles his
>   dogs up
> he whistles his Jews out and orders a grave to be dug in the earth
> he commands us now on with the dance

6. Paul Celan, "Ansprache," in *Ausgewählte Gedichte* (Frankfurt am Main: Suhrkamp Verlag, 1968), pp. 128–29. Translation mine.

Black milk of daybreak we drink you at night
we drink in the mornings at noon we drink you at nightfall
drink you and drink you
A man in the house he plays with the serpents he writes
he writes when the night falls to Germany your golden hair Margarete
Your ashen hair Shulamith we are digging a grave in the sky it is
      ample to lie there

He shouts stab deeper in earth you there you others you sing and
      you play
he grabs at the iron in his belt and swings it and blue are his eyes
stab deeper your spades you there and you others play on for the
      dancing

Black milk of daybreak we drink you at night
we drink you at noon in the mornings we drink you at nightfall
drink you and drink you
a man in the house your golden hair Margarete
your ashen hair Shulamith he plays with the serpents

He shouts play sweeter death's music death comes as a master from
      Germany
he shouts stroke darker the strings and as smoke you shall climb to
      the sky
then you'll have a grave in the clouds it is ample to lie there

Black milk of daybreak we drink you at night
we drink you at noon death comes as a master from Germany
we drink you at nightfall and morning we drink you and drink you
a master from Germany death comes with eyes that are blue
with a bullet of lead he will hit in the mark he will hit you
a man in the house your golden hair Margarete
he hunts us down with his dogs in the sky he gives us a grave
he plays with the serpents and dreams death comes as a master
      from Germany

your golden hair Margarete
your ashen hair Shulamith[7]

The poem is enveloped by a contradiction of colors, which serve
as both parallel and contrasting images and define—or, less
explicitly, suggest—the two realms that interweave throughout its

7. In Michael Hamburger and Christopher Middleton, eds., *Modern German Poetry,
1910–1960: An Anthology with Verse Translations* (New York: Grove Press, 1962),
pp. 318–21. The translation of "Fugue of Death" is by Christopher Middleton.

lines. Blackness poisons the whiteness and purity of milk just as the ominous ashes corrupt the golden beauty of hair, and it finally seems as if the milk and the gold, with all their connotations of youth, pleasure, and glory, are intruders in a darker universe, accidental interlopers whose presence only magnifies the enormity of the evil committed in their presence. They do not belong in such a world, but by including them Celan undermines the possibility of melodrama and disarms the charge of madness or pure villainy which might "rationalize" the situation in the poem. The unspeakable paradox of a reality that permits the suffering of Shulamith to exist in the same breath as the apparent innocence of a Margarete, or acknowledges that the same man can "whistle his Jews up" and write love-letters home to Germany, hovers on the brink of dissolution, as the reader's sensibilities try to encompass both. The subtle modulations of tone and juxtaposition of imagery refuse to permit a reconciliation of disparate feelings: thus, at least on first glance, "the stars glitter" seems a misplaced image of natural splendor, diverting our attention from the central horror, just as "and blue are his eyes" momentarily seems to beguile us from our hostility toward the brutal attitude and raucous voice of their possessor; though on a more complex level the German *blitzen* ("glitter") may carry a vague note of threat, just as the blue eyes, with their clear connotation of Aryan superiority, confuse rather than clarify one's response, especially when we consider the ominous "blue" of death's eye in a later allusion. The poem repeatedly violates the idea of unity and prompts disunity of impression, apparently defeating its own end.

But unity of impression is precisely what the Holocaust experience cannot evoke, and in this sense, in duplicating its contradictions without providing an opportunity for "ordering" one's reactions or assembling them into a meaningful pattern, Celan has invented a poetic form singularly appropriate for the substance of his vision. The art of atrocity is a stubbornly unsettling art, indifferent to the peace that passeth understanding and intent only on reclaiming for the present, not the experience of the horror itself, since by common consent of the survivors this is impossible to do vicariously, but a framework for responding to it, for making it *imaginatively* (if not literally) accessible. And this is what Celan must have meant when he declared that the challenge facing him after the war was to shape a reality for himself by wresting from silence the language that had survived its fearful events but lacked the eloquence and precision of a vocabulary to describe it.

Celan's "Fugue of Death," however, involves more than vocabulary. The opening strophe introduces the initial tension between a communally anonymous "we," the victims, and a "he," the executioner, several times identified, with increasing irony, simply as a "man." At first their realms are distinct, though within each a further contradiction intervenes: for the sufferers, metaphorically imprisoned by the black milk that poisons their lives in an unbroken cycle of oppression, and literally engaged in digging their own graves, nevertheless initially find cause to hope in this desert of futility: "we are digging a grave in the sky it is ample to lie there" ("da liegt man nicht eng")—an illusion of relief after death that is gradually but implacably eroded in the course of the poem.

Similarly, their persecutor, and ultimately their murderer, is introduced simultaneously as a lover, with a girl in Germany as the repository of his devotion (and it is unlikely that German readers would be insensitive to the fact that Goethe's Gretchen in *Faust* is also named Margarete, a clear echo of one ideal of national womanhood). But love, like hope, slowly becomes an echo of a disappearing world, muted and almost—but not quite—drowned out by the thundering tones of death, which eventually dominate the orchestration of the poem. Man as murderer dispenses with hope in accents of mocking cynicism—"as smoke you shall climb to the sky/then you'll have a grave in the clouds it is ample to lie there"—a theme virtually without variations; yet the mere addition of the image of smoke transforms hope into terror and the grave in the sky (now ominously become clouds) into a fate that answers prayer with silence and leaves the victims with no resources other than the naked face of fear.

With the introduction in the fourth strophe of the explicit theme that has been implied from the beginning—"death comes as a master from Germany"—the dominant motif of the poem appears, and from here to the end it resounds with ever more frightening intensity, casting a pall of gloom and futility over the themes which "accompany" it. The marching anapestic rhythms of the original German—"der Tod ist ein Meister aus Deutschland" (which occurs four times in the original without inversion of any kind), with its severe dentals enclosing a core of gentle sibilants, subtly reproduces a central paradox of the poem: the impulse to normalcy within a framework of terror and doom. Soiled by a halo of ashes, the golden hair of Margarete will never be the same; nor is it conceivable how the same reality could breed both: ashes and gold, love and death, any hope in the midst of such futility.

If poetry could actually achieve the condition of music, then the final two lines should sound simultaneously in the imagination (as if they were superimposed on each other on the printed page); for "your golden hair Margarete/your ashen hair Shulamith" do not constitute a sequence in time or in logic or in moral cause and effect (which may also be said of all the other images and "ideas" in the poem); rather, in their simultaneity, in their paradoxical and often contradictory coexistence, their inexplicable participation in one civilization ("culture" and "extermination" merging into a culture of extermination), they delineate an ambiguity which nothing in our prior experience, or in humanity's prior experience, can illuminate.

Nevertheless, the ambiguity is there, the dubious, literal fact of black milk has become an imaginative truth, an "impossible" metaphor fuses grim sorrow with life's most common nourishment, spreads across the landscape of the Holocaust, and transforms its reality into a bitter gall that nevertheless retains a faint savor of its original taste, just as the voices in the poem *sound* human even as they articulate—perhaps the supreme paradox—an inexpressible, almost unintelligible inhumanity. If language can serve such unholy ends in life, what exertions must the poet submit to in order to make it serve the holier ones of art!

Yet the critical sensibility has expressed reservations about the artist's ability to overcome this dilemma. To resurrect through art, not a dead age, but an unspeakable one whose atrocities nurtured a landscape of violence and an image of man unprecedented in the annals of history or of the literary imagination—such a task, to some, has seemed insurmountable. Taking his cue from Adorno, George Steiner, in *Language and Silence*, has provided the most searching analysis of this position, and though it is unlikely that he would still defend all of his premises and conclusions today, his ideas were so persuasively developed that, even where they failed to convince, they illuminated many of the issues that writers (like Celan) concerned with the reality of the Holocaust had to confront themselves. His conceptions are fruitful as formulations of the tensions that afflicted the artist despite the fact that they led Steiner himself to negative judgments on the possibility of an art of atrocity. For Steiner argues that the reality of the Holocaust addresses the contemporary mind most effectively with the authority of silence. His fundamental objection is appealing on emotional as well as intellectual grounds: "The world of Auschwitz lies outside speech as it lies outside reason." [8]

No one intimately acquainted with the nature of Auschwitz can dispute the second half of this proposition, which haunts the creative faculties of every artist who has ever tried to assimilate into his work a reality that includes Nazi concentration camps. Steiner acknowledges this even more eloquently when he confesses: "We cannot pretend that Belsen is irrelevant to the responsible life of the imagination. What man has inflicted on man, in very recent time, has affected the writer's primary material—the sum and potential of human behavior—and it presses on the brain with a new darkness." Indisputably. But as Paul Celan has contended, what dims the light of creation need not extinguish the lamps of language, though it may compel us to reconsider the sources of efficient illumination. Steiner, however, insists that the horrors of modern history have so stunned the imagination of the artist that it has been paralyzed: history collaborates with invention to produce—silence. "It is as if the complication, pace, and political enormity of our age had bewildered and driven back the confident master-builder's imagination of classic literature and the nineteenth-century novel." [9] But the allusion to Ibsen and other literary titans of his age only accentuates the abyss which atrocity has riven between their reality and ours; and if, as Steiner insists, the "ineffable lies beyond the frontiers of the word," [10] is he saying any more than that, by analogy, one cannot expect open-heart surgery to be performed with the antiquated (though for certain limited ends still effective) instruments of an earlier era? To be sure, the conventions and the rhetoric of nineteenth-century literature are inadequate for the representation or evocation of the physical, moral, or psychological chaos of a reality that one survivor, David Rousset, has definitively

8. George Steiner, "K," in *Language and Silence* (New York: Atheneum, 1966), p. 123.
9. Steiner, "Humane Literacy," in *Language and Silence*, pp. 4, 7.
10. Steiner, "The Retreat from the Word," in *Language and Silence*, p. 12.

labeled *l'univers concentrationnaire;* the "classic forms of statement and metaphor" are like unyielding clay to the sculptor of atrocity, who in his search for new forms and metaphors (consider, by comparison, what Dickens could have made of ashes and chimneys —or Balzac) to express his vision, learns as his foremost lesson that the great masters—Dostoevsky and Kafka are qualified exceptions —have little or nothing to teach him. Before the gas chambers and ovens of Auschwitz, a Dickens and even a Melville might have stood mute. But one must dispute Steiner's ancillary observation that "in the presence of certain realities [i.e. *l'univers concentrationnaire*] art is trivial or impertinent." [11] The authors included in this study offer weighty evidence to the contrary.

But in all fairness, the problem is more complex than I have yet made it sound. Many of Steiner's attitudes toward the relationship of language to silence derive from an idea, as much emotional as theoretical, that he later modified: that under Nazism "words were committed to saying things no human mouth should ever have said and no paper made by man should ever have been inscribed with," and that the use of the German language to dehumanize man for twelve years had pushed it beyond the breaking point and finally exhausted its resiliency and usefulness for art. Steiner touches on a crucial issue here, to which, as we have already seen in the case of Celan, many of the writers considered in this study were especially sensitive; but he weakens an otherwise valuable critical insight by interjecting a variation of the pathetic fallacy: "Everything forgets. But not a language." [12] At the risk of oversimplification, perhaps it is worth emphasizing that language is in fact only a thing, without memory, perception, or conscience, a tool controlled by the carver in words, and when writers were prepared to employ it once again in the name of imaginative truth, the German language proved as adequate to the challenge as any other national idiom, limited only by the talent and resourcefulness of the "carver." Insufficient time and perspective, the youth and literary inexperience of many aspiring authors among the survivors, together with a reticence bred by the traumas of survival, are the real sources of difficulty in the gradual growth of an art of atrocity; but by the late 1950s and early

11. Steiner, "K," p. 123.
12. Steiner, "The Hollow Miracle," in *Language and Silence,* pp. 99, 108.

1960s, when the relevant essays in Steiner's *Language and Silence* were written, its substance was already so abundant that his remarks are still rather surprising.

Certain experiences lend themselves more readily to verbal expression by the artist than others—an axiomatic and perhaps obvious assumption. As Dante struggled to capture ineffable bliss at the end of his *Paradiso*, so the artist of atrocity seeks to recreate unspeakable horror. Steiner feels no compunctions over the first half of this proposition but hesitates unaccountably over the second—though they represent two sides of a single coin. "By exhaustive metaphor," he agrees, "by the use of similes increasingly audacious and precise—we hear the prayer in the syntax—Dante is able to make verbally intelligible the forms and meanings of his transcendent experience." [13]

But if for Dante what "lies beyond man's word is eloquent of God," [14] why can there not be, for the artist whose "spiritual" nucleus is Auschwitz rather than heaven, a focus eloquent of Nothing, a demonic nihilism, or merely a blank and meaningless chaos? The challenge to the artist of atrocity is analogous to Dante's, though we must read *transcendent* in a different way, since the premises of medieval Catholicism, no matter how refined or developed by Dante, were still universally available to his readers, whereas *l'univers concentrationnaire* was a unique mansion of—a suitable word eludes us, since even "hell" was too rigidly conceptualized by Dante's *Inferno*—a unique mansion of contemporary reality, let us say, whose inhabitants could not draw comfortably on the collective imagination of their readers, as could Dante, since its customs and furnishings were literally exclusive, unavailable to the imagination *except insofar as they could make it so*. But this is only to define their task, not to negate it: making "verbally intelligible the forms and meanings" of the experience of the Holocaust challenges the artist's use of language, not the language itself, and if he abandons this challenge to silence, he simply admits his own inadequacy to discover the resources of language necessary to capture his vision. Steiner's suggestion that Auschwitz created serious problems for the literary artist is sound enough; but its

13. Steiner, "Silence and the Poet," in *Language and Silence*, p. 40.
14. Ibid., p. 39.

extension—that "the political inhumanity of the twentieth century and certain elements in the technological mass-society which has followed on the erosion of European bourgeois values" [15] have done irremediable damage to language and imposed an enforced silence on the artist—is an intellectual formulation not borne out by the literary evidence.

Distrust of language—and rhetoric—has in fact been a commonplace of our century at least since Woodrow Wilson announced that we must make the world safe for democracy. The naked simplicity of Kafka's style—even when parodistically employed in the service of a bureaucratic milieu—is as much a response to the historical circumstances generated by World War I as the bare prose of understatement chiseled into a fine art by Ernest Hemingway. The relationship of Kafka to the events of atrocity that followed within a decade of his death is, to be sure, no simple matter; but to assert, as Steiner does, that "Kafka heard the name Buchenwald in the word *birchwood*," and that he "prophesied the actual forms of that disaster of Western humanism" we call the Holocaust, might tempt hasty readers to ignore the spectres Kafka did *not* perceive in the shadows of his dark wood.[16] We will apprehend the art of atrocity more clearly if we keep in mind what Kafka *failed* to anticipate (and why), as well as what he prophesied. An intricate maze leads from the claustrophobic Law Court Offices to the gas chambers, and though winding corridors may indeed connect the two, neither Joseph K. nor his creator ever trod them. The exact nature of Kafka's prescience is arguable and perhaps ultimately indeterminable, even from the luxury of a postwar perspective never afforded Kafka himself; and whether he finally despaired of language's power to express his vision or not, we have only his words, not his silences, to serve as our Ariadne's thread.

Steiner's invaluable assistance in focusing our thinking on a subject virtually ignored by critics before him reaches a climax in his discussion of a poet who symbolically chose silence through suicide in her kitchen gas oven: "The question of whether the poet

15. Ibid., p. 49.
16. Ibid., p. 50. Steiner is guilty of a curious oversight here, since *Buchenwald* literally means "beech wood" and not "birch wood." He may have been thinking of Birkenau (Birken = birch trees), the extermination camp associated with Auschwitz. Elsewhere in *Language and Silence* (p. 122), he does observe that "Kafka came on Buchenwald in the beech wood" (Steiner, "K," p. 121).

should speak or be silent, of whether language is in a condition to accord with his needs, is a real one. 'No poetry after Auschwitz,' said Adorno, and Sylvia Plath enacted the underlying meaning of his statement in a manner both histrionic and profoundly sincere." Using her death as an example, Steiner asks whether our civilization "by virtue of the inhumanity it has carried out and condoned" has "forfeited its claims to that indispensable luxury which we call literature? Not for ever, not everywhere, but simply in this time and place" [17] (1966!—of the place we cannot be sure, but presumably Steiner means Western civilization).

But Sylvia Plath's fate illustrates a vital dilemma of the poet, not of the poet's language; until her death she had found words adequate for her art, and left behind her numerous poems which sought to express the agony implied by Auschwitz for "this time and place." And of course Steiner knows this, since in an essay on " 'Dying is an Art' " written a year earlier, in 1965, he asserted—in apparent contradiction to his "later" view—that in "Daddy" Plath had written "one of the very few poems I know of in any language to come near the last horror." [18] But this would make Adorno's aphorism "after Auschwitz no poetry" itself a histrionic verbal gesture, unless we take it to signify—and here we get to the very heart of Steiner's critical position, and the real point of departure for a study of the literature of atrocity—unless we take it to signify that, after the unutterable horrors represented by Auschwitz no one should wish to, no one should be encouraged or permitted to evoke with the mere instrument of language, the indescribable torment of the victims, or the insane "rationality" which led up to it.

We get our deepest glimpse into the critic's cry for silence— which, if heeded, would indeed stifle a multitude of richly imaginative voices—in the following revealing comment: "Was there latent in Sylvia Plath's sensibility, as in that of many of us who remember only by fiat or imagination, a fearful envy, a dim resentment at not having been there, of having missed the rendezvous with hell?" These are perhaps the most honest words spoken on the subject by Steiner, who in another moving essay calls himself "a kind of survivor"; but they represent autobiography, not

17. Stener, "Silence and the Poet," p. 53.
18. Steiner, " 'Dying is an Art,' " in *Language and Silence*, p. 301.

literary criticism, and they allow the conclusion that makes possible his elaborate theory on the necessity for silence: "Perhaps it is only those who had no part in the events [of the Holocaust] who *can* focus on them rationally and imaginatively; to those who experienced the thing, it has lost the hard edges of possibility, it has stepped outside the real." [19] Steiner's genius for expressing significant half-truths on this theme reaches a climax here, since many of those directly involved in the experience of atrocity asked themselves this very question and later became writers, or used their literary talent, precisely because they arrived at a conclusion directly contrary to Steiner's. Authors like Elie Wiesel, Jakov Lind, André Schwarz-Bart, Ilse Aichinger, Jerzy Kosinski, and others, all of whom, in one way or another, were more intimately involved in the Nazi catastrophe than either Steiner or Sylvia Plath, recognized from the beginning that their experience would have to be recorded, if it were to be authentic, as something truly beyond "the hard edges of possibility," as events that had "stepped outside the real." Haunted by their private visions of disaster, they had returned from their varied encounters with hell—though their descent into an un-Dantesque Inferno had been without benefit of Virgil, without expectation of Purgatory or the blessed intercession of Beatrice—alone, bereft of everything but memory and the consciousness that irrationality and unreality were the very essence of *l'univers concentrationnaire* and must somehow be incorporated into their art.

Whether writers who did *not* possess empirical evidence of this universe could recreate its atmosphere convincingly is another debatable question—Anthony Hecht's "More Light! More Light!" and Sylvia Plath's "Daddy" suggest that the possibility exists, though neither poem has the intensity of vision of Celan's "Fugue of Death." But anyone seriously concerned with the literature of atrocity must devote his primary attention to those writers who were more closely allied with the events of the Holocaust even when they were not literally survivors, since they were the ones, notwithstanding intermittent moments of despair, who were destined to recreate in their art a unique portion of contemporary reality. For the first time in history human beings found themselves

19. Ibid., p. 301.

confronted with a situation totally incommensurate with their capacity for hope (a recognition that extinguished the light in the "blue Polish eye" of Hecht's poem); and the result was a nightmare of fantasy that coexisted daily with the possible, the familiar, and the real. This sounds very much indeed like the world of Franz Kafka, which lacked only the concrete threat of dehumanized extermination to make him the authentic forerunner of the literature of atrocity—the distinction so often claimed for him.

Perhaps one difference between Kafka's world (rather than his works) and the world of his successors, is comparable to the difference between violence and atrocity, between the horrors that we have long been familiar with, like the Inquisition, and the unique horror we call the Holocaust. The distinction is difficult and controversial, and must remain tentative; yet Picasso's *Guernica*, perhaps the first valid example of an art of atrocity in our time, for all its roots in his earlier work, laid the foundations for a fresh way of perceiving—and conceiving—reality, as a direct result of the incomprehensible historical action of the decimating of a helpless town, the victimizing of its women and children, for no apparent reason other than the desire (and need?) to terrorize and destroy. As never before, the pressures of the *hideous* penetrated the consciousness of the literary imagination, forcing it to reconstitute reality in shapes and images that reflect a fundamental distortion in human nature, while compelling us to revise our conception of what is normal in human character and to see aberration and the grotesque as standards from which the rest of reality deviates.

No apparent reason—the catastrophe in life we call the Holocaust, which these words characterize, bred upheavals in the art I call the literature of atrocity, which these words help to define. *No apparent reason*—doesn't the distinction between violence and atrocity lie here?—for an act of violence, however unattractive to the civilized mind, however unjustifiable in its form or nature, is an explicable event, in the sense that a cause and effect exist, the connection between agent and victims is clear (though, as I say, it may horrify us, as Claudius's cold-blooded murder of Hamlet's father horrifies us), and suffering somehow seems to be a direct (though not necessarily equivalent) consequence of the impetus behind it. Atrocity, on the other hand, is analogous to sentimentalism or melodrama—consequences in excess of the situations that inspired them; but because its literary expression is rooted in a historical reality that haunts the reader, we cannot dismiss it as we might some of the more extravagant passages in Dickens or Poe. The mind resists what it feels to be imaginatively valid but wants to disbelieve; and the task of the artist is to find a style and a form to present the atmosphere or landscape of atrocity, to make it compelling, to coax the reader into credulity—and ultimately, complicity. The fundamental task of the critic is not to ask whether it should or can be done, since it already has been, but to evaluate *how* it has been done, judge its effectiveness, and analyze its implications for literature and for society.

It may seem presumptuous, but perhaps it is time to begin thinking of such literature and such writers as a "movement," and to speak, however hesitantly, of an aesthetics of atrocity. Aristotle may have felt presumptuous when he began to deduce certain principles of drama from the corpus of plays available to him, principles which gradually grew into an art of poetry, a poetics. But in so doing he helped to lay the foundations of literary criticism, and—the real service of the critic—he furnished a perspective for appreciating the sources of the appeal which these plays had for an audience. If later critics hardened his plastic ideas into the marble of dogma, this was none of Aristotle's doing. Greek dramatists drew on a common reservoir of myth and invented original ways of presenting it; and "Greek tragedy," with Aristotle's help, became a standard designation for a particular kind of art. Similarly, during the Middle Ages, poets drew on a common semilegendary heritage —familiarly known today as the "Matter of Britain" and the "Matter of France"—and the medieval romance, in all its infinite variety, was born. Will critics in a half-century, or less, look back on the "Matter of Auschwitz" and speak as familiarly of an "art of atrocity" (or, as David Rousset has named it, a *Littérature Concentrationnaire*)? I believe so; and during the past twenty-five years enough significant work has appeared to enable us to begin making critical generalizations about it today.

The need for such generalizations is confirmed not only by the shifting and ambiguous attitudes of George Steiner about the relationship of the writer to the experience of atrocity, but by the honest confusion of a poet (and critic) like Stephen Spender, who shares with Steiner the feeling of alienation of a writer who was not a participant in the events of the Holocaust. Reviewing—appropriately—Nelly Sachs's *O the Chimneys*, Spender draws a vital distinction between "outsiders" and "insiders," and comments indirectly on the problems afflicting each:

> One terrible aspect of our century is that fantasies horrible as the worst nightmares of writers like Baudelaire and Dostoevsky in the previous century have become literally true, realized in world wars, mass murder, genocide, concentration camps. They have come true in the minds of all of us, and in the lives and deaths of the victims.
>
> It is almost impossible though, to those of us for whom the truths are things we read about, even to imagine the realities of tormentors and victims. A result of this is that it has become a problem for the writer to relate the small circle of his private experience to the immense circumference of contemporary human violence and suffering. A good many writers refuse perhaps to admit that there is such a problem. But I think they feel it deep down; and the very refusal to admit it usually takes the form of insisting that individual experience is all that matters and that there is no such thing as general suffering. . . .
>
> The conditions in which it is possible for writers to do their work—their writing, simply—nearly always preclude their entering by their own experience into the centers of "the destructive element." Most writers gaze at the furnace through a fire-proofed window in a thick wall. Necessarily so, because they have to preserve the conditions in which their sensibility can act without becoming damaged; and to experience in its intensity the horrors of our time almost inevitably means being maimed or destroyed by it.[20]

Fantasies have become literally true—a principle, as we shall have occasion to see, that was to have a profound shaping effect on the writer's conception of his world. Fantasy, of course, had been employed for centuries by artists, for its own sake and to offer commentary on the human scene—Bosch populated his canvases with creatures of fantasy; and the records of myth and literature, from the Minotaur to the Houyhnhnms and beyond, are crowded with comparable distortions of reality—sometimes comic, sometimes tragically earnest—and though the reader or observer is often

20. Stephen Spender, "Catastrophe and Redemption: *O the Chimneys*. By Nelly Sachs," *New York Times Sunday Book Review Section*, 8 October 1967, pp. 5, 34.

absorbed by these universes of the imagination, he never mistakes them for literal reality. Similarly, in our time the Surrealist, for whom reality was in a sense the denial of the impossible, could turn to pure invention, and paint clocks dripping human toes hanging in an egg-filled sky, and the spectator might feel bemused (and amused), but would never confuse these fanciful distortions with recognizable reality. But when fantasies become literally true, the artist, the writer, must record a reality that has become an *expression* of the impossible, at the same time convincing his audience that whatever distortions he employs do not negate, but *clarify* reality and subject it to an illuminating metamorphosis.

But if, as Spender confesses, it is almost impossible for most writers even to imagine this reality, who is to transform it? Celan, as we have seen, for one; and for another, Nelly Sachs, a poet, according to Spender himself, "who writes out of a life immersed in the horror of the actual nightmare, the deaths of those who were burned in ovens. . . . One feels at once that here is a writer who does not make poetry out of material which she imagines from afar. Her poetry is the lived material itself." [21] If it is true, as Spender argues, that most writers "gaze at the furnace [of the horror of modern reality?] through a fireproofed brick wall," it is equally true, as he implicitly admits when speaking of Nelly Sachs (a Jew who escaped from Germany to Sweden in 1940), that an exclusive few have been able (like Melville's Ahab) to "strike through the mask" of that brick wall because they have survived the furnace themselves (though only vicariously, in Nelly Sachs's case), with sensibilities seared, perhaps, but still intact. Although the poems of Nelly Sachs are vital testimony to the ability to do so, Spender paradoxically feels compelled to add, in virtual contradiction to himself, that experiencing such horror "almost inevitably means being maimed or destroyed by it." What he wants to say, apparently (and he must feel it deeply himself), is that such experience *ought to* do irreparable damage to the creative imagination, and that writers instinctively shield the eyes of the mind against its blinding implications (readers too, one might add, though Spender does not).

All the more urgent, and all the more fascinating, then, should be a study of those who have plunged to the center of Spender's new

21. Ibid., p. 5.

destructive element, the heart of darkness of our time, in an attempt to make their private experience the metaphorical focus of "the immense circumference of contemporary human violence and [public] suffering," and to use their injured sensibilities as the source of a fresh creative vision. For them, the concentration camp, the gas chamber, the crematory oven have *become* the destructive elements of the twentieth-century nightmare, they have made "the realities of tormentors and victims" their own (for many, they literally were), they inhabit this world—they need not search the avenues of the imagination for a suitable entry.

A far more pressing problem—though Spender does not mention this—is *not* the relation of the alienated writer to this special world, but of the initiated writer to his audience outside. The irony of his experience may be its very exclusiveness, and though he has pledged himself to explore the universal implications of his unholy vision, he has recognized better than any critic the difficulties of metamorphosing unmitigated horror into the enduring forms of art, especially when the images he must draw on to animate the emotions and situations inherent in his vision—chimneys and furnaces, corpses and ashes, blood and agony—represent portions of reality from which the human imagination intuitively withdraws. More so than even Spender's writers, the reader shields his eyes from the demonic counterpart of Dante's beatific Rose.

At the beginning of this chapter I examined briefly Anthony Hecht's attempt to absorb both "mitigated" and what I have called unmitigated horror into the language of verse, and discussed some of the distinctions between the two, based on Hecht's juxtapositions in the poem. A more complex example of the explicit use of "unmitigated horror" in verse was Celan's "Fugue of Death." Far less direct an illustration of the metamorphosis of the events of the Holocaust into the language of poetry, but equally vivid, is Nelly Sachs's "What Secret Cravings of the Blood," whose concentrated imagery haunts the mind with a mood and a vision that no naked literal description could ever conjure up:

> What secret cravings of the blood,
> Dreams of madness and earth
> A thousand times murdered,
> Brought into being the terrible puppeteer?

Him who with foaming mouth
Dreadfully swept away
The round, the circling stage of his deed
With the ash-gray, receding horizon of fear?

O the hills of dust, which as though drawn by an evil moon
The murderers enacted:

Arms up and down,
Legs up and down
And the setting sun of Sinai's people
A red carpet under their feet.

Arms up and down,
Legs up and down
And on the ash-gray receding horizon of fear
Gigantic the constellation of death
That loomed like the clock face of ages.[22]

The poet takes items of nature like earth and hills, horizon and moon, customary sources of consolation in romantic (or even sentimental) verse, and which indeed must have formed much of the visual milieu of the camp inmates, and identifies nature in its familiar guise with unfamiliar, unexpected, improbable emotions and substances: "madness and earth," "horizon of fear," "hills of dust," and "evil moon," for example—a strategy that unites a mood of uneasiness and bizarre horror with traditional images and finally undermines the spirit's confidence in the durability of the reality which has always supported it.

The poem begins with a question which is never answered, which is, by any measure men know—isn't this one response the poem seeks to evoke?—unanswerable. *Why* is displaced by *what*, as if to suggest the irrelevance, even the impossibility, of discovering causal relationships in a fundamentally irrational situation. Under a sinister ash-gray light, a weird catastrophe is enacted, with automatic gestures ("Arms up and down, / Legs up and down") that fuse the enervated despair of the victims with the twisted limbs of the corpses they were to become. And "the terrible puppeteer," the author of all their woe, more animal ("foaming mouth") than human, directs this wooden drama on the stage of history for

22. Nelly Sachs, *O the Chimneys*, trans. Michael Hamburger, Christopher Holme, Ruth and Matthew Mead, Michael Roloff (New York: Farrar, Straus and Giroux, 1967), pp. 16–17. "What Secret Cravings of the Blood" is translated by Michael Hamburger.

reasons that are never disclosed. As in Anthony Hecht's poem, the failure of light (here "the setting sun") introduces the dark night of the spirit, draws a curtain of blackness across the future of an entire people, and ominously leaves behind only a carpet of blood to guide their uncertain steps. The desolation of the scene is immeasurably intensified by the departure of nature from its usual role of witness and solace to human suffering, to become a participant, in this instance, in the Holocaust itself. The language and imagery of the poem make nature and man conspirators in their own destruction— or in the destruction of the humanistic attitudes that have nurtured our conceptions of them for centuries. In the poem all portions of reality, including nature, collaborate in the fearful spectacle of murder—with this word, at least, Nelly Sachs is unambiguous— until even the stars cease to illuminate possible universes beyond our own and are absorbed into the gigantic "constellation of death" to whose blandishments and supremacy everything in creation submits. Death merges with time and eternity in the final image of the poem, drawing to itself the blood, the madness, the fear, the evil, the dust that define it as the climax of the poem's experience and establish it as a hallucinatory omnipresence that dwarfs the possible significance of any other events in the lives of victims or persecutors, past or future.

What light can ever flow out of this darkness, what rebirth follow so looming a triumph of death? Stephen Spender says that Nelly Sachs's poetry "enables the reader to enter into an attitude uniting catastrophe with redemption." [23] "What Secret Cravings of the Blood" offers no hint of redemption, but other poems make tentative—more tentative, perhaps, than Spender suggests—gestures in that direction; and although this is not the place for an exhaustive survey of Sachs's verse, a brief inspection of a representative poem of the latter type may provide us with an insight into the limits of the literature of atrocity, the evocation of total despair on the one hand, and on the other a cry from those who have returned from beyond the symbolic grave and wonder how to reestablish contact with the living—if they ever can. If "What Secret Cravings" is a painful litany to the exterminated, the following poem, "Chorus of the Rescued," is a desperate hymn from the survivors:

23. Spender, "Catastrophe and Redemption," p. 5.

We, the rescued,
From whose hollow bones death had begun to whittle his flutes,
And on whose sinews he had already stroked his bow—
Our bodies continue to lament
With their mutilated music.
We, the rescued,
The nooses wound for our necks still dangle
before us in the blue air—
Hourglasses still fill with our dripping blood.
We, the rescued,
The worms of fear still feed on us.
Our constellation is buried in dust.
We, the rescued,
Beg you:
Show us your sun, but gradually.
Lead us from star to star, step by step.
Be gentle when you teach us to live again
Lest the song of a bird,
Or a pail being filled at the well,
Let our badly sealed pain burst forth again
and carry us away—
We beg you:
Do not show us an angry dog, not yet—
It could be, it could be
That we will dissolve into dust—
Dissolve into dust before your eyes.
For what binds our fabric together?
We whose breath vacated us,
Whose soul fled to Him out of that midnight
Long before our bodies were rescued
Into the ark of the moment.
We, the rescued,
We press your hand
We look into your eye—
But all that binds us together now is leave-taking,
The leave-taking in the dust
Binds us together with you.[24]

Although many of the same ominous presences appear in this
poem, death here represents not journey's end but memory's

24. Sachs, *O the Chimneys*, pp. 24–25. "Chorus of the Rescued" is translated by Michael
Roloff.

beginning, as "We, the rescued" in plaintive refrain seek to strengthen the tenuous thread that binds their fabric to the garments of the living. "Dead" and absent souls cry out for rejuvenation, for light, for human affection, but the palpable burden of their past echoes from the wings, with an appeal that refuses to be silenced—the "mutilated music" that death's bow has stroked on the sinews of the survivors. Spirits reach out across a chasm of suffering and a vision of chaos that cannot be shared, yearning to leave behind their "sealed pain" but ever conscious of the difficulty, perhaps the impossibility, of doing so. Time drips blood instead of sand, and nooses block the sun from the blue air; nature and eternity are permanently stained, but human creatures continue to grope for the open contact ("We press your hand / We look into your eye") that will earn them, if not the redemption that Spender speaks of, at least the certainty that they have rejoined a familiar reality.

But the survivors' long traffic with a "midnight" past undermines the durability of the present, casts a shadow on the "ark of the moment" which constitutes their only temporal base, and raises for us the question of whether reality can ever be "familiar" again. Leave-taking has become a principle of their existence, dust the element that shrouds all mankind in the community of human pain, so that the unresolved tension at the end of the poem leaves us poised over an abyss of meaning, anxious to leap, uneasy about the vision that awaits us on the other side. Have the rescued, though sad, finally rejoined the living? or will the living, drawn into the perimeter of the rescued by hands actually seeking escape, succumb at last to the inescapable power of their unexorcised past? Hope wrestles with despair on a battleground of art; or, in the imagery of the poem, birdsong and wellwater vie with worms of fear and buried constellations, while the dust of our mortality—remnants of ashes?—darkens the scene, making it increasingly difficult for us to interpret the armistice of meaning with which it concludes.

But that interpretation is increasingly necessary, since the "mutilated music" of the poem resonates with tones and intensities which ask to be harmonized, and which no historian or reporter of mere facts is capable of reproducing. Art may be no more satisfactory than history for solving the desperate and by now persistent questions of how and why the Holocaust occurred—but this has never been the province of art. The significance of the literature of atrocity is its ability to evoke the atmosphere of monstrous fantasy that strikes any student of the Holocaust, and simultaneously to suggest the exact details of the experience in a way that forces the reader to fuse and reassess the importance of both. The result is exempted from the claims of literal truth but creates an imaginative reality possessing an autonomous dignity and form that paradoxically immerse us in perceptions about that literal truth which the mind ordinarily ignores or would like to avoid.

Form and dignity—odd terms to use in conjunction with *monstrous* and *atrocity*. Can art indeed conjure a reality that itself must remain forever unredeemable? It has made the attempt, groping toward a possibility that tests its resourcefulness and perhaps defines its limitations. In a world of absurdity, says Elie Wiesel, echoing Camus but speaking from a personal experience whose spiritual desolation Camus never approached, "we must invent reason; we must create beauty out of nothingness." [25] To create beauty out of nothingness—this is the dark challenge facing the human spirits who sought expression, if not renewal, by translating the agony of annihilation into the painful harmonies— and discords—of an art of atrocity.

25. "Jewish Values in the Post-Holocaust Future," *Judaism* 16 (Summer 1967): 299.

2: ACQUAINTED WITH THE NIGHT

Who will write us new laws of harmony?
We have no further use for well-
tempered clavichords. We ourselves
are too much dissonance.

Wolfgang Borchert

In the beginning there was the Holocaust.
We must therefore start all over again. . . .
What it was we may never know; but
we must proclaim, at least, that it was,
that it is.

Elie Wiesel

The journey from documentation to art, from the gross horrors of the Holocaust to their imaginative realization in literature, is a devious and disconnected one, full of unexpected detours through terrain scarcely surveyed by earlier critical maps. Writers themselves have gone astray in this uncharted landscape, a circumstance best illustrated, perhaps, by Peter Weiss's *The Investigation*, an attempt to create with a minimum of alteration from the testimony of witnesses at the Auschwitz trial in Frankfurt between 1963 and 1965 a series of dramatic scenes which would convey the authentic reality of that experience by using only the language of history, the words of the men and women who themselves endured—as victims or tormentors—its fearful tenure in time.

The result on the stage is singularly undramatic, notwithstanding the loose verse form of the monologues and dialogues of the characters—the chilling evidence in its pages rarely rises above the cold, harsh surface of mere factual truth. By duplicating the details of history without embellishing them, while at the same time being highly selective in his use of them, Weiss eliminates any perspective which might offer his audience an entry into their implications; oddly, and certainly unintentionally, the result is not a new aesthetic distance, but an aesthetic *indifference*, a failure of the artist's imagination to seduce the spectator into a feeling of complicity with the material of his drama. *The Investigation*

confirms more powerfully than any theoretical argument the
need for a dimension in the literature of atrocity beyond the
poetic distillation of court records, for something comparable to
the wedding of history and innovation that made Weiss's own
Marat/Sade (in its fullest stage version) such a brilliant success.[1]

Anyone present in the courtroom in Germany during the trial
which furnished the substance of Weiss's Auschwitz play might
have seen and heard impressive evidence of the human mind's
inadequacy to absorb—to say nothing of perceiving the implications
of—the naked facts of atrocity:

> The witness remembers one particular day in November, 1944:
> "Jewish children were brought to Auschwitz. A truck came and
> stopped for a moment in front of the Political Section. A little boy
> jumped off. He held an apple in his hand. Boger and Draser [SS men]
> were standing in the doorway. I was standing at the window. The
> child was standing next to the car with his apple and was enjoying
> himself. Suddenly Boger [one of the guards on trial] went over to the
> boy, grabbed his legs, and smashed his head against the wall. Then he
> calmly picked up the apple. And Draser told me to wipe 'that' off the
> wall. About an hour later I was called to Boger to interpret in an
> interrogation and I saw him eating the child's apple."
> Nobody can quite believe that he has heard right, but the witness
> reiterates the description of this insane act.
> "You saw it with your own eyes?"
> "I saw it with my own eyes."
> "You can swear to it in good conscience?"
> "Absolutely." [2]

Later the judge summons the witness back to the stand: "Is what
you have told us the absolute truth?" Replies the witness: "I swear
it is." [3]

Between the incomprehension of judge and jury and the certitude
of the witness, the groping for a response and the incontrovertible
facts of Auschwitz, lies that nocturnal realm which the writers I
examine in this study inherited as their reality. Since such evidence

---

1. I base this judgment partly on my response to the New York City stage production of
The Investigation. The Berlin production, which I have not seen, is said to have been far more
imaginative.

2. Bernd Naumann, *Auschwitz*, trans. Jean Steinberg (London: Pall Mall Press, 1966),
p. 133.

3. Ibid., p. 138.

clearly *dis*orients whatever human faculty might respond to it, piling atrocity on atrocity in the manner of *The Investigation* without providing an imaginative orientation for the development of this faculty could only paralyze it further. The writer bequeathed this evidence can deny it (surely the witness is lying); or he can ignore it (an aberration, totally uncharacteristic of modern reality); or he can accept its challenge, concede that the familiar structure of reality has crumbled, forge a path between incomprehension and response, and finally rebuild from the rubble of such testimony a grotesque literary edifice that will leave its inhabitants, like the judge and jury, incredulous and dismayed, but also, unlike the audience, better equipped to enter into the literal revelation through the avenue of accessibility laid out by the imagination of the artist.

"Normal men," insists David Rousset, whose *L'Univers Concentrationnaire* has given one name to the nocturnal realm just described, "do not know that everything is possible. Even if the evidence forces their intelligence to admit it, their muscles do not believe it. The concentrationees do know. . . . They are set apart from the rest of the world by an experience impossible to communicate." This recurrent notion, which we have encountered before and will meet again, expressed most often by writers who, like Rousset, nevertheless go on to "tell about" what they know only a few initiates will comprehend, illuminates the discontinuous and dislocated nature of their vision perhaps even more than the divided impulses driving them simultaneously to speech and silence, and culminates most fruitfully in the search for a metaphorical language to sustain the tensions that inspire it.

Thus, Rousset imagines this incommunicable experience as one ripe with decay that "shrivels away within itself" though it "still lives on in the world like a dead planet laden with corpses." [4] His grim simile aptly illustrates a vital paradox afflicting many writers themselves intimately involved with the Holocaust: for just as "surviving corpses" palpably contradicts our sense of a reasonable reality, so Rousset's language graphically summons up the very atmosphere of death-in-life that lay at the heart of his private

4. David Rousset, *The Other Kingdom*, trans. Ramon Guthrie (New York: Reynal & Hitchcock, 1947), pp. 168–69.

experience. It conjures the writer to dredge from the mute abyss of anguish verbal tokens of that woe, even as it warns of the dangers that threaten to stifle the voice of the intruder who dares to wander through its depths.

One of the first to venture in this direction was Wolfgang Borchert, a young German who returned from the war maimed in spirit and ailing in body, conditions to which he shortly succumbed —in 1947 he was dead at the age of twenty-six. His most famous work, the play *Draussen vor der Tür (The Man Outside)*, dramatizes the disillusionment of a soldier arriving in his homeland to find it drained of all meaning, hollow compensation for the years of senseless agony. But more important for our purposes are the stories and short prose pieces—half essay and half rhapsody—that Borchert left behind him. These illuminate the inner duality which the earliest writers in the tradition of atrocity seem to have experienced, the conviction that language was powerless to evoke their nightmare visions and the urgent need to find words to do so—a nightmare, as one commentator has suggested, which "imposes silence even while it demands speech." [5]

In a lyrical essay of late 1946 or early 1947, entitled "In May, In May Cried the Cuckoo" (intensifying the paradox, since May represents the crest of spring, the time of renewal, and also the month of the Third Reich's final collapse and war's end in Europe), Borchert struggles with the familiar question of "after such horrors, what language?" deeply tormented as he is by the writer's inability to draw on his customary treasury of words to express his vision of what men have committed and endured. Mourning the writer's isolation, he invokes the mocking cry of the cuckoo as a reminder of the abyss which history has sunk between the poet and his art:

> Cry, bird of loneliness, make fools of the poets, they lack your mad syllables, and their lonely distress becomes drivel, and only when they're dumb do they do their best, bird of loneliness, when mothercry hunts us through sleepless May nights, then we do our most heroic deed. The unspeakable loneliness, this icy male loneliness, we live then, we live without your mad sounds, brother bird, for the last, the ultimate cannot be put into words.[6]

5. "Jewish Values in the Post-Holocaust Future," *Judaism* 16 (Summer 1967): 267.
6. Wolfgang Borchert, "In May, in May cried the Cuckoo," in *The Man Outside*, trans. David Porter (London: Calder and Boyars, 1966), pp. 189–90.

Borchert makes the cuckoo a surrogate spokesman for "the true sounds of the world" which the helpless writer, overwhelmed by the enormity of the "truths," regards with frustration. In so doing, he himself becomes a spokesman for all those who looked out on their shattered world with dazed eyes and numbed memories and wondered how they would ever organize their sensations into meaningful verbal patterns.

The proposition that before 1939 imagination was always in advance of reality, but that after 1945 reality had outdistanced the imagination so that nothing the artist conjured up could equal in intensity or scope the improbabilities of *l'univers concentration-naire*—this proposition, offered by several writers in the tradition of atrocity, is a crucial one, sustained by Borchert's own response to the postwar scene:

> For who among us, who then oh, who knows a rhyme for the rattle of lungs shot to pieces, a rhyme for the scream at the gallows, who knows the metre, the rhythm, for rape, who knows a metre for the bark of machine-guns, a sound for the new-smothered scream of a dead horse's eye, in which no further heaven is mirrored, not even the blazing of villages, what press has a sign for the rust-red of goods-trucks [i.e. *Güterwagen* = freight cars or box-cars, used for deporting Jews and other prisoners to concentration camps], this world-in-flames red, this dried-up blood-encrusted red on white human skin? Go home, poets, go into the forests, catch fish, chop wood and do your most heroic deed: Be silent! Let the cuckoo cry of your lonely hearts be silent, for there's no rhyme and no metre for it, and no drama, no ode and no psychological novel can encompass the cry of the cuckoo, and no dictionary and no press has syllables or signs for your wordless world-rage, for your exquisite pain, for the agony of your love. . . . Since for the grandiose roar of this world and for its hellish stillness the paltriest words are lacking. All we can do is: to add up, collect the sum, count it, note it down.[7]

But even while demanding silence, Borchert labors to discover a speech, a voice to express his "wordless world-rage" and "exquisite pain," to recapture the lost eloquence of the poet's tongue. Notwithstanding his demurral, his catalogue of the items of atrocity is more than a notation: the rust-red of box-cars and "dried-up blood-encrusted red on white human skin" are not statistics of

7. Ibid., p. 190.

death, adding up, collecting, and counting, but stark suggestive images of atrocity which draw on a landscape of extreme horror not wholly familiar to his readers, even though it is an inescapable part of the reality of their time. Untroubled by his apparent self-contradiction (which by now we can recognize as a symptom of the literature concerned with this problem), Borchert in the same passage proclaims: "We must make a note of our misery"—though he agrees that sparse illustration, never detailed explanation, is all one can hope for, with two hundred printed pages serving as a commentary on "the twenty thousand invisible pages, on the Sisyphus pages which make up our life, for which we know no words, no grammar and no punctuation. But on these twenty thousand invisible pages of our book stands the grotesque ode, the ridiculous epic, the most prosaic and bewitched of all novels: Our crazy spherical world, our quivering heart, our life! That is the book of our mad, bold, fearful loneliness on night-dead streets."[8]

Grotesque, ridiculous, crazy, mad—terms that do not describe an ordered world, or even a readily visible one. Perhaps the most convincing evidence that certain writers following World War II felt themselves confronted by a unique situation for which earlier literary traditions had not prepared them is the fundamental difference between Borchert's response and the reaction of writers to World War I. They shared with Borchert his shock and disillusionment, and were vividly aware of a rupture in historical tradition (and to some extent, in traditions of literary style), but neither Dos Passos nor Hemingway nor Erich Maria Remarque felt totally disabled by his experience—each turned willingly to a kind of literary realism that could satisfactorily echo "the true sounds of the world" of war and violence, as they had experienced it. Their sensibilities were jarred by the disjunctions between the rhetoric of peace and the brutal events of war, but this became the *basis* of their vision, not a barrier against it. Hemingway's aim was to describe "the way it was"; Borchert realized the futility of such an ambition, since the "ultimate" was indescribable.

Yet Borchert tried, and since his time a generation of writers has invented a new fictional grammar, or several, all designed to make each written page evoke ten unwritten ones. One of the peculiari-

8. Ibid., pp. 190–91.

ties of the literature of atrocity is that (far more than Hemingway's literature of understatement) so much of it is a literature of innuendo, as if the author were conspiring with his readers to recapture an atmosphere of insane misery which they somehow shared, without wishing to name or describe it in detail. Borchert experimented with such a technique in a tale of 1946, called "Billbrook," about a Canadian airman walking at war's end through a dead and utterly demolished section of Hamburg. The landscape presents a desolation scarcely evokable; yet the precisely chosen images communicate horrors far in excess of their fragmentary nature. For example:

> He was standing at a big cross-roads. He looked back: No child? No dog? No car? He looked to the left: No child. No dog. No car. He looked to the right and in front: no child and no dog and no car. He looked along the four endless roadways: No house. No house? Not even a cottage. Not even a hut. Not even an isolated, still-standing trembling, tottering wall. Only the chimneys, like the fingers of corpses, stabbed the late afternoon sky. Like the bones of a giant skeleton. Like tombstones. The fingers of corpses, clutching at God, threatening heaven. The bare, bony, burnt, bent fingers of corpses. In whichever direction he looked, and he had the feeling that from the cross-roads he could see for miles in each direction: No living thing. Nothing. Nothing living.[9]

For the writer in quest of a new idiom, this scene provides a startling challenge; indeed, the specific physical image of the crossroads is invested with unusual metaphorical significance. The familiar sounds of civilization have abruptly disappeared—the cry or laugh of a child, a dog's bark, the whine of an auto engine—to be replaced by a stark visual silence that conveys its implications through a series of ominous and sinister similes of extermination. Borchert is "only" describing his native Hamburg, but the association of chimneys with corpses inescapably wakens memories of scenes which Borchert may never have witnessed, but which were absorbed by his imagination and transformed into a kind of archetypal symbolic presentation of the inconceivable annihilation —the literal reduction to nothingness—that we identify with the Holocaust. It is a landscape without figures, an eerie, frozen *danse*

9. Borchert, "Billbrook," in *The Man Outside*, p. 58.

macabre of inert forms sculptured against a background of silence—
and through all this wanders the Canadian airman, from the town of
Hopedale in Labrador, whose naïve and peaceful eyes survey this
fantasy of death with fascinated incomprehension, as his comfortable assumptions succumb to the suasions of a reality too terrible to
behold. The passage is saturated with negatives, in a desperate
attempt to suggest presence by representing absence; the few
chimneys projecting from the earth are metamorphosed into the
pleading, accusing arms and fingers of corpses which suddenly
clutter the barren landscape and assault the imagination with
remembrances of things past that populate the desolate scene with
the vividness of a waking dream. Yet Borchert has actually
mentioned almost none of this.

Nothing is unaffected by this metamorphosis, including nature.
For Hemingway nature usually provided solace and escape, at least
temporary respite from disillusioning human reality. But (as in
Nelly Sachs's poems) Borchert's story is encompassed by a landscape of horror, merges with it, and finally shares its grotesque
atmosphere of gloom. The development comprises a remarkable
demonstration of prose persuasion. The passage begins with a
suggestion of the effect of this unholy pilgrimage on the airman
himself: "He gazed stubbornly before him at the earth. But he could
not recover his lost premature pride and his high-spirited mood.
Lost, crumbled, dead." Then:

> Suddenly he saw that there was indeed something living in this dead
> houseless noiseless corpse-fingered city: grass. Green grass. Grass as in
> Hopedale. Normal grass. Millions of blades. Insignificant. Scanty. But
> green. And alive. Alive like the hair of the dead. Dreadfully alive.
> Grass, as everywhere in the world. Sometimes a little too gray, too
> dewy, too crumpled, dusty. But still green and alive. Everywhere
> living grass. He grinned. But the grin froze, because his brain thought
> of a word, a single word. The grin grew gray and dusty, like the grass
> in several places. But iced with too much hoar-frost. Graveyard grass,
> thought his brain. Grass? Good, grass, yes. But graveyard grass. Grass
> on graves. Grass of ruins. Gruesome ghastly gracious gray grass.
> Graveyard grass, unforgettable, full of the past, saturated with
> memory, eternal grass on graves. Unforgettable, shabby, mean:
> unforgettable gigantic grass carpet, over the graves of the world.[10]

10. Ibid., pp. 59–60. (I have slightly modified the translation.)

Perhaps the ultimate cannot be put into words, but Borchert here
has managed to envelop civilization in a shroud through which its
spectral death-mask weirdly shines; his grim ironic hymn to the
"greenness of the grass" is comparable to Melville's celebrated
chapter on the "Whiteness of the Whale." As in Melville, the visible
world of green gives way to the invisible spheres of gray, and by
applying to inanimate matter epithets like "dreadfully," "gruesome," and "ghastly"—epithets that should properly be reserved for
the *human* atrocities committed upon the grasses of the world
during the period of his apprenticeship to life—Borchert (again like
Nelly Sachs) forces all of reality into complicity with death, with the
unforgettable agonies that haunt the memory of the past and
permanently alter the physical, the spiritual, the psychological, and
the emotional landscape of the present.

The gradual erosion of familiar reality, its displacement by a
different, scarcely recognizable, threatening, amorphous externality
providing no reassurance or support for the tottering spirit of the
victim, is a theme which Borchert's successors would repeatedly
exploit. To the protagonist of Borchert's tale, born in Hopedale, the
grass at first offers a cause for relief, if not rejoicing: in the city of
the dead, at least the green grass is alive. But in the passage quoted,
a remarkable counterpoint is established between the expectations
of Borchert's character and the direction in which the prose
compels the reader. To the young airman, the grass seems
"normal"; to the reader, it is transformed gradually into a sinister
reminder that never again, or not for a long time, will he be able to
contemplate grass without seeing it, as it were, under the influence
of the graveyard, alive "like the hair of the dead." Perhaps the
contrast is too stark, but the metamorphosis in attitude is under-
scored when we recall Walt Whitman's use of the identical image in
Leaves of Grass. One is tempted to suggest, indeed, that Borchert
offers a grim rejoinder to the innocent question of Whitman's child:
"What is the grass?" The reality of Borchert's immediate past,
pressing with obstinate gloom on the imagination, casts ineradicable
shadows on Whitman's cheerful alternatives ("I guess it must be the
flag of my disposition, out of hopeful green stuff woven," or "I guess
it is the handkerchief of the Lord"); Whitman's association of grass
with death ("now it seems to me the beautiful uncut hair of graves")
only confirms the distance we have traveled from transcendental

conviction to the bizarre uncertainties of a post-atrocity era. Ironically, Whitman almost supplies writers like Borchert with an epigraph that describes the core of their vision—"And to die is different from what any one supposed"—"almost" because Whitman adds "and luckier," [11] a supplement which must leave a bitter taste on the tongue of anyone who has sampled the ingredients with which writers like Borchert season their literary brews.

One of these writers was Ernst Wiechert, who never properly joined the fraternity himself but anticipated several of its problems and expressed them with extraordinary clarity and insight for his younger successors. A German novelist with an established reputation before the war broke out, Wiechert was arrested by the Gestapo in 1938 and eventually wound up in Buchenwald, where he spent five months before the efforts of his wife and friends (he was not Jewish), aided apparently by his fame as a writer, secured his release. During the war Wiechert wrote a brief account of his experiences in the concentration camp, which was published in 1947 as *The Forest of the Dead (Der Totenwald)*. The prologue to the work is gravely prophetic:

> This report is meant to be no more than a prelude to the great Symphony of Death which will some day be written by hands more competent than mine. I have but stood in the doorway and looked at the dark stage, and I have recorded not so much what my eyes have seen as what my soul has seen. The curtain had risen only part of the way, the lamps were dim yet, the great actors were still standing in the dark. But the spokes of the horrible wheel had already begun to turn, and blood and terror were dripping from it as it circled flashing in the dark.
>
> I was called upon, and now my voice must speak. Others will be called, and they will speak. But behind them all the Great Voice will be swelling from beyond, saying "Let there be night!" [12]

Actually, the book progresses slowly from what the "soul" has seen to what the "eyes" have seen, as Wiechert first assesses the influence his "new" life must irrevocably exert on his former one,

11. Walt Whitman, "Song of Myself," in *Leaves of Grass and Selected Poems* (New York: Rinehart & Co., 1949), pp. 27–29.

12. Ernst Wiechert, *The Forest of the Dead*, trans. Ursula Stechow (New York: Greenberg Publishers, 1947), p. 1.

then tries to realize visually, through the precision of language, the exact nature of this "new" vision of experience, and finally confesses—we almost anticipate it—his inability to record what words were never designed to describe, or eyes in fact to behold, or human creatures to suffer, thus reaffirming the barrier between art and reality which the unique nature of the Holocaust (with its attendant experiences) created whenever it touched the sensibilities of the writer.

In an effort to gain detachment and probably greater universality in *The Forest of the Dead*, Wiechert assumes the guise of an inmate named Johannes, but the autobiography is thinly veiled, and Johannes plays the role of a sensitive mind stunned by a reality it was unprepared to encounter:

> It is hard to describe the emotions which had stirred Johannes from the moment of arrival in the camp. It was not so much terror, or bewilderment, or a half-conscious numbness. It was more the sensation of an ever-growing coldness that spread gradually from deep within until it filled his entire being. It was as if the life he had lived up to now, and his whole world were freezing to numbness in this chill. As though he was gazing through a thick sheet of ice at very distant things. And in that distance moved the noiseless and unreal spirits of his past; the people he had loved, his books, his hopes and plans, all of them marked now, bearing the germ of death, and given to disintegration, without a purpose in a world in which these sons of pastors were now the ruling men ["sons of pastors" = SS guards]. He felt the cold break down his dream as frost breaks a flower stem. He felt a crack run through God's image, a crack that would not ever heal.[13]

Imagery of insulation abounds in the literature of atrocity—insulation separating two worlds, as here the comfortable past and inconceivable present of Johannes, or Borchert's once-vital grass "iced with too much hoar-frost"; and we recall Spender's writers hesitating to plunge into the modern centers of the "destructive element," gazing rather "at the furnace through a fire-proofed window in a thick wall." Fire and ice—Robert Frost was not the last to offer us these dismal alternatives, though his waspish humor traditionally excludes him from the ranks of those who have had genuine acquaintance with the night.

13. Ibid., p. 63.

Most important in the Wiechert passage, however, is the effect of the present on the past: ice separates, it chills and freezes, but it does not preserve; it is here literally another destructive element, disintegrating the substances of memory ("people," "books," "hopes," "plans,")—customary companions to human solitude— and leaving a vacuum of values, a paralyzing, frozen, meaningless and inconsolable despair. And the last concession is the most difficult, but Wiechert submits to its promptings with a painful honesty: the crack in God's image sunders man from his spiritual heritage and destiny and returns us to Wiechert's own ominous echo of the Great Voice: "Let there be night!" A world darkened by the withdrawal of spiritual possibility is unusual, though not unique, in the history of literature; but the demonic powers that trod this God-abandoned landscape, and the acts carried out at their behest and under their supervision, tinted everything with an unfamiliar hue of death that even Dante's Inferno failed to reflect.

This is precisely what required the writer to devise a new palette of colors, and Wiechert added his voice—though in point of time his was one of the first—to the chorus of those who announced the futility of the endeavor, even while he experimented with shades and tones for sketching visions of the unspeakable. His evocation of prisoners huddled forlornly on the *Appelplatz*—the area where roll call was held—is all the more remarkable when we consider that he is drawing on recollections of 1938, when Buchenwald was a comparatively "mild" prelude to the extermination camps that were to follow:

> When late in August, in the gray light of dawn, those thousands gathered for early roll call, bent down and freezing, in pouring rain, mud on the drill ground reaching above their ankles, many leaning on tall sticks to hold themselves upright, some in a serious condition clinging to the shoulders of their comrades, some on crude stretchers; when the wind drove puffs of fog about the columns, enveloping and then revealing them in the pale light; when at the foot of one of the trees or a light pole a man lay dying, half in the other world already, with his face open to the light of dawn, then all this was a picture of the damned arisen like a specter from Hades, or a vision out of Hell, beyond the brush of the greatest painter, beyond the needle of the greatest etcher, because no human phantasy or even the dreams of a

genius can measure up to this reality, which has not had its like in centuries, perhaps never.[14]

The fog-shrouded atmosphere drives the spectator to rub his eyes to see whether or not he is dreaming, to deny what his vision confirms, to draw comparisons—as does Wiechert, instinctively searching for a literary vindication at the very moment of his consciousness that none could possibly exist—almost helplessly with the traditional Hell or Hades, which are clearly recognized as inadequate similes; and finally, as the fog rolls in and out of the scene, to retreat in awed silence. But Wiechert's prediction that no human fantasy and no dreams can "measure up to this reality" is premature, though he shrewdly defines the perspective which later writers will have to use in their approach to that reality: for "human phantasy" is precisely the combination of real and unreal that can evoke the moral and physical chiaroscuro Wiechert speaks of; and the atmosphere of dreams, already familiar to readers of Kafka, afforded an entry to the world of the Holocaust that was denied the advocates of literal realism.

To establish an order of reality in which the unimaginable becomes imaginatively acceptable exceeds the capacities of an art devoted entirely to verisimilitude; some quality of the fantastic, whether stylistic or descriptive, becomes an essential ingredient of *l'univers concentrationnaire*. Indeed, those who recorded details painstakingly in an attempt to omit none of the horror may have been unwittingly guilty of ignoring precisely the chief source of that horror—existence in a middle realm between life and death with its ambiguous and inconsistent appeals to survival and extinction, which continuously undermined the logic of experience without offering any satisfactory alternative. It is scarcely accidental that those who testify most intensely to the dilemma are writers who themselves were somehow intimately acquainted with the "reality" of the era, since they are the ones best equipped to understand the layers of apparent fantasy which obscured it. And perhaps the most singular appeal of their literary efforts is that the distortions wrought by their veils of fantasy only illuminate the terrors of the "reality" with an unholier glow.

Inevitably, writers concerned with the aesthetic interplay of fantasy and reality would turn to those phenomena of the half-

14. Ibid., p. 70.

conscious life where the two are tightly intertwined—the world of dreams. More concretely, the influence of the reality of atrocity on the dreams of those who endured it—whether victims or spectators —forms a fascinating study in itself, and indeed at least one brief study of the subject has already appeared, which, though limited in scope *and* inference, offers some relevant background for the literature we are concerned with. Charlotte Beradt's *The Third Reich of Dreams* examines recurrent dreams of selected Germans between the years 1933 and 1945 (though the author herself fled Germany in 1939, returning after the war to complete her research). She is less interested in what the dreams reveal about the individual personalities of the dreamers than in what they disclose about the inner tension of a people collectively trapped (some willingly, others not) by an environment of "total authority" in which the "normal" development of character through the free expression of ideas and impulses is forbidden.

In other words, she explores the impact of a more broadly public and less explicitly brutal and repressive *univers concentrationnaire* on the psychic life, the realm of dreams, of the ordinary inhabitant of the Third Reich; and the results of her investigation are of special interest to us because they suggest and clarify some of the problems of characterization and style which novelists exploiting this material will have to confront: the creation of characters with divided and often uncomplementary sensibilities, or personalities so passive as to be virtually extinguished, or individuals with exaggerated impulses (like an extraordinary capacity for cruelty), which in a traditional setting would be acceptable only in surrealistic or ultramelodramatic literature. Thus, it is not surprising that in the dreams recorded the dreamers are usually involved in situations inconsistent with the expectations of logic or reason. According to Miss Beradt, a major value of these dreams is what they expose about the emotional states and motives of men when they become cogs in a giant machine; and though we dare not confuse the workings of that machine inside and outside the concentration camp, the dreams it inspired among nonvictims help to clarify the nature of the reality imposed on those who suffered a harsher fate. For example:

> When a person sits down to keep a diary, this is a deliberate act, and he remolds, clarifies, or obscures his reactions. But while seeming to

record seismographically the slightest effects of political events on the psyche, these dreams—these diaries of the night—were conceived independently of their authors' conscious will. They were, so to speak, dictated to them by dictatorship. Dream imagery might thus help to describe the structure of a reality that was just on the verge of becoming a nightmare.[15]

The transfer and expansion of such visions into sustained works of the imagination has been the delicate and difficult task of the writers considered in this study, who almost uniformly acknowledged that the material of their art must somehow include a sense of a reality not merely on the verge of becoming a nightmare, but already become one.

The uncanny resemblance between the dreams recorded in Miss Beradt's book (and the very language she employs to describe them), and the substance of the literature of atrocity indicates an imaginative affinity that reaches far deeper than the accidental fulfillment of certain scattered dreams in real experience. It is by no means merely a matter of prophetic intuition, she suggests:

These dreams are indeed reminiscent of mosaics—often surrealistic ones—whose single pieces had, as it were, been chipped from the reality that was the Third Reich. This justifies interpreting them as contributions to the psychology of totalitarianism, and permits one to apply them to the concrete situation they illuminate. . . .

Set against a background of disintegrating values and an environment whose very fabric was becoming warped, these dreams are permeated by a reality whose quality is unreal [irreale Realität]—a combination of thought and conjecture in which rational details are brought into fantastic juxtapositions and thereby made more, rather than less, coherent; where ambiguities appear in a context that nonetheless remains explicable, and latent as well as unknown and menacing forces are all made a part of everyday life.[16]

Although "unreal reality" is intended as a description of dream-content, it serves equally well as an exact commentary on the paradoxical quality of the experience attested to by some of the witnesses mentioned in this chapter. Perhaps "irrealism" would be a more valid description of certain techniques that sought to enlarge on their testimony.

15. Charlotte Beradt, *The Third Reich of Dreams*, trans. Ariadne Gottwald (Chicago: Quadrangle Books, 1968), p. 9.
16. Ibid., pp. 16, 17.

Dreams, of course, have long been literary devices for probing the unconscious motives and tensions of characters, but never before has their provenance been so clearly a moral and emotional reality shared by large masses of people. The private nightmares of Lady Macbeth or Dostoevsky's Svidrigaylov arise from situations afflicting only themselves or those closest to them: total strangers could not make much sense of Lady Macbeth's obsession with cleanliness or the rodents and spiders that haunt Svidrigaylov. The literature of atrocity, however, like the dream images in Miss Beradt's study, draws on a nonimaginative reality available to anyone familiar with even the barest details of the historical past it alludes to; accordingly (and unlike literary tragedy), it is compelled to employ the implications of fact to create its unique aesthetic appeal.

Thus, Miss Beradt is not far off when she observes "how closely the means employed in these dreams to describe life under the Third Reich coincide with the techniques contemporary German writers use to convey a dark past that eludes them when they approach it in a realistic fashion," or that the atmosphere of total if inexplicable oppression they exude resembles some episodes and parables from Kafka. In fact, she astutely continues, slipping unconsciously from dream analysis to literary criticism,

> the line between the comic and the tragic often becomes blurred as their authors struggle to express the inexpressible. They describe phenomena typical of the period in the form of parables, parodies, and paradoxes. And situation is heaped on situation in a succession of snapshot images from which the echo of daily life reverberates with frightening loudness or with equally frightening softness, emerging radically simplified but also radically exaggerated.[17]

The dreams thus become commentaries on a reality that insinuates itself into the sensibility of the dreamer (or the writer) and through some kind of ambiguous transformation is altered into "a reality whose quality is unreal" but simultaneously more vivid and—perhaps most inexplicable of all—more tolerable and accessible to the imagination. This atmosphere seems appropriate for such fiction because in these dreams (as in the experience of totalitarian reality that inspired them) the rigid framework of familiar values has

17. Ibid., pp. 17–18.

disintegrated, and a world appears where recognizable fears are masked by eccentric behavior—obliterating, as Miss Beradt points out, the boundaries between tragedy and comedy and thus laying the foundations for the possibility of the absurd which, following a tributary not far distant from the literature of atrocity, led to the drama of Beckett and Ionesco. Just as the moral enormities committed (and suffered) during the Holocaust required these authors to revise their conception of human character and of what represented "normal" behavior, so they had to alter their notion of literary setting, substituting for the traditional environments of fiction a complex amalgamation of reality and unreality that gradually displaced previous norms and itself became the measure of what once was considered "normal."

Since the genesis of these authentic dreams may be traced to a reality akin to (but by no means identical with) the one that later stimulated the literature of atrocity, it is hardly surprising that some of them read like condensed anecdotes from their pages. To glance at only one or two by way of illustration: a twenty-two-year-old girl who felt her crooked nose identified her as a member of the "inferior" race dreamed in the early years of the Hitler era:

> "A peaceful family outing. Mother and I had brought along some cake and the folder containing our genealogy. Suddenly a shout: they're coming. Everyone in the garden restaurant there on the Havel River knew who 'they' were and what our crime was. Run, run, run. I looked about for a hiding place high up. Perhaps up the trees? Atop a cupboard in the restaurant? All at once I found myself lying at the bottom of a pile of corpses with no idea how it got there—at least I had a good hiding place. Pure bliss under my pile of bodies, clutching my papers in their folder." [18]

The omissions here are as significant as the included details: the introduction of the threatening force without explanation (everyone "knew who 'they' were"); the abrupt transition from familiar routine to macabre flight, without any attempt to establish a logical connection between the two; the reduction of tragedy by the absurd failure of the victim to respond to her dilemma with intense emotion (further compounded by the grotesquely comic sensation of "pure bliss" in the security of the death heap); and the

18. Ibid., pp. 80–81.

remarkable anticipation of a later reality, which retrospectively, given our knowledge of the mass exterminations, controls the reader's response in a way that compels him to view what is "only" a dream through the shuddering (and partially distorting) lenses of historical fact. The mad-sane fictional universe of Jakov Lind is not far off.

One other example must suffice to illustrate the ingredients that constitute the unfamiliar yet never entirely unrecognizable reality of *l'univers concentrationnaire*, a hybrid of the nerve-wracking bewilderments of a Kafkan anti-hero and the spiritual futility of Dante's infernal sufferers:

> "While out for a walk we heard a rumor in the streets that people should keep away from their apartments because something terrible was going to happen. We stood across the street and looked longingly up at our apartment where the blinds were drawn as if no one lived there.
>
> We went to my mother-in-law's apartment, the last place left to go—up the stairs, but we discovered strange people living there now—could it be the wrong building?
>
> We went up the stairs in the building next door, but it, too, was the wrong one—a hotel. We came out by another door and tried to find our way back, but now we couldn't even find the street any more.
>
> All at once we thought we'd found the house we so badly needed, but it was only the same hotel that had confused us once before. After we'd gone through this unnerving run-around for the third time, the woman who owned the hotel told us, 'It won't do you any good even if you do find that apartment. This is what is going to happen. . . .' And in the manner of Christ's curse on Ahasuerus [the legendary Wandering Jew], she pronounced:
>
> > 'There comes a law:
> > They shall dwell nowhere.
> > Their lot shall be
> > To wander ever through the streets.'
>
> Then she changed her tone and, as if she were reading out some proclamation, droned: 'In conjunction with said law, everything previously permitted is now forbidden, to wit: entering shops and stores, employing craftsmen. . . .' Right in the middle of this horrifying scene something trivial occurred to me—now how was I to have my new suit made up?

We left the hotel and went out *forever* into the dismal rain." [19]

The tension between the normal ("how was I to have my new suit made up?") and the abnormal (literally displaced persons, doomed to wander without cause forever in the rain) was a basic constituent of reality during the Holocaust. The departure from the "safe" and familiar apartment into an unspecified but threatening future (for which no one is prepared—the common response was to "walk around the corner," as it were, expecting to find the old apartment, the former security, with nothing changed) is an astonishing anticipation of the fate of millions (considering that the dream was recorded in 1935!). But the most revealing and useful detail, insofar as the later development of character and setting in fiction is concerned, is the preponderance of what we might call nostalgia over apprehension, the inability of the victims to confront the sudden events with concrete action, or even reflection, because nothing in their past was commensurate with the possibilities of physical and spiritual annihilation that lay before them. And since the dreamers themselves were relatively unselfconscious about the implications of their dreams (in this instance, the dreamer wasn't even Jewish, though her husband was), they are valuable to us chiefly as evidence of the influence the Third Reich had on the unconscious life of those affected by it, and as the raw material for a clearer understanding of the relationship between "irrealism" and "realism" as literary techniques for portraying the world of the Holocaust.

The raw material approaches the more finished forms of art—if not the final version—in dreams recounted by self-conscious authors who sought to articulate some of the tensions between the normal and abnormal alluded to earlier, and who therefore commented more elaborately on the implications of their dreams and the problems these implications posed to the literary imagination. One of these, a young Italian Jew named Primo Levi, spent a year at Buna-Monowitz, a munitions labor-camp associated with the main extermination camp at Auschwitz-Birkenau. Like so many others, Levi retrospectively acknowledged that the ordeal suffered by him and his fellow prisoners would never be erased from their consciousness, but would afflict their sensibilities permanently and transform their responses to life, awake and in dreams:

19. Ibid., pp. 138–39.

So for us even the hour of liberty rang out grave and muffled, and filled our souls with joy and yet with a painful sense of pudency, so that we should have liked to wash our consciences and our memories clean from the foulness that lay upon them; and also with anguish, because we felt that this should never happen, that now nothing could ever happen good and pure enough to rub out our past, and that the scars of the outrage would remain within us for ever, and in the memories of those who saw it, and in the places where it occurred, and in the stories that we should tell of it.[20]

Levi goes on to describe the effects this "awful privilege" of his generation has had on the lives of himself and his contemporaries: like modern ancient mariners, they must plunge back into the "inexhaustible fount of evil" they have survived, but which has indelibly stained their future reality, and narrate to trapped but fascinated bridegrooms the "incurable nature of the offense" to humanity which they have endured and which "spreads like a contagion" across the landscape of contemporary history.

The permanently corrupting influence of such experiences inspired survivors, too, with recurrent collective dreams that later provided many writers with material for an imaginative universe existing between the bounds of fantasy and reality. Elsewhere Levi has commented on one peculiarity of the dream-phenomenon in *l'univers concentrationnaire*:

My dream stands in front of me, still warm, and although awake I am still full of its anguish: and then I remember that it is not a haphazard dream, but that I have dreamed it not once but many times since I arrived here, with hardly any variations of environment or details. I am now quite awake and I remember that I have recounted it to Alberto [a fellow inmate] and that he confided to me, to my amazement, that it is also his dream and the dream of many others, perhaps of everyone. Why does it happen? Why is the pain of every day translated so constantly into our dreams, in the ever-repeated scene of the unlistened-to story?[21]

Levi's dream-state is a "ladder between the unconscious and the conscious," in which he tries to explain to friends and members of

20. Primo Levi, *The Reawakening*, trans. Stuart Woolf (Boston: Little, Brown, 1965), pp. 12–13.
21. Primo Levi, *Survival in Auschwitz*, trans. Stuart Woolf (New York: Collier Books, 1961), p. 54.

his family the essential truth of his camp experience—the railway cars, the train whistles, the hard wooden beds, the hunger, the lice, the beatings, the blood; but his listeners do not follow him, "they are completely indifferent: they speak confusedly of other things among themselves, as if I was not there." The gulf between the two worlds, not the poverty of language, is what imposes silence here, as if the speaker in the dream had not yet recognized the need for finding new ways of communicating his painful sense of a "different" reality to those still dwelling in the familiar and normal past. "This is the most immediate fruit of exile, of uprooting," Levi concludes: "The prevalence of the unreal over the real. Everyone dreamed past and future dreams, of slavery and redemption, of improbable paradises, of equally mythical and improbable enemies; cosmic enemies, perverse and subtle, who pervade everything like the air." [22]

As in the poems of Nelly Sachs and the passages by Wolfgang Borchert, the cosmic enemy becomes life itself, absorbed into the landscape and the atmosphere, pervading everything, an indefinable *threat*, always there to disturb one's waking hours and hover over one's dreams, announcing the impossibility of an episode at the very moment it occurs, deceptively reassuring at the instant of extremity, when the options of oblivion and eternity disrupt the "real" until the imagination can no longer acknowledge what it once considered "real." Many of these qualities are incorporated into a kind of archetypal dream of Levi's (as the dream was incorporated into his own future waking hours), adding an imperishable quality of apprehension to the consciousness of contemporary humanity, altering every prior conception of reality and chafing the imagination of those writers who have chosen to devote a part of their talent to the imaginative recreation of atrocity:

> It is a dream within a dream, varied in detail, one in substance. I am sitting at a table with my family, or with friends, or at work, or in the green countryside; in short, in a peaceful relaxed environment, apparently without tension or affliction; yet I feel a deep and subtle anguish, the definite sensation of an impending threat. And in fact, as the dream proceeds, slowly or brutally, each time in a different way, everything collapses and disintegrates around me, the scenery, the

22. Levi, *The Reawakening*, pp. 107–08.

walls, the people, while the anguish becomes more intense and more precise. Now everything has changed to chaos, I am alone in the center of a grey and turbid nothing, and now, I *know* what this thing means, and I also know that I have always known it; I am in the Lager [i.e. concentration camp] once more, and nothing is true outside the Lager. All the rest was a brief pause, a deception of the senses, a dream; my family, nature in flower, my home. Now this inner dream, this dream of peace, is over, and in the outer dream, which continues, gelid, a well-known voice resounds: a single word, not imperious, but brief and subdued. It is the dawn command of Auschwitz, a foreign word, feared and expected: get up, *"Wstawàch."* [23]

It is as if the *Angst* introduced to the modern era by Kierkegaard, Kafka, and their successors had finally acquired a local habitation and a name; certainly the "dawn command of Auschwitz" resembles the inaugural knell of Kafka's nightmare world, for "getting up" opens the odyssey into unreality of both Gregor Samsa and Joseph K. And in both instances, in Levi and Kafka, awakening signifies the termination of the "dream of peace" which for us represents conventional reality: the consolations of friends, family, nature, normalcy, a world whose irrevocable disappearance into an unrecapturable past is a premise of the art of atrocity. *Das wandlose Leben*, life without walls, in the graphic phrase of Charlotte Beradt—a life inflexibly shadowed by a particular kind of threat, permanently deprived of a particular kind of security, has begun. "Nothing is true outside the Lager" now represents reality; all the rest, says Levi, was the "real" dream. And it is not merely a clever but ephemeral slogan; even when it is not literally applied, as in the succeeding account of a dream-become-literature, it symbolizes a portion of the universe entrenched in the modern imagination.

Hermann Kasack's novel, *The City Beyond the River* (*Die Stadt hinter dem Strom*, 1947), represents one of the earliest fictional attempts to create a literary mise-en-scène commensurate with this universe, though his account of its genesis is far more relevant to our purposes than the result, which is only moderately successful. According to Kasack, the germ of the novel was a vision he had in 1942, in which he saw "the expanses of a ghostly ruined city, that disappeared into infinity and in which people moved about like troops of imprisoned puppets." The vision, Kasack confesses

23. Ibid., pp. 221–22.

(perhaps naïvely), may have been inspired by the war and the Nazi years, but he considers this (naïvely too) irrelevant. It is also connected, he says, to a dream of the previous year. In any event, Berlin (where he was living) was still intact, and he had not yet seen any place that had been touched by the war. His vision, he concludes, must have been an anticipation of reality; it inspired him to begin the novel, without knowing where it might lead.[24]

The novel, whose chief limitation is probably a *total* reliance on the descriptive techniques of realism to evoke an unrealistic atmosphere, takes a young man on a train journey across a river into a realm populated by strange figures, some known to him, who behave with a passivity he cannot comprehend, and who, we suspect sooner than he (and with an ease that minimizes the tension of the fiction), are actually dead. "At first," Kasack writes in his retrospective account, "I intended to get by with a few pages, in order to capture the vision of a life grown ghostlike. But the increasingly uncanny reality of the time repeatedly summoned up new images." Gradually, the content of his original vision became a reflection of the real world, one that "in its social, spiritual, and cultural structure appeared just as dubious and fragile, just as false and insecure" as the houses of German cities, which everywhere tottered on the brink of collapse. Then a strange thing happened, which temporarily convinced Kasack that he would be unable to finish his book: "Something occurred that completely paralyzed me, though I should have foreseen it:—reality had caught up with my vision. The reality which I had foreshadowed had become the arena of general existence—including the most bizarre details." [25]

When the landscape of life begins to resemble the landscape of art, and the work of the imagination becomes a retrospective prophecy, then the usual creative process is reversed, and the writer must reorient his own attitude toward experience. As Germany turned into the kingdom of the dead that he had supposedly anticipated in his novel, Kasack realized that "reality had not overtaken my vision, but had only confirmed it." This recognition— a slow process of nearly a year, according to Kasack—liberated him

24. Hermann Kasack, "Die Stadt hinter dem Strom: Eine Selbstkritik," in *Mosaiksteine: Beiträge zu Literatur und Kunst* (Frankfurt am Main: Suhrkamp Verlag, 1956), pp. 350, 351. Translation mine.

25. Ibid., pp. 351, 352.

from his imaginative paralysis; after 1945—by then the war was over, and the full extent of the human desolation it had bred in Germany and beyond its borders was public knowledge—he completed his novel. Later, Kasack could describe its milieu in detail as an intermediate realm "where men exist only as images of life, without participating in it in the fullest sense, and where at the same time they are touched by death, without falling senseless into its lap." Human creatures whose mechanical gestures belie their reality, signs of civilization promising a vitality that dissolves as one approaches, the familiar giving way to the threatening, the individual consciousness sinking into anonymity—"when I searched for a fixed place," says Kasack, "where the images of our reality had settled, this middle-realm of the dead offered itself poetically as the clearest answer."

All this suggests that features of *l'univers concentrationnaire* reached beyond their barbed-wire boundaries to the imagination of writers, whose intimations of disaster floated in an atmosphere of apprehension until history gave substance to these "images of our reality" and persuaded a novelist like Kasack that, for his generation at least, death was less occult than life. He had begun his account of his novel's origin by admitting the possible influence of the Nazi regime on his vision; he ended on a far less ambiguous note: "Terror and the horrible should not be evaded. It is useless to cling to an idyllic attitude that the convulsions of the present are not prepared to acknowledge." [26]

The problem of writing about experience under circumstances in which death is more "real," a more accurate measure of existence— gruesome as that may sound—than life, was anticipated by Borchert in his landscape of a mutilated city whose corpselike rubble assumes a vitality of its own, and by Anthony Hecht in "More Light! More Light!" where the grave becomes the habitation of man and human creatures climb in and out of it in a grisly game of "house." It was foreseen in Ernst Wiechert's *Totenwald* (*Forest of the Dead*), where the germ of death infected his past life, freezing (and disintegrating) all values, cracking God's image, "as frost breaks a flower stem." Hermann Kasack preserved in detail—in fact, published during the war—the dream he alluded to earlier as preceding and helping to

26. Ibid., pp. 352, 353, 354.

shape his subsequent vision of the "middle-realm" of death, and it provides an even sharper insight than Kasack's own commentary into the displacement of life by death as an imaginative framework for understanding the literature of atrocity. Not unexpectedly, Kasack calls his version *"Der Totentraum"*—the Dream of Death.

The account of the dream is so vivid, its treatment of the illogic of reality in a death-dominated atmosphere so artful, that one deplores all the more Kasack's inability to sustain this mood in his novel. In the dream, Kasack finds himself among the dead, having gained entry to their realm by committing a crime punishable by decapitation. He has been convicted and sentenced for slandering the gods of the state in public (this in the printed version; Kasack admits that in the actual dream, the "gods of the state" were the leaders of the Nazi party—reenforcing the curiously literal quality of the dream, in which apprehensions generated by reality are not very much distorted or disguised); the execution, similarly, was carried out before the eyes of all. But the abyss between life and death does not appear, the victim does not quickly lose consciousness, he feels no bodily pain but simply stands there with his blank neckstump: "a single sharp cut had separated [him] from life on earth, [leaving him] still in the midst of the enraged, heaving mob and at the same time in the place of death." In his dream, Kasack is surprised but not overwhelmed by the contradictions between his expectations and his experience: according to the laws of anatomy, the unity of head and body has been destroyed; but someone simply set his head on his neck "like a helmet," [27] and he continues to function. The reader is gradually induced to accept the impossible as plausible by a matter-of-fact style that belies what it is describing (somewhat in the manner of Kafka). Like the dreamer, he clings to the memories of normality even as reality alters its usual visage: as the two worlds drift apart, the inhabitant of the realm of death makes vain efforts to communicate with the vanishing universe of "life," from which his "crime" has sundered him forever.

Thus, at first the dream-figure remains visible to those who had demanded his execution (as they remain visible to him), including his wife, his children, and his friends, and his instinct is to establish contact with the latter, to reassure them (and to assure himself) that

27. Kasack, "Der Totentraum," in *Mosaiksteine*, p. 355.

the dead do not depart, but "observe everything on earth, as if they
still belonged to the sphere of living creatures." The initial response
of the "dead," then, is to refuse to accept the possibility that a
permanent metamorphosis in their condition (and in the nature of
reality) has occurred: "I told [them] of this strange intermediate
state in which I found myself, but soon noticed that my voice made
no more sound (because my organs had been severed); I noticed
that no one heard me." Writing a message proves equally futile, as
the letters dissolve before the eyes of the "living" before they can
be deciphered: "everything seemed to have been written with
water, nothing remained but some scarcely meaningful scratches of
a broken pen, empty furrows on an empty sheet of paper." One is
reminded of Joseph K's desperate attempt tp prove that nothing has
changed by pulling out his identity papers and thrusting them
before the eyes of his mysterious accusers. In his dream, Kasack
gradually acknowledges his changed environment, without abandoning hopes of reestablishing contact with normality, until he is
literally split into a kind of Dostoevskeyan double, in the manner of
Ivan Karamazov, uncertain which is his real "self," caught between
two physical (and, symbolically, spiritual) realities:

> I continued to imagine myself visible on the surface of the earth,
> even though parts of me were drawn down to unfathomable depths
> and were condensed there into a phantom which I saw moving about
> like an external image of myself. I was already assigned to other
> prisoners of this hell, and noticed the shapes of guards approaching
> suddenly like cardboard figures, which reached gigantic proportions
> as I looked. The landscape of lava-like rocks in irregular layers
> stretched endlessly into the distance.[28]

Primo Levi's principle that "nothing is true outside the Lager" is
transposed by Kasack into a dramatic illustration of his less specific
conviction that terror and the horrible should not be evaded by the
writer who has lived under their influence. At first the realities of
death (the more "normal" condition, symbolically, one is tempted to
say the "Lager-truth") appear in distorted form; the atmosphere of
fear and desolation (the threatening shapes of the guards, for
example) belongs to an alien environment. But anyone familiar with
the uninitiated prisoner's initial response to his entry into a

28. Ibid., pp. 356–57.

concentration camp will detect a remarkable imaginative sympathy between the actual accounts and Kasack's dream-vision, ostensibly not concerned with that experience at all—as if the threat of repression at home (Kasack's dream, after all, was unconsciously inspired by a desire to rebel against the sources of power in the state) possessed a secret kinship with the facts of oppression in the camps, the unreal reality of the authentic experience.

For example: Kasack's dream-figure receives advice and information which—given certain differences in emphasis to be expected of a dream—many an actual inmate might recognize:

> From one of the dead who had already been in this circle of the underworld for some time I learned that some guards were friendlier, but most were increasingly fierce and malicious. He gave me many suggestions: for example, how I could avoid drinking at meals the hot brew that was like molten lead. By a clever turn of the hand I could unobtrusively pour out the contents of the bowl, without being noticed by the guards. But I was never able to ascertain this way of holding it.[29]

From the center of "the destructive element," events assume a strange logic—the question of self-protection and survival was always uppermost in the minds of the real prisoners—yet the will of the dreamer is still reluctant to assent to what experience proclaims (his inability to learn the "rules" of the death-realm); rather, he feels a compulsion to announce to those he left behind that the transition from life to death is continuous, not abrupt, that in death as in life there is "a way of torment leading to purification," and especially he feels a need to correct some of the misconceptions about death that he himself had expressed while still alive. Again one is reminded of the two worlds of Joseph K., the one in which he protests his innocence, and the one in which he seems unable to ignore the vague accusations which alter his life. The imagery of Kasack's dream supports such a schizophrenic reality: "I saw everything as one views a distant event through glass, approaching and drawing one towards it." First, verbal communication fails; then written messages; finally, visual contact grows dimmer, until what was once real becomes questionable, and all contact between the realms of life and death is broken off—the displacement is complete:

29. Ibid., p. 358.

But now I was compelled to notice that I myself, as earlier the handwriting and the paper, faded more and more from the eyes of my family, more and more withered away into invisibility, even though in death I remained physically embodied, so that I could hardly seem only a shadow to them.

For a while I saw them anxiously running back and forth seeking me or some trace of me. But then they went about their usual business, without acknowledging my presence. And since they no longer thought of me, the bond that joined me to the life of the past gave way, and my dead visage lost sight of their forms. I still saw only the guards, who pressed toward me like a gray wall, and this time it was the wickeder ones who seized me. Then the earthly part of me was extinguished, and I knew nothing more of my death, because I had forgotten life.[30]

When life seems superceded by a condition of existence that the word or concept "death" insufficiently describes, a condition which perhaps we should call an eternal moment of apprehension fused with terror, then the artist has come close to defining the rational-irrational atmosphere that flourishes in most literature of atrocity, a broadly imaginative equivalent to Primo Levi's "dawn command of Auschwitz," which similarly banished his past life into the realm of unreality as "a brief pause, a deception of the senses, a dream"; in Kasack as in Levi, an immediate threat, however incredible in its implications, variously embodied, dissipates the familiar world and compels the mind and the senses to accept its replacement, if only because the single alternative is to return to a void. To salvage some fragment of his past—a gesture, a memory, some token that an "awakening" must follow this interminable sleep—this is the aim of Kasack's dream-figure. His failure is also a failure of his "forgotten life" (of which he himself, of course, was once a part, and which in the dream he tries so desperately to contact); his reluctance to abandon the attempt reflects the difficulty with which the modern mind (and the creative imagination) accepts the fact that the events culminating in the Holocaust have altered that "forgotten life" beyond recognition; and the futility of his efforts, signified by the hiatus in his memory, suggests that anyone determined to communicate the profoundest implica-

30. Ibid.

tions of this rupture will have to find uniquely convincing ways of rejoining and revitalizing the two alien worlds.

But like the survivors in Nelly Sachs's "Chorus of the Rescued," "leave-taking" may be the only legacy to facilitate such a rehabilitation, a dubious eventuality indeed: perhaps all the artist can do is clarify the reality that lies behind such a rupture. No one will ever isolate the single most crucial crisis for the individual implicit in the Holocaust experience, but certainly included among a list of them must be a new association, or more precisely, a new and unprecedented alliance, with death. Ernst Wiechert's *Forest of the Dead*, Kasack's "Dream of Death," Borchert's spectral landscape of death in his native Hamburg, the young girl who dreamt of lying beneath a pile of corpses—these and countless other illustrations confirm the significance to the imagination of a realm whose features were subtly transforming the familiar contours of life and finally undermining their very stability. The traditional descents to the underworld recorded in the epic poets and Dante always culminated in a return to the living characterized by a spiritual strengthening, a celebration of the future, perhaps a temporary nostalgia (in some instances) for the departed, but never a permanent mood of despair. But the various landscapes of death we have encountered, physical or spiritual, are encompassed by gloom and shrouded with the melancholy fact that nothing—not love or understanding, not memory or hope—will ever again be the same.

An archetypal example of the fiction resulting from these circumstances, assimilating as it does many of the extraordinary responses to the reality of the Holocaust examined in this chapter, is Pierre Gascar's novella *The Season of the Dead*, a tale that begins with the idea of death—"Dead though they may be, the dead do not immediately become ageless"—and ends with the fact of death—"After a moment I wiped away my tears and went back to my dead." Death insinuates itself into the substance of the narrative until it no longer represents merely the termination of life, but the very marrow of existence, the secret at its heart. It is as if the narrator had reversed the direction of the pilgrim Dante's voyage and concluded the journey in the depths of the Inferno face-to-face with a secular incarnation of the negation of spirit, a truth far more mournfully essential than the radiant divine Rose of Paradise—that hunted man, haunted by fear, condemned to extermination, is reduced to nullity.

As a French soldier, not a Jew, who spent five years in German prisoner-of-war camps, Gascar must have been in a position, like his narrator, to observe the process whereby the mind moves imperceptibly toward the content of this vision, unaccustomed as it may be at first to the literally buried horror at the end of the ordeal. For the controlling metaphor of *The Season of the Dead*, the setting of the story, is a cemetery adjoining the French prisoner-of-war camp in the Ukraine, and the chief task of the narrator and his associates is to offer decent interment to those of his comrades who die, from whatever cause, during their imprisonment. A grave-digger (and prisoner) assigned to bury the "war dead," the narrator quickly realizes that this formula "had lost its heroic sense without becoming obsolete" [31]; and thus, in the beginning he unconsciously drifts into the role of reinterpreting, or rediscovering, the meaning of that traditional epithet, "war dead," to penetrate, as it were, the euphemism of death shorn of its heroic associations but as yet lacking a concrete image, an embodiment in the action of the narrative, to add moral and emotional flesh to this discovery.

Just as the men have entered their "second captivity" in this disciplinary prisoner-of-war camp (having previously attempted several abortive escapes), so the narrator slowly penetrates to a "second" sense of his own reality, and all men's, a sense in which death plays a new part, not only as a persistent threat, which is expected in wartime, but as a phenomenon that disfigures his attitude toward himself and the bond that links him to life. The feeling spreads to the other members of the cemetery detachment, who live, Gascar suggests, from "death to death," which distinguishes them from the other prisoners: "We belonged to another world, we were a team of ghosts returning every morning to a green peaceful place, we were workers in death's garden, characters in a long preparatory dream through which, from time to time, a man would suddenly break, leaping into his last sleep" (p. 185). Their routine, given the circumstances, may *seem* ordinary, but fortified by imagery like that in the passage above, which animates

31. Pierre Gascar, "The Season of the Dead," in *Beasts and Men and The Seed*, trans. Jean Stewart and Merloyd Lawrence (New York: Meridian Books, 1960), pp. 175–76.

associations beneath the surface level of the narrative, it exercises a
stealthy effect on our conception of their labor, and finally on the
narrator's conception of it too.

The transition, as so often in the literature of atrocity, is made
possible by the fate of the Jews, whose suffering, even in narratives
like the present one (Kosinski's *The Painted Bird* and Semprun's *The
Long Voyage* are other examples), where it does not constitute the
central theme of the work, catalyzes the imagination as it expands
to symbolic dimensions and ultimately magnetizes the narrator's
attention with its fascinating and inscrutable appeal. For in their
closely supervised confinement the only escape is for the eyes, and
the only horizon, the endless trains of Jewish deportees from the
Ukrainian town adjoining the prison camp and the cemetery; until
finally, in a silent communion with victims more irrevocably
doomed than they, they read in the fate of the Jews a dramatic
pantomime of their own destiny as men.

An unspoken bond unites the two groups, as if "some final inner
process of preparation was taking place" (as indeed it was), though
as yet their future is still a matter of anticipation, of intellectual
formulation, rather than concrete and visceral fact. One morning,
however, the prisoners make a discovery that approaches (though it
does not yet quite reach) the intensity of an epiphany:

> we saw a man lying dead by the roadside on the way to the graveyard.
> There was no face; it was hidden in the grass. There was no
> distinguishing mark, save the armlet with the star of David. There was
> no blood. There is practically no blood in the whole of this tale of
> death. [pp. 189–90]

Death anonymous but embodied, a paradigmatic emblem of the
mystery locked in the narrator's experience, with no assurance of a
solution other than the visible testimony before his eyes—the
challenge then as now is to transform the hidden features into a
human identity and to distill some significance from this ominous
death of the Jew. Groping for an attitude consonant with the
grotesque truth implicit in the discovery of the corpse, the narrator
concludes that "every death invents death anew," a harsh, unconsoling, even terrifying principle, since it stifles the prospect of life's
renewal after the impulse to destroy has exhausted itself, as if death
extended its stranglehold beyond the last act of the tragedy,

preventing catharsis and poisoning the future—much in the spirit of the conclusion of *King Lear*.

As if to seal the finality of the rift between the idea of the tragedy of death as man's earthly lot and the grim principle enunciated by the narrator, the narrator together with his German guard visits the ancient Jewish cemetery of the Ukrainian district, where in a dramatic confrontation they explore familiar and unconventional attitudes toward the dead. The German, a pastor in peacetime who himself spent two years in a concentration camp for his "subversive" moral views, then was assigned to this comparatively safe post, traces the letters on the gravestones, reads out the Hebrew dates, and finds solace in the conviction, preached by his religion, that "death belongs to the past."

The narrator, on the other hand, intrigued by the strange breaking branch carved on most of the gravestones, converts its symbolism into the vexing inquiry: "when death has come, has one finished dying?" His subsequent reflection echoes the language and the very imagery of Nelly Sachs's poem: "Perhaps we are doomed to a perpetual leavetaking from that which was life and which lies in the depth of the night, as eternal as the patient stars"—a fearful constellation, illuminating each man's life with a kind of darkness visible, and casting a lurid glow on the ambiguous insight that every death invents death anew. If, as the narrator meditates aloud, "the moment of death is never over" (pp. 198–99) then life may be an immortality in reverse, a "demortality"—to coin a term in the absence of a vocabulary to describe his response—and the unidentified Jewish corpse, like his ancestors in the cemetery, are merely ultimate extensions of a condition that now must define the living as well as the dead.

Absorbed by these unorthodox but increasingly relevant premises, the mind finds it more and more difficult to accommodate itself to the old idea of a world where vitality and survival take priority as human values, and where the persistence of nature assures a hopefully recurring cycle of day following night and spring the winter:

> There was still the sky, the sky between the branches when you raised your head, an unyielding sky, still heavy with threats. Daylight is up there. I must be dreaming. It was as if when you pushed open

the shutters after a night full of bad dreams the influx of light proved powerless to dispel the terrifying visions of the darkness from your eyes. And yet everything is there, quite real. [pp. 203–04]

Waking is dreaming, light is darkness, life is death: contradictions grow logical in this universe *if* we can adjust to the perspective of abnormality (from the point of view of our own safe normalcy) that Gascar's imaginative vision slowly unfolds before our eyes. Seeking to rescue experience from the shackles of a random chaos, the narrator reveals the possibility of a deeper secret meaning behind the facade of our comfortable reality:

These things were on the scale of a cosmogony. Or worse: they took you into a universe which perhaps had always existed behind the solid rampart of the dead, and of which the metaphors of traditional rhetoric only gave you superficial glimpses: where . . . one could not keep body and soul together, where one really was bled white and died like a dog. [p. 214]

Thus, Gascar incorporates into his narrative the very dilemma which has inspired so much critical controversy—a *univers concentrationnaire* which refuses to be subjugated by the rules of traditional rhetoric, but which asserts the essential realities of its hell in spite of the dry husks of verbal formulae which contain or express them. The reader participates in the struggle, as the narrator concedes (like George Steiner) that monstrous orders disfigure a language, but insists that language did not present an insuperable barrier between the human imagination and the horror that beckoned beyond the solid ramparts of the dead. The vitality of that horror lurks in the imagery with which Gascar clothes his idea: "In those days the German language was like a landscape full of ravines, from the depths of which rose tragic echoes" (p. 215). One of these ravines is the treacherous transvaluation of values which experience daily confirms, for the French narrator quickly learns that any expression of compassion for the Ukrainian Jews threatens his own safety: "fraternization had become conspiracy" (p. 216).

The German guard, on the other hand, the former pastor, authorized by the camp commandant to make some "human" approaches to the doomed Jews, desperately mouths the platitudes of his faith in a vain effort to salvage his own crumbling humanity in the presence of their fate: "This is the last form of priesthood open to me . . . the last power I've got. It's inadequate and clumsy, it needs to be exercised upon a living object, a single object" (p. 217). Unwilling to accept the axiom that the Jews are no longer living objects in any meaningful sense, the German utters the last gasp of a dying principle of love in the midst of an encroaching spiritual anarchy, and the narrator's response provides an apt climax to this little conversational parable on language and values, or more precisely perhaps, language and silence: "His lips went on moving. I said nothing. I would not have known what to say" (p. 217).

The failure of language and of the traditional values it expresses is one discovery impressed on the imagination of the narrator. But his education has far to go, for when he abandons the "way" of Ernst, the German pastor turned camp guard who preaches love even as he executes the heartless authority of his masters, the narrator has nothing but the graveyard to assure his identity, the "only innocent place" left, as he calls it, offering him a kind of immunity, though from what he does not specify—certainly, at least, from the delusions of language. Having spoken earlier of the German language as a landscape full of ravines, Gascar seems to transmute the metaphor into the subsequent activity of his narrator, a dramatic incarnation of the principle that the concreteness of the Holocaust repudiates the abstractness of the words used to describe it. For instinctively he is drawn away from life on the surface, to death in the depths, as he and his companions unite in a kind of "cult of the grave," whose weeds, in a phrase reminiscent of Borchert, "are the white hair of the dead" concealing some terrifying knowledge, some "haunting dream of underground" still to be disclosed to them (p. 218).

They decide to dig a trench from the nearby forest to the cemetery to drain off the rainwater that is scoring the graves, and in the process they are lured into physical labyrinths of extinction beyond the most extravagant excursions of the imagination, notwithstanding their prior experience with the anonymous corpse. For the ditch-diggers "accidentally" uncover, in a quest that merges the literal and the symbolic layers of the tale, a clandestine, subterranean charnel-house, a mass grave of half-decayed, hastily buried bodies—apparently Jews executed secretly before their arrival in the camp. They are naturally horrified by the spectacle, but the episode reaches far profounder dimensions, becoming a kind of parable of the Holocaust for all humanity, representing as it does the fundamental truth which the imagination must face with absolute immediacy, ungraced by any mitigating idea or deed—for Gascar, the grand metaphor of *l'univers concentrationnaire* is the kind of death suffered by the Jews, and here language plunges into the ravine as conviction wrestles with disbelief:

> This was death—these liquifying muscles, this half-eaten eye, those teeth like a dead sheep's; death, no longer decked with grasses, no longer ensconced in the coolness of a vault, no longer lying sepulchered in stone, but sprawling in a bog full of bones, wrapped in a drowned man's clothes, with its hair caught in the earth.

The narrator is forced by the discovery to distinguish between "the idealized dead," the inherited, civilized conception of what it means to die, and "the state of insane desolation to which we are reduced when life is done." The perception is equally essential for anyone seeking entry to the realms of the literature of atrocity, for it reverses the customary growth toward insight that fiction has trained the imagination to expect by transforming death into a vital image and reducing life to an aborted journey, "wreckage stranded in the cul-de-sac of an unfinished tunnel" (pp. 220–21).

For Gascar has created a pattern to complete the scheme of reality toward which the authors discussed earlier in this chapter were groping: the stench of the exhumed corpses gradually permeates the landscape (inner and outer) inhabited by the narrator and his friends; the grisly site of previous slaughter proclaims the appalling notice from underground that history has arrived at a unique stage in its cycle, foretold earlier in the title of the story—a season of the dead. No one can predict its duration, but its temporary triumph is undeniable; the pastor himself finally confesses to the narrator, "we ought to realize that there can't be any true life afterwards for us, who have endured these sights" (p. 227). But even such professions of disillusionment, like professions of faith, are suspect, because their rhetoric introduces an inescapable barrier between lips and imagination. True as the guard's statement may be, it cannot rival in potency of response the final insight of the prisoners themselves, caretakers in the cemetery of the world, who on "the fringe of the war, on the fringe of the massacres, on the fringe of Europe . . . seemed like hollow-eyed gardeners, sitters in the sun, fanatical weeders, busily working over the dead as over some piece of embroidery" (p. 233). In a world decimated of value, of the echoes of life, no other fruitful activity seems to remain; this is one of the most difficult lessons for the initiate into *l'univers concentrationnaire* to accept, since its consequences are so somber, the opportunities it offers for growth so limited—the mind instinctively recoils from the responsibilities it imposes.

Yet Gascar unerringly finds the dramatic equivalent for this melancholy conclusion in the last scene of *The Season of the Dead*, where against a background of rumbling convoys of mechanized death the narrator learns that the possibility of death as a personal tragedy has been eliminated from the universe, and that this in turn has altered the meaning of living, of survival itself. A spare grave is always kept empty, awaiting its corpse, and one morning his companion discovers that during the night it has been occupied by a living tenant, obviously a Jew from the town hiding from the Germans to escape deportation, who has another place of concealment during the day; and gradually, in a symbolic, silent communion with the grave through a series of laconic, surreptitious exchanges of notes—literally notes from underground this time—they identify him as one Lebovitch, whom the narrator had in fact met briefly in the nearby village earlier in the story. Thus, the unidentified corpse of a Jew who had inaugurated their initiation into the unreal reality of the underworld is ironically resurrected; and though he remains invisible to the end, he is given, in a grisly parody of human identity that is characteristic of the literature of atrocity, a local habitation and a name, which only make his doom seem more terrible than the fate of the faceless corpse, identified simply by his Star of David.

For Lebovitch—actually, in his brief notes he uses his initials, I. L., which the narrator is able to recognize—is the last hope of the principle of life in *l'univers concentrationnaire*, and though the prisoners grow obsessed with the challenge of keeping him alive, concealing provisions in the grave during the day that are gone the following morning, they are really paying homage, in a modern ritual of appeasement, to a power already dominating their souls: "our continual contact with death was beginning to open for us a sort of wicket gate into its domain" (p. 242). Before our eyes a replacement for Dante's Inferno is born, a creation of the Holocaust, shorn of allegorical trappings and theological dimensions, a literal hell that nevertheless treads on the boundaries of myth ("We continued to offer food to this Egyptian tomb," p. 244). In such an environment man is a victim even when he seems to control his actions; when a prisoner dies and Lebovitch's haven is occupied by an actual corpse, the narrator and his friend dig another spare grave alongside it, but with the uneasy feeling that they "were preparing to bury an unseen friend" (p. 245)—their affirmative efforts are governed by the force they think they are resisting. From his charnel-house Lebovitch offers his message to an unresponsive world, to a world which, given the opportunity, could respond only with silence: "They've killed them all . . . killed them all! What is loneliness?" (p. 245).

But Lebovitch is a man as well as a prophet, announcing the new apocalypse while simultaneously longing for his own survival, and his complementary question to his associates "beyond the tomb"— "Are there any exemptions?"—confirms the reluctance of the imagination to assent to a principle of existence that shatters the established limits of reality and utterly destroys the nostalgia of hope. Lebovitch's loneliness is undefinable, incommunicable—the traditional idea of society as the locale of man's destiny or as an impetus to the growth of moral values seems utterly ludicrous here—and as the narrator tries to comprehend how such a forlorn and abandoned victim could still think in terms of "exemptions," he furnishes a glimpse into the "locale" that would replace this shattered reality, now declared bankrupt by the Holocaust: "I was beginning to find out how rich and full was insanity's account compared with the meager bankbooks of reason" (p. 246). At this point, to approach life with the resources of reason and all the attitudes behind this noble concept is equivalent to embracing madness, given the nature of the narrator's milieu; but embracing madness is equally futile, and the only other option, honestly if sadly acknowledged by Gascar, is a lucid recognition of how events have disfigured human values and condemned men to inhabit a landscape permanently consecrated to death, a doom accurately prefigured in the harrowing image of Lebovitch the Jew and the paradox of his simultaneously occupied and empty grave.

All that remains is epiphany, but not one ripe with the promise of future life and spiritual redemption. In few other works of this sort does the profusion of imagery reach so insistently across the abyss of

language to lure the imagination into the labyrinths of its unfamiliar
world. If the experience of the narrator alienates him from himself,
his own reservoir of usable values, what effect must it have on his
audience? Hence Gascar chooses his metaphors and similes as
weapons to assault the sensibilities and break down any remaining
reluctance on the part of the reader to accept the "abnormal" world
of his fiction as an accurate reflection of modern reality. As autumn
darkens the Ukrainian countryside and slows down the cycle of
nature, it is

> less like the morning after a bad dream or the lucid astonishment of
> life than the final draining away of all blood, the last stage of a slow
> hemorrhage behind which a few tears of lymph trickle, like mourners
> at life's funeral. Autumn brought a prospect of exhausted silence, of a
> world pruned of living sounds, of the reign of total death. [p. 247]

And we are invited, induced, persuaded to join the procession of
mourners and share with the narrator his loss of the last two vestiges
of hope that might preserve at least a faint gleam from the fading
security of the past: the life of Lebovitch, and—it sounds almost
weird in the context of the story—the love of a woman.

The first hope is of course vain: although the narrator confesses
that the precarious existence of the Jew became for him "the last
remaining symbol of a denial of death" (p. 247), he arrives one
morning at the cemetery to find the planks of the spare grave
thrown aside, and is greeted by a stark image that should waken
memories of an earlier experience: "At the bottom of the grave
there lay a black jacket without an armlet" (p. 248). Only this
solitary and mute shred of evidence beckons the imagination toward
the truth that "I. L." has vanished without a trace and "would
never come back" (p. 248), a dismal symbolic affirmation of what
the narrator had hoped desperately to deny, leaving only unanswered questions in the empty space of the grave—an epitaph of
silence. And when soon afterwards the convoys cease to rumble
across the plain, the epiphany expands into the remaining spiritual
vacuum, as I. L.'s private doom merges with the desolate fate of an
entire race. Now, the narrator acknowledges, autumn has really
arrived, the season of the dead is defined, and only the prospect of
winter looms: spring, like love, has apparently perished with the
victims of *l'univers concentrationnaire*.

Thus, when a love-theme is abruptly introduced near the end of the narrative, it is already anomalous, its resolution almost predictable: what have the emotions generated by this kind of feeling to do with a milieu like the one Gascar has portrayed? One evening the narrator notices a young Polish girl passing near the cemetery, and in a surge of the human in the very midst of its opposite, he clings to her image as a last refuge for his own withering "normal" affections. Her appeal—she is a stranger, and the narrator himself admits that he "knew nothing to suggest that she was worthy" (p. 240) of his devotion—remains a mystery; but in the rhythm of the story she introduces a faint echo of human promise against the reverberating crescendos of the negations of death. The girl, whose name is Maria and whose voice, we are told, could still express joy, temporarily disappears from the tale during the Lebovitch episode, but returns with autumn and bears with her in that austere landscape the possibility of romantic longing; and some deep independent impulse of the imagination, an unconscious "will-to-life" in the midst of all this terrible chaos of fear and suffering, seems to justify her presence at this crucial moment in the narrator's emotional existence.

Gascar has conjured up a dramatic confrontation between pre-Holocaust reality and *l'univers concentrationnaire,* but only to confirm what we have already suspected, what the narrator's experience has made inevitable: the irrevocable incompatibility of love and death. For as Maria visits the burial-ground and the narrator (with the sentimental guard's permission) rushes to the verge of the forest to embrace her in the sinister setting of a darkening sky and a rising wind, their fleeting union is only the prelude to a more enduring, eternal separation. The very language with which the narrator describes his bliss undermines its stability, as he equates the "ultimate salvation" of Maria's arms with an instant of "blindness" and "oblivion." In a world consecrated to death, the traditional rhetoric of love and religion (the implications of the name "Maria" are unavoidable) is confused with the vocabulary of nihilism, as words fail and only the image can express the tensions with which Gascar concludes *The Season of the Dead*:

It was the only refuge within which to break the heavy, clipped wings that thought had set growing on one's temples, the only place where the mind, like a heavy-furred moth dazzled by the great light of death, could for an instant assuage its longing to return to the warm, original darkness of its chrysalis. [p. 249]

Alien to the narrator's universe, frightened by the urgency of his gestures, Maria kisses him and flees, but his instinctive effort to follow her is futile: "Within me and about me a great silence had fallen. After a moment I wiped away my tears and went back to my dead" (p. 249).

There is really no choice, as Gascar's grotesque metaphors assert; the tug of the chrysalis is inescapable, and clipped wings cannot, given what the narrator has endured, soar to a heaven of love. In an ironic reversal of the living epic hero's inability to embrace the spirit of his departed companion in the underworld, Gascar's unheroic narrator enters into his heritage of death-in-life while the still vital spirit of Maria fades into the hopeless distance. The immediacy of his proximity to death, to such death, imprisons his awareness and sensibility, destroying, for the present at any rate, the possibility of love. In the wake of the failure of its ultimate salvation floats the ultimate revelation that for him, as for I. L. and his fellow Jews, there is no exemption, and that he must now enact in his own destiny the answer to Lebovitch's horror-stricken question, "What is loneliness?" (p. 245).

Thus Gascar adds impressive imaginative testimony to Primo Levi's more restricted principle that, for him, "nothing was true outside the Lager," that all the rest was "a brief pause, a deception of the senses, a dream." The conception of two such worlds, disproportionate, estranged, coexistent but barred from communion by the unreconcilable quality of their assumptions, is an essential premise of the literature examined in the following pages. The gross distinctions between these worlds are by now clear, but subtle and elusive ones exist that are more difficult to explain. The role of death is a major source of confusion, and Gascar has done much to clarify it.

Some complementary and highly original insights are added in a unique and remarkable work, still untranslated, by Jean Améry, *Jenseits von Schuld und Sühne (Beyond Guilt and Atonement)*, in which the author tries to define the attitude of intellectuals like himself toward the wholly unanticipated ordeal of torture and humiliation which he endured in Auschwitz and other camps. For example, in a single lucid (and slightly sardonic) formulation, Améry illuminates (quite unintentionally, of course) the Maria episode in *The Season of the Dead*: "In the concentration camp there was no Tristan music to accompany death, only the bellowing of the SS and the Kapos [brutal inmates, often criminals, in charge of certain prison barracks]." But most significantly, Améry makes explicit a theme that Gascar and other authors considered in this study explore, without formulating it as precisely as Améry does.

Améry observes that one consequence of the camp experience was the "total collapse of the aesthetic idea of death." The intellectual, especially one of German training (Améry, an acrostic for Mayer, was himself Austrian), nourished by Schopenhauer, Wagner, Mann, and Rilke, was suddenly confronted with a reality that left him paralyzed and without resources, groping for a response: "There was no place in Auschwitz for death in its literary, philosophical, or musical forms. No bridge led from death in Auschwitz to 'Death in Venice.' "[32] But traditionally, "death in its literary, philosophical, or musical forms" has provided the imagination of all men, not merely intellectuals, with metaphors for confronting and understanding our ultimate fate; art and metaphysics have collaborated in the past to derive eschatologies that make human destiny, even under the most adverse circumstances, endurable to the individual. In his striking antithesis between death in Auschwitz and "Death in Venice," Améry articulates what unwilling victims of *l'univers concentrationnaire* must have encountered with a mute dismay, and in the process discloses a major legacy of the camp experience, one that enriched the literary mind long before it reached the perceptions of the historian.

For after the empirical invalidation of the "aesthetic idea of death" which had fortified the prisoner against adversity in his "normal" life, he was left defenseless; and if in spite of this he tried to establish a spiritual or metaphysical attitude toward death, he stumbled once more, in Améry's words, "against the reality of the camp [*Lagerrealität*], which condemned the hopelessness of such an

32. Jean Améry, *Jenseits von Schuld und Sühne* (Munich: Szczesny Verlag, 1966), p. 33. Translation mine.

attempt." As a result—and here Améry contributes an invaluable distinction for anyone seeking to appreciate the literary imagination's use of *l'univers concentrationnaire*—the intellectual, like his nonintellectual comrade, concerned himself "not with death [*Tod*], but with the *process of dying [Sterben]*." [33]

Améry cites the example of an SS-man who slit open a prisoner's belly and filled it with sand, and suggests that, given such possibilities, an individual would scarcely occupy himself with *whether* one must die, or *that* he must, but *how* it would happen. Thus, a primary ingredient of the tragic vision is eliminated for the artist, who is faced with the challenge of infusing literature with a sense of "dying" commensurate with the *Lagerrealität* and creating an art beyond tragedy, where death in Auschwitz is translated into "Death in Auschwitz"—an art capable of incorporating implications about human experience unimaginable in the pre-Holocaust perfection of "Death in Venice." Where dying was omnipresent, Améry concludes, death withdrew.

Améry's analysis not only illuminates retrospectively the climax and other episodes in Gascar's *Season of the Dead*, but also sheds necessary light on the obsessive quality of the literature discussed in subsequent chapters. For a reader accustomed to the secure terrain of *Tod*, with its assumptions about cause and effect in human experience and the consolations of tragedy it makeṣ available, inevitably feels an uncanny and often intolerable disquiet when cast adrift on the uncertain sea of *Sterben*, especially when we recollect that this "simple" dichotomy represents an estrangement vastly more far-ranging than the terms themselves imply. Perhaps the discomfort engendered by this situation accounts for some of the psychological and emotional rejection frequently provoked by the content of the literature of atrocity.

For as this literature usurps the bulwarks of our civilization—childhood, family, love, a sense of the human spirit, reason, an idea of the will as a faculty that shapes if it does not always control the future, and a durable faith in the uninterrupted processes of time and history—as this displacement occurs, the reader finds himself unconsciously maneuvered into an alien territory devoid of familiar landmarks; and if he persists, he becomes himself a temporary

33. Ibid., p. 34.

inhabitant of *l'univers concentrationnaire*, recreating, in collaboration with the artist, the features of a reality that history has declared extinct but which continues to haunt the memory and imagination with echoes of an unquenchable despair.

*The most frightening aspect of our
present world is not the horrors in
themselves, the atrocities, the
technological exterminations, but the
one fact at the very root of it all: the
fading away of any human
criterion. . . .*

Erich Kahler

*. . . a man can cross the threshold of
death before his body is lifeless.*

Alexander Solzhenitsyn

Death too can be a way of life.

Jakov Lind

True art, says Erich Kahler, expanding Erich Auerbach's idea of
"mimesis" or imitation, is and has to be

> an act of conquest, the discovery of a new sphere of human
> consciousness, and thereby of new reality. It lifts into the light of our
> consciousness a state of affairs, a layer of existence, that was dormant
> in the depth of our unconscious, that was buried under obsolete
> forms, conventions, habits of thought and experience. And by showing
> this latent reality, by making it visible to us, open to our grasp, the
> work of art actually *creates* this new reality as a new sphere of our
> conscious life. There is no true art without this exploratory quality,
> without this frontier venture to make conscious the preconscious, to
> express what has never been expressed before and what heretofore
> had seemed inexpressible.[1]

Once we recognize that critical dogmas of this sort are not to be
measured for their "truth"—if this were the case, most critical
principles would cancel each other out—but for their relevance,
their appropriateness, their consistency with a given body of
material—once we recognize this, then Kahler's definition of art
proves singularly applicable to the literature of atrocity. All serious

1. Erich Kahler, *The Tower and the Abyss* (New York: The Viking Press, 1967), p. 151.

art undoubtedly aspires toward the revelation of a new sense of reality, but the literature we are concerned with possessed the curious advantage of having such a "new" reality already available, pressing with equal force on the conscious and (as we have just seen) the preconscious life of the artist, and seeking only a way of being convincingly presented to an audience of contemporary readers. Normally, nonfiction is excluded from such definitions of art, since by its very nature it seeks to reflect a historical reality without manipulating or distorting details, drawing on the very conventions and habits of thought and experience that Kahler excludes. Most autobiographies, for example, orient us toward the past rather than shaping fresh visions of the future. Yet Kahler's terms are broad enough, and the nature of the Holocaust experience sufficiently unique, to permit autobiography to be included in his definition of art—if one could be found.

Most of the autobiographies concerned with *l'univers concentrationnaire* numb the consciousness without enlarging it and providing it with a fresh or unique perception of the nature of reality, chiefly because the enormity of the atrocities they recount finally forces the reader to lose his orientation altogether and to feel as though he were wandering in a wilderness of evil totally divorced from any time and place he has ever known—a reality not latent in, but external to, his own experience. The most impressive exception to this general rule is a work that has already become a classic in our time, an autobiography which, in its compressed imaginative power and artful presentation of the circumstances of the author's internment in Auschwitz, yields the effect of an authentic *Bildungsroman*—except that the youthful protagonist becomes an initiate into death rather than life—Elie Wiesel's *Night*.

A reader confronted with this slim volume himself becomes an initiate into death, into the dark world of human suffering and moral chaos we call the Holocaust; and by the end he is persuaded that he inhabits the kind of negative universe which Lear invokes when he enters with Cordelia dead in his arms: "Thou'lt come no more; / Never, never, never, never, never," and is prompted to intone together with Lear: "No, no, no life"—a final rejection of love, of family, of the past, of order, of "normality"—that lies dead on the stage at his feet. Wiesel's *Night* is the terminus a quo for any investigation of the implications of the Holocaust, no matter what the terminus ad quem; on its final page a world lies dead at our feet, a world we have come to know as our own as well as Wiesel's, and whatever civilization may be rebuilt from its ruins, the silhouette of its visage will never look the same.

Night conveys in gradual detail the principle that Hermann Kasack had evoked in his dream: death has replaced life as the measure of our existence, and the vision of human potentiality nurtured by centuries of Christian and humanistic optimism has been so completely effaced by the events of the Holocaust that the future stretches gloomily down an endless vista into futility. The bleakness of the prospect sounds melodramatic but actually testifies to the reluctance of the human spirit to release the moorings that have lashed it to hope and to accept the consequences of total abandonment. Disappointed in a second coming, man has suffered a second going, a second fall and expulsion, not from grace this time but from humanity itself; and indeed, as we shall see in one of the most moving episodes in his harrowing book, Wiesel introduces a kind of second crucifixion, consecrating man not to immortality but to fruitless torture and ignominious death. Yet one is never permitted to forget what is being sacrificed, what price, unwillingly, the human creature has had to pay for *l'univers concentrationnaire*, what heritage it has bequeathed to a humanity not yet fully aware of the terms of the will.

Works like *Night* furnish illumination for this inheritance, an illumination all the more necessary (especially if one is to go on to explore the literature succeeding it) when we consider how unprepared the human mind is to confront the visions it reveals. A book like *Anne Frank: The Diary of a Young Girl*, incontestably more popular and influential than Wiesel's *Night*, by its very widespread acceptance confirms our unpreparedness to respond to the grimmer realities and the imaginative re-creations of the literature of atrocity. In many respects *Anne Frank* is the reverse of *Night*—in its premises, in the nature of the experiences it narrates, and in its conclusions; in fact, it draws on the very "obsolete forms, conventions, habits of thought and experience" which, in Erich Kahler's formulation, the writer must burrow through if he is to create for his reader the new reality we dignify by the name of art.

Of course, the comparison is meant to be objective rather than invidious; Anne Frank was indeed a young girl, and her eventual fate was more terrifyingly final, if no more fearful, than Wiesel's. But her *Diary*, cherished since its appearance as a celebration of human courage in the face of impending disaster, is in actuality a conservative and even old-fashioned book which appeals to nostalgia and does not pretend to concern itself with the uniqueness of the reality transforming life outside the attic walls that insulated her vision. Bruno Bettelheim long ago provoked angry criticism for suggesting the limitations in the tactics of the Frank family; whether or not it was justified is irrelevant here, but it further confirms the sentimentality of an audience that pursues Anne's reality—like Anne herself—only to the arrival of the "green police," that is unable or unwilling to peer beyond the end of her tale to the "new" reality symbolized by her wretched death in the barracks of Bergen-Belsen.

Anne Frank's *Diary* was written in the innocence (and the "ignorance") of youth, but its conclusions form the point of departure for Wiesel's *Night* and most authors in the tradition of atrocity; indeed, their work constitutes a sequel to hers and ultimately challenges the principle that for her was both premise and epitaph—"In spite of everything, I still think people are good at heart"—a conception of character which dies hard, but dies pitilessly, in *Night* and in literature of atrocity in general. The optimism which nurtured her faith in humanity is symbolized by her family's quarantine from reality during their years of hiding; their real story, and the story of the transformed world that determined their destiny, began after Anne's diary ended. The values it preserves—love, devotion, courage, family unity, charity—are mocked by the fate she suffered (mocked too, one is inclined to add, by the fate of Lear and Cordelia), and to the informed reader only dramatize the inadequacy of heart-warming terms to describe the soul-chilling universe that destroyed her.

Yet Elie Wiesel recognized, as Anne Frank could not, that the values she celebrated might form an indispensable core for creating a magnetic field to attract fragments of atrocity, so that a permanent tension could be established between the two "forces" —a similar tension exists in some of the dreams we examined—a kind of polarity between memory and truth, nostalgia and a landscape of horror eerily highlighted by the pale reflection from vacant moral spaces. The literary effect is that memory ceases to offer consolation but itself becomes an affliction, intensifying the torment of the sufferer. Or rather, the usual content of memory is replaced by the harsh events of life in the concentration camp, until the past loses the hard edge of reality and the victim finds that both past and future, memory and hope—the "luxuries" of normal existence—are abruptly absorbed by an eternal and terrifying present, a present whose abnormality suddenly becomes routine. At this moment, life becomes too much for man and death assumes the throne in the human imagination.

A prospect like this must have led Camus to begin *The Myth of Sisyphus* with the statement that the only truly serious philosophical problem is suicide. In fact, Camus offers a lucid description of the consequences for man of his familiar world disappearing (consequences which Elie Wiesel presents in greater detail in *Night*):

> in a universe suddenly divested of illusions and lights, man feels an alien, a stranger. His exile is without remedy since he is deprived of the memory of a lost home or the hope of a promised land. This divorce between man and his life, the actor and his setting, is properly the feeling of absurdity.[2]

Too lucid, perhaps: Camus built intellectual defenses against a universe ruled by atrocity and the irrational in an attempt to prevent man's total defeat at its hands; Wiesel's relationship to *l'univers concentrationnaire* was far more tentative, and he was concerned no less with its effect than with its essence. The unreal reality of *Night* and most literature of atrocity exists in a world halfway between Camus's alternatives of suicide or recovery.

Perhaps even *essence* is an inexact word for Wiesel's appeal to the imagination as well as to the intelligence of the reader: asked some years after the liberation if he himself believed what had happened in Auschwitz, he replied, "I do not believe it. The event seems unreal, as if it occurred on a different planet." Even more paradoxically, he commented on the difficulty of coming to terms, not with the Holocaust—"one never comes to terms with it"—but with its tale:

> The full story of the Holocaust has not yet been told [1967!] All that we know is fragmentary, perhaps even untrue. Perhaps what we tell

2. Albert Camus, *The Myth of Sisyphus*, trans. Justin O'Brien (New York: Vintage Books, 1959), p. 5.

about what happened and what really happened has nothing to do one with the other. We want to remember. But remember what? And what for? Does anyone know the answer to this? [3]

What this ambiguity conceals we may never know, but it emphasizes the difficult struggle between language and truth that every author must engage in when he turns to this theme; and the important distinctions it draws between the Holocaust itself and its tale, "what really happened" and "what we tell about what happened," explains why Wiesel's autobiographical narrative reads more like fiction than "truth," since the power of the imagination to evoke an atmosphere does far more than the historian's fidelity to fact to involve the uninitiated reader in the atmosphere of the Holocaust.

Night is an account of a young boy's divorce from life, a drama of recognition whose scenes record the impotence of the familiar in the face of modern atrocity; at its heart lies the profoundest symbolic confrontation of our century, the meeting of man and Auschwitz (a meeting reenacted by Rolf Hochhuth in the culminating episode of *The Deputy*)—and this confrontation in turn confirms (as in Anthony Hecht's "More Light! More Light!") the defeat of man's tragic potentiality in our time, and the triumph of death in its most nihilistic guise. The book begins with the familiar, a devout Jewish family whose faith supports their human aspirations and who find their greatest solace—and assurance—in the opportunity of approaching, through diligent study, the divine intentions implicit in reality. The premises behind these aspirations are clarified for the boy narrator by Moché the Beadle, a humble, sagelike man-of-all-work in the Hasidic synagogue in the Transylvanian town where the boy grows up:

> "Man raises himself toward God by the questions he asks Him. . . . That is the true dialogue. Man questions God and God answers. But we don't understand his answers. We can't understand them. Because they come from the depths of the soul, and they stay there until death. You will find the true answers . . . only within yourself." [4]

With this counsel, says the narrator, "my initiation began"; but the kind of questions one asks in his dialogue with God are determined

3. "Jewish Values in the Post-Holocaust Future," *Judaism* 16 (Summer 1967): 283; 285.
4. Elie Wiesel, *Night*, trans. Stella Rodway (New York: Hill and Wang, 1960), p. 16.

by tradition and education and assumptions that have withstood the assault of adversity. Moché's wisdom is tested when he is deported, together with other foreign Jews from the small Hungarian town. One day (having escaped, miraculously, from his captors), he reappears with tales of Jews digging their own graves and being slaughtered, "without passion, without haste," and of babies who were thrown into the air while "the machine gunners used them as targets" (p. 18). The joy was extinguished from his eyes as he told these tales, but no one believed him—including the young narrator.

The inability of humanity to accept the version of reality proclaimed by Moché the Beadle brings us once again to the world of despair transcending tragedy inhabited by King Lear. For just as Lear attributes to the symbols of royalty more power than they possess, and stubbornly refuses to believe that his daughters are capable of the monstrous behavior and attitudes which his situation confirms, so the citizens of Sighet, the narrator's town, depend on the material "items" of their civilization, almost as if they were sacred talismans, for security. Their abandoned possessions, after their deportation, become symbols of a vanished people, a forgotten and now useless culture.

Throughout *Night*, Wiesel displays a remarkable talent for investing the "items" of reality, and of the fantastic "irreality" that replaces it, with an animistic quality, and then setting both on a pathway leading to an identical destination: death. For example, in this description of a landscape without figures, crowded with things but devoid of life—less macabre than Borchert's bomb-ruined Hamburg but equally devastating to the imagination—in this passage, presided over by an indifferent nature, symbols of an exhausted past turn into harbingers of a ghastly future:

> The street was like a market place that had suddenly been abandoned. Everything could be found there: suitcases, portfolios, briefcases, knives, plates, bank-notes, papers, faded portraits. All those things that people had thought of taking with them, and which in the end they had left behind. They had lost all value.
>
> Everywhere rooms lay open. Doors and windows gaped onto the emptiness. Everything was free for anyone, belonging to nobody. It was simply a matter of helping oneself. An open tomb.
>
> A hot summer sun. [p. 28]

Just as Lear undergoes a physical disrobing and a spiritual denudation before he gains a measure of self-knowledge and a more valid conception of reality, so the fifteen-year-old narrator of *Night* is gradually deprived of the props which have sustained him in his youth; but his experience is such that self-knowledge (as ultimately for Lear) becomes more of a burden than a consolation, and "a more valid conception of reality" sounds like a piece of impious rhetoric.

The displacement of life by death as a measure of existence is metaphorically reinforced in *Night*—as it is in some of Nelly Sachs's poems—by imagery that has become standard fare for much literature of atrocity, imagery facilitating the transition from one world to the other—the box-cars, for example, in which victims were transported:

> The doors were closed. We were caught in a trap, right up to our necks. The doors were nailed up; the way back was finally cut off. The world was a cattle wagon hermetically sealed. [p. 35]

"Liberation" from this hermetic world upon arrival in the camp, however, changes nothing; the "way back" ceases to have meaning, and man must turn his attention to absorbing the nature of the fearful "way ahead," and of finding methods to survive in spite of it, though the price he must pay for his survival is not calculable in figures inherited from the familiar past. He must somehow accommodate himself to an environment dominated by the macabre images of furnace and chimney, of flames in the night and smoke and reeking human flesh; and he must further acknowledge, against all his human impulses and religious training, the authenticity of this harsh, incredible fate:

> "Do you see that chimney over there? See it? Do you see those flames? (Yes, we did see the flames.) Over there—that's where you're going to be taken. That's your grave, over there. Haven't you realized it yet? You dumb bastards, don't you understand anything? You're going to be burned. Frizzled away. Turned into ashes." [p. 40]

The narrator's response introduces a tension that permeates the literature of atrocity: "Surely it was all a nightmare? An unimaginable nightmare?" With a desperate insistence he clings to a kind of emotional nostalgia, as if the stability of his being depends on an affirmative answer; but a subsequent experience shatters that stability permanently, and his efforts henceforth are devoted to making the reader relive the nightmare that continues to haunt him.

His world crumbles—as did Ivan Karamazov's—over the suffering of little children: his first night in the camp he sees babies hurled into a huge ditch from which gigantic flames are leaping:

> I pinched my face. Was I still alive? Was I awake? I could not believe it. How could it be possible for them to burn people, children, and for the world to keep silent? No, none of this could be true. It was a nightmare. . . . Soon I should wake with a start, my heart pounding, and find myself back in the bedroom of my childhood, among my books. . . . [p. 42]

The waking dream, haunted by the omnipresence of death, filled with "truths" unacceptable to reason but vivid, nevertheless, in their unquestionable actuality, leads first to a disorientation—the new inmates of the camp begin reciting the Jewish prayer for the dead *for themselves*—then to an attempt, at least by the young narrator, to discover mental attitudes commensurate with what the mind initially finds incomprehensible. The ritual incantation which marks his inauguration into *l'univers concentrationnaire* inverts the traditional pattern of autobiography and *Bildungsroman* by beginning with a repudiation that depletes the possibilities of life scarcely after it has begun; it signifies not only a boy's despair, but the exhaustion of meaning in a world henceforth unlike anything men have ever encountered:

> Never shall I forget that night, the first night in camp, which has turned my life into one long night, seven times cursed and seven times sealed. Never shall I forget that smoke. Never shall I forget the little faces of the children, whose bodies I saw turned into wreaths of smoke beneath a silent blue sky.
> Never shall I forget those flames which consumed my faith forever.
> Never shall I forget that nocturnal silence which deprived me, for all eternity, of the desire to live. Never shall I forget those moments which murdered my God and my soul and turned my dreams to dust. Never shall I forget these things, even if I am condemned to live as long as God Himself. Never. [pp. 43–44]

When the author of these words said a decade later that the events seemed unreal, that he did not believe they had happened t him, he emphasized not only their uniqueness, but also the paradoxical situation that life goes on even after it has "stopped," that Wiesel the man survives and talks about what happened—or remains silent—while Wiesel the writer, certainly in *Night*, has transcended history and autobiography and used the imagery of atrocity and his own experience to involve the nonparticipant in the essence of its world. With due respect to the suffering of the victims, one may repeat what has often been reported by students of the Holocaust—after a particular point, catalogues of brutalities and lists of statistics cease to affect the mind or the imagination, *not* because what they seek to convey lacks significance, but because the mind and imagination lack a suitable context for the information. Hence Wiesel's gradual shift in focus to the *implications* of the events, and his dramatic juxtaposition of carefully selected—though always genuine—scenes and feelings, create an indispensable vestibule for anyone wishing to venture farther into the mansion of Holocaust fiction.

When the first night ends, the narrator presumably has left normality behind, and death has infected his future: "The student of the Talmud, the child that I was, had been consumed in the flames. There remained only a shape that looked like me. A dark flame had entered into my soul and devoured it." The flame illuminates a vision of the self which under ordinary circumstances might be called self-knowledge, but here leads to a futility that negates tragedy and prefigures an exile more complete than anything Camus ever conjured up, a human condition that will have to create new terms for its existence, since Auschwitz has irrevocably breached any meaningful alliance between it and the past:

> Those absent no longer touched even the surface of our memories. We still spoke of them—"Who knows what may have become of them?"—but we had little concern for their fate. We were incapable of thinking of anything at all. Our senses were blunted; everything was blurred as in a fog. It was no longer possible to grasp anything. The instincts of self-preservation, of self-defense, of pride, had all deserted us. In one ultimate moment of lucidity it seemed to me that we were damned souls wandering in the half-world, souls condemned to wander through space till the generations of man came to an end, seeking their redemption, seeking oblivion—without hope of finding it. [pp. 45–46]

Even *oblivion* and *redemption*, once the sacred and universally recognizable alternatives in Dante's *Inferno* and *Paradiso*, are goals consigned to the limbo of language, words drawn from memory because reality affords no exact vocabulary for what Wiesel wishes to describe; Wiesel's "half-world," in many of its features remarkably like Hermann Kasack's purely imaginary *Totentraum* or Dream of Death, responds to evocation through vague images rather than specific ideas. Language is not reduced to silence, but it must be used more sparingly, and its range of allusion is governed by concrete experiences rather than by abstract conceptions: for example, the word *furnace*, which was not, says Wiesel, "a word empty of meaning: it floated on the air, mingling with the smoke. It was perhaps the only word which did have any real meaning here" (p. 48).

For Stephen Dedalus, words—"A day of dappled seaborne clouds," for instance—unlocked the mysteries of reality and disclosed vistas of beauty that inspired him to affirm his spirit before a hostile or indifferent world and trust his powers of creation to shape the future. In *l'univers concentrationnaire* of Wiesel's narrator, a diametrically opposite principle of negation prevails, whereby events silence the creative spirit, destroy the longings of youth, and cast over reality an all-embracing shadow of death.

One of the dramatic pinnacles of *Night* illustrates with unmitigated horror this reversal of the *Bildungsroman* formula: three prisoners, two men and a young boy, have been "convicted" of sabotage within the camp and are sentenced to be hanged before thousands of inmates. One imagines the boy, a "sad-eyed angel" on the gallows in the middle, the older victims on either side of him, a grotesque and painful parody—though literally true—of the original redemptive sufferer; the sentence is executed, and the prisoners are forced to march by the dangling bodies, face to face with their own potential fate:

> The two adults were no longer alive. Their tongues hung swollen, blue-tinged. But the third rope was still moving; being so light, the child was still alive. . . .
> For more than half an hour he stayed there, struggling between life and death, dying in slow agony under our eyes. And we had to look him full in the face. He was still alive when I passed in front of him. His tongue was still red, his eyes were not yet glazed.

Behind me, I heard [a] man asking:
"Where is God now?"
And I heard a voice within me answer him:
"Where is He? Here He is—He is hanging here on this gal-
lows. . . ."
That night the soup tasted of corpses. [p. 71]

More than one boy's life and another boy's faith is extinguished
here, and more than soup loses its familiar taste—a rationale for
being, a sense of identification with the human species (as well as a
divine inheritance), all the feelings which somehow define our world
as a "civilized" place of habitation, are sacrificed on this gallows-
crucifix, until it is no longer possible to establish a connection
between one's intelligence and its apprehension of surrounding
reality. The ritual of death, the agonizing struggle between living
and dying which always has one inevitable outcome, even if some
fortunate few should literally survive—for a time—the ritual of
death ungraced by the possibility of resurrection, becomes the focus
of existence and shrouds reality in an atmosphere of irrational,
impenetrable gloom—"Our senses were blunted," as Wiesel wrote
earlier; "everything was blurred as in a fog."

Under such circumstances men learn to adopt toward totally
irrational events attitudes that one would expect only from insane
or otherwise bewildered human beings: the result is that the
incredible assumes some of the vestments of ordinary reality, while
normality appears slightly off-center, recognizable, one might say,
"north-north-west." Neither total confusion nor absolute comprehension, neither a mad world in which men behave sanely, nor a
reasonable one in which human conduct seems deranged—this is
the schizophrenic effect Wiesel achieves in his autobiographical
narrative. It is scarcely necessary to arrange literal episodes or
invent new ones to create the nightmare atmosphere which
imaginative works in the tradition will strive for—such is the unique
nature of reality in l'univers concentrationnaire. For example,
shortly after the episode of the hanging of the boy, the Jewish New
Year arrives, and Wiesel establishes a counterpoint between the
traditional celebration of the inmates, who offer the familiar prayers
of praise—"All creation bears witness to the Greatness of God!"—
and his own religious disillusionment, which makes him resemble a

solitary shrub on a desolate island of faith, which itself appears diminutive and even slightly ludicrous in an endless sea of atrocity:

> My eyes were open and I was alone—terribly alone in a world without God and without man. Without love or mercy. I had ceased to be anything but ashes, yet I felt myself to be stronger than the Almighty, to whom my life had been tied for so long. I stood amid that praying congregation, observing it like a stranger. [pp. 73–74]

Nevertheless, a short time later the apostate narrator seriously debates with fellow inmates living in the shadow of the crematorium whether or not they should fast on Yom Kippur, the Day of Atonement. No participant in this discussion could appreciate more intensively than the innocent, horrified spectator-reader the scathing irony, not to say the insane logic, of this situation: starving men choosing not to eat. The narrator ultimately nibbles his bread and feels a void in his heart, a void intensified by the futility of religious values in a universe that not only refuses to acknowledge them, but is built on premises so cynical that such values mock the men who espouse them.

For the victims who seek sustenance in their faith are reduced to a more degrading role by the subsequent episode, a "selection"—which in plain language meant that some men, usually those physically weaker, were periodically designated for death in a ritual that resembled the weeding-out of defective parts in a machine-assembly plant. Men who know in advance that their life depends on the opinion of an SS "doctor" run past this official, hoping that their numbers will not be written down; most pass the "test," but a few are aware that they "fail," that in two or three days they will be taken to the "hospital" and never be seen again. After such knowledge, what humanity? What logic or reason or connection between what men do and what they suffer, can prevail in one's conception of the universe? In one's conception of one's self? For the narrator, existence is reduced to an elemental struggle between acquiescence to death—"Death wrapped itself around me till I was stifled. It stuck to me. I felt that I could touch it. The idea of dying, of no longer being, began to fascinate me." (p. 90)—and the need to live, in order to support his weakening father, broken in health and spirit by the rigorous discipline of the camp.

Ultimately, the contest between Death and the Father, the one

representing *l'univers concentrationnaire* with its insidious and
macabre dissolution of reasonable longings, the other all those
familiar inheritances which constitute the basis of civilized existence—ultimately, this contest assumes symbolic dimensions, as if
normalcy in its dying gasp makes one final effort to assert its
authority over the gruesome power seeking to dispossess it. But
when death intrudes on the imagination to the point where memory
and hope are excluded—as happens in *Night*—then this rivalry,
with the accompanying gesture of resistance, proves futile; a kind of
inner momentum has already determined the necessary triumph of
death in a world disrupted beyond the capacity of man to alter it.
The extent of the disruption, and the transformation in humanity
wrought by it, is painfully illustrated by the cry of SS guards to the
prisoners being transported westward in open cattle-cars from
Auschwitz (because of the approaching Russian troops) to Buchenwald: "Throw out all the dead! All corpses outside!"—and by the
response of those still surviving: "The living rejoiced. There would
be more room" (p. 100).

Thus disinherited, bereft of any value that might permit him to
confront the inevitable death of his father with at least the dignity
of an illusion, and compelled in the depths of his heart to accept the
desolate rule of *l'univers concentrationnaire*—"Here there are no
fathers, no brothers, no friends. Everyone lives and dies for himself
alone." (p. 111)—the narrator helplessly watches his last living link
with the familiar world of the past expire and learns that grief has
expired with him. Not only have normal feelings lapsed—plunging
us into a shadowy realm where men cease to respond to reality by
following any predictable pattern—but they have been replaced by
attitudes which a "normally" disposed reader, still bound by the
moral premises of pre-Holocaust experience, would characterize as
verging on the inhuman. But to the reader who has himself
submitted imaginatively to the hallucination-become-fact of this
experience, the narrator's reaction to his father's death can more
accurately be described as one illustration of what happens when
human character is pressed beyond the limits of the human: "in the
recesses of my weakened conscience, could I have searched it, I
might perhaps have found something like—free at last!" (p. 113).

At this moment, to follow Camus's language, man is divorced
from his life, the actor from his setting, and the son (in a manner

quite different from the conventional *Bildungsroman*) severed from his patrimony and thrust forth onto a stage which requires the drama of existence to continue, though without a script, *sans* director, the plot consisting of a single unanswerable question: How shall I enact my survival in a world I know to be darkened by the shadow of irrational death, before an audience anticipating a performance that will be illuminated by the light of reason and the glow of the future? Out of some such query as this, representing a paradox of private existence, is born a principle of schizophrenic art, the art of atrocity.

The final, haunting moment of *Night* occurs when the narrator, Wiesel himself, following his liberation, gazes at his own visage after lingering between life and death (a result of food poisoning):

> One day I was able to get up, after gathering all my strength. I wanted to see myself in the mirror hanging on the opposite wall. I had not seen myself since the ghetto.
>
> From the depths of the mirror, a corpse gazed back at me.
>
> The look in his eyes, as they stared into mine, has never left me. [p. 116]

An unrecognizable face from the past and a living death-mask—variations on this confrontation, spanning two worlds with a current linking regret to despair, characterizes the literature that grew out of the nightmare of history which transformed a fifteen-year-old boy into a breathing corpse.

Wiesel's account is ballasted with the freight of fiction: scenic organization, characterization through dialogue, periodic climaxes, elimination of superfluous or repetitive episodes, and especially an ability to arouse the empathy of his readers, which is an elusive ideal of the writer bound by fidelity to fact. His narrative approaches fiction in its ability to evoke rather than describe the two worlds that eventually create a Karamazov-like "double" in the narrator on the final page. It demonstrates more clearly than any other literal account of the Holocaust how powerfully the paradoxes of this historical horror will challenge and exasperate the imagination of the artist—the painter as well as the writer, one might add—who tries to create a form appropriate to its jagged revelations. The young boy who stared at the inarticulate knowledge and suffering in the eyes of his reflection at that crucial moment in his life was destined to become a novelist himself, though his fictional concern with the implications of his ordeal—understandably enough, perhaps—would be more philosophical than dramatic; but the *sensibilité concentrationnaire*, roused by similar knowledge, if not always similar suffering, drew this portion of history into the unlimited aspirations of literary art, and gave it a resonance and universality which only imaginative literature could achieve.

For example, it would seem—and generally it was so—that of all the stylistic techniques available for representing the experience of atrocity, naturalistic dialogue would be the least effective, since the subject itself was so unnatural, so extraordinary, so resistant to the graphic efforts of unmanipulated prose. Yet as we have seen, even in the concentration camps the sun rose daily, men and women awoke to face their ordeal—and if some did not, but died quietly (or noisily) in their sleep, this too came to be part of an expected routine. Most accounts of the Holocaust—quite properly—emphasize the abominations, though these would seem even more execrable if they could be highlighted by a kind of verbal chiaroscuro, in which horror is embedded like chips of mosaic in a clay of commonplace behavior.

A brief passage from a story by Tadeusz Borowski called "Auschwitz. Our Home (A Letter)" will illustrate the possibilities inherent in this theme when developed by an accomplished writer (himself a survivor of Auschwitz). In the scene, which concludes the story, the narrator (who has undergone "training" in the camp as a medical orderly) encounters a familiar inmate he has not seen for some time. They exchange pleasantries:

> "Ah, it's you! Want to buy anything? If you've got some apples . . ."
>
> "No, I haven't any apples for you," I replied affectionately. "So, you're still alive, Abbie? And what's new with you?"
>
> "Not much. Just gassed up a Czech transport."
>
> "That I know. I mean personally?"
>
> "Personally? What sort of 'personally' is there for me? The oven, the barracks, back to the oven . . . Have I got anybody around here? Well, if you really want to know what 'personally'—we've figured out a new way to burn people. Want to hear about it?"
>
> I indicated polite interest.
>
> "Well then, you take four little kids with plenty of hair on their

heads, then stick the heads together and light the hair. The rest burns by itself and in no time at all the whole business is *gemacht*."

"Congratulations," I said drily and with very little enthusiasm.

He burst out laughing and with a strange expression looked right into my eyes.

"Listen, doctor, here in Auschwitz we must entertain ourselves in every way we can. Otherwise, who could stand it?"

And putting his hands in his pockets he walked away without saying goodbye.

But this is a monstrous lie, a grotesque lie, like the whole camp, like the whole world.[5]

The casual interchange—"And what's new with you?" "Not much. Just gassed up a Czech transport." "That I know. I mean personally."—leaps with chilling effect from the page in a kind of verbal counterpoint, as the harmony of conversational tone is constantly disrupted by the dissonance of its theme: "A new way to burn people." The difficulty, perhaps the impossibility, of sustaining this delicate balance is accentuated by the explicit—too explicit—coda, the final line in which the intelligence of the author penetrates the point of view of the narrator, as if the horror of the subject finally bursts the limits of art and an extraneous voice feels compelled to shatter the illusion of the fiction.

Like Camus, Borowski is outraged by man's acquiescence to forces that dehumanize, humiliate, and ultimately destroy him; but in this passage he appears even more apprehensive over the possibility of the reader's failing to recognize the implications of such acquiescence—hence his angry outburst. It is almost as if he feared too great a success for his literary art: the ostensible indifference in the tone of the speakers inculcates a comparable detachment in the reader, and creates the danger of his "passing by" without acknowledging the insidious change that has been wrought in the characters. The "monstrous" and "grotesque lie" that Borowski denounces, abruptly compels us to face the horrible fact that we too may have been seduced into accepting the abnormal as normal, intellectually conscious of the atrocities in the background but emotionally relieved that they happen to "others," not the characters we are concerned with (nor, by psychological

5. Tadeusz Borowski, *This Way for the Gas, Ladies and Gentlemen*, trans. Barbara Vedder (New York: The Viking Press, 1967), p. 122.

extension, with ourselves)—abruptly we are wrenched from the detachment of contemplating a narrative, to an awareness of the narrative's roots in history: and with a shock we rub our imaginative eyes and try to sort out our responses, half literary, half real.

For in the literature of atrocity, no fiction can ever be completely that—a fiction; however extraordinary the imaginative efforts of the writer to disguise his theme with the garments of literary invention —and as we shall see, some of these efforts are extraordinary indeed—he can never totally conceal the relationship between the naked body and the covering costume, the actual scars of the Holocaust and the creative salves that often only intensify pain. Like many experimental poets and dramatists of the past decade, these writers have as a major aim, immersing their readers in the experience of their art, vanquishing the detachment which Borowski, perhaps, feared he had overemphasized; yet unlike these experimenters they have the singular "advantage" of a portion of actuality we call *l'univers concentrationnaire* to work with, an actuality that does not require specification because its gruesome features already dwell within the consciousness of the potential audience. On the other hand, one premise of the art of atrocity is the inadequacy of this supposedly "common consciousness"; perhaps never before in the history of literature have authors had to fight a reader reluctance based not on an inability to understand what they are about—this had been the initial fate of *Ulysses, The Sound and the Fury,* and *Waiting for Godot,* for example—but on the alleged assumption of the reader that he understood it only too well, that there is little need to burden the human imagination with further morbid explorations of a horrible reality which anyone with a long memory or a diligent curiosity is already acquainted with.

Thus, numerous readers recoil from works like Wiesel's *Night* with the demurral that they couldn't finish them, they were too "terrible" (not too difficult or too dull—reasons one might understand, if not approve), too "terrible" because they evoke a part of contemporary experience that the mind instinctively consigns to silence. The whole subject of "reader reluctance" would seem trivial and scarcely worth raising were it not for the insight it offers into the literature itself, which has as one of its goals (and indeed as one of its themes) the conquest of this very inability of the mind to contend with the recollections, the emotions, the apprehensions

that *l'univers concentrationnaire* evokes. Wiesel himself enacts this
frustration in his imaginative autobiography, and in so doing he
creates (perhaps unconsciously) an important principle for his
successors in the tradition. Simply stated, it is this: a tension exists
between events as they actually happened and the implications of
these events for individual fate and the destiny of humanity. The
former (the events) dwell (and hence disappear) in time, victims of
temporality; the latter (the implications), rescued from oblivion by
memory and imagination, endure in a realm—in the case of the
literature of atrocity—that is partly invented and partly recreated
from episodes which themselves appear too fantastic to be anything
but fiction.

One of the main problems—and confusions—in assessing such
literature is the failure to distinguish between the two terms of this
"tension"—*actuality* (events that literally occurred, the slow stran-
gulation of the boy or the hurling of infants into a pit of flames in
Night, for example), and *reality*, the attempts of the mind to absorb
such events into a literary harmony or to compose a new dissonance
that will make them endurable and meaningful to the imaginative
"ear." Heinrich Böll, whose *Billiards at Half-Past Nine* impinges
significantly on the tradition we are discussing, makes a similar and
useful distinction between "actuality" (or, literally, "the topical")
and "reality" (recalling Paul Celan's remarks on his need to design a
new reality for himself), a distinction he illustrates by an event not
unrelated to the subject of atrocity. Böll alludes to the Japanese
fishermen who unwittingly sailed into a proscribed atomic testing
area and were contaminated by nuclear fallout. Perhaps postdating
the occasion—should this attribution not be reserved for the victims
of the Holocaust?—he describes them as "the first martyrs of a new
reality of death." (This "new reality" is what transformed the young
Elie Wiesel into a "living corpse," just as it stimulated the vision of
human experience which culminated in what I have called the art of
atrocity.) Böll then continues:

> For several days they were "topical"—a brief wave of terror swept
> around the world, and people began to suspect what had happened
> there: the possibility of humanity's collective suicide became appar-
> ent for the first time. The fishermen, and what happened to them,
> were "topical," as much is "topical" for days. But what *really*
> happened that day was scarcely apparent: the rain that falls on us, the

air that we breathe, can contain this new death. The baker, without knowing it, can knead this new death in bread, the postman can bring it into the house with the mail.[6]

The artist of atrocity is concerned with what "really" happened, what is scarcely apparent, and part of his task is to rouse his audience into a recognition of the ease with which one confuses Böll's "topical" with his "real." The power of imagination, Böll observes, is the key to such discrimination, a power which enables us to create images that vivify the "static" episodes, however macabre, of history—an image, for example, such as nuclear death baked in a loaf of bread, which the "topical" fate of the fishermen scarcely evokes; or an image like the following, in which Böll projects an atmosphere of nightmare we have encountered before:

> Contemporary man is like a traveler who climbs into a train at his home station and sets out in the night for a destination whose distance is unknown: in the darkness he is often startled out of a half-doze and hears from the loudspeaker of an unknown station the announcer telling him where he is at the moment: names are mentioned that he doesn't know, that appear unreal to him, names from an alien world that seems not to exist: a fantastic episode, that is nevertheless absolutely real. The real *is* fantastic—but we must understand that our human imagination always moves within the real.[7]

The unfamiliar names that challenge the reality of this journey might be way-stations to Auschwitz, where "a fantastic episode" which was "nevertheless absolutely real" awaited the travelers. Much of the "reality" of the Holocaust belongs to the period of such night voyages, and even to the days and months before they began, when the prospective victims, filled with suspicion and fear, reluctant to admit the awful fate awaiting them at journey's end, used the power of the imagination to contend with that fate, with the threat of a terrifying, impersonal Death that hovered over the images they created to personify or disguise the destination that was too real to be fantastic, too fantastic to be real—the "unreal reality" which infected the dreams of men during the years of the Third Reich.

6. Heinrich Böll, "Der Zeitgenosse und die Wirklichkeit," in *Hierzulande: Aufsätze zur Zeit* (Munich: Deutsche Taschenbuch Verlag, 1963), pp. 64–65. Translation mine.
7. Ibid., p. 66.

When the symbolic "night" of which Wiesel wrote permeated the waking hours of men too, men for whom the daily "actualities" still provided a deceptive measure of protection against the impending "darkness," then a situation was created in which characters and author conspired to reorient the reader's conception of experience, though often the characters only slowly recognize their role in the fictional conspiracy. Such a sorting out of an ordinary individual's responses to the possibilities and implications of *l'univers concentrationnaire* is the theme of Ladislav Fuks's *Mr. Theodore Mundstock*, a novel which seeks to dramatize at length the consequences of the difficult question formulated earlier in this chapter: How shall I enact my survival in a world I know to be unalterably darkened by the shadow of irrational death, before an audience anticipating a performance that will be illuminated by the light of reason and the glow of the future?

But Fuks does not invest his fictional creation with the intense sensitivity of the boy in *Night*. As one might expect of an autobiography like Wiesel's, the collaboration between author and his retrospective image of himself is nearly complete; in Fuks's novel, however, Mr. Mundstock knows the "question," but his reactions, his "answers," are deliberately plunged by his creator into an intermediate realm between ambiguity and clarity, insight and delusion, so that we can only speculate about his understanding of the world which threatens him. Can reality achieve such a condition of disorientation for some men (in this instance, for the Jews in a town in occupied Czechoslovakia during wartime) that all attempts at orientation must fail? Or more precisely: what happens when the equivalent of Böll's puzzled voyager (in the train-image cited earlier) discovers that the "real *is* fantastic" but at the same time tries to assert the principle that "our human imagination always moves within the real"?

As a Jew, the scope of Mr. Mundstock's expectations have shrunk to the dimensions of his letter box, which he inspects daily for the official "summons" that will request him to appear at the railroad station for deportation and "resettlement" (the Holocaust, as both Böll and Fuks understood, had invested the train-journey with a new and fearful vitality as a literary image). But as his story begins, he receives—to his relief—a "summons" of another sort, addressing him with a human appeal rather than a demand that he keep a dehumanizing appointment—a letter from Mrs. Stern, whose family of five, old friends of his, similarly await their fate in helpless anxiety: "Mr. Mundstock," writes Mrs. Stern, "I'm crying all the time, wherever I go, though I don't let myself think of the horrors ahead of us. I don't even dare to remember there is anything of the sort. Have you got any reliable news? Do come soon, please." [8]

Mrs. Stern's request for a visit is a thinly veiled plea for moral sustenance from Mr. Mundstock, whose personal dilemma is dramatized by the inner tensions liberated by her letter. Mr. Mundstock's only companions are a ragged bird he affectionately calls "chicky" and an elusive "shadow" he calls Mon, an alter ego vaguely reminiscent, in the role it plays in the novel, of Ivan Karamazov's "devil" and Lear's Fool: for Mon is a mocking and often cynical presence, irritably persistent in his attempts to undercut the illusions which Mr. Mundstock invents to convince the Stern family (and perhaps himself) that things are bound to get better. "Every one of us can expect the summons any day," says Mr. Mundstock in colloquy with his pet, "only there's no need to be afraid, they say once you get to the concentration camp you get dulled to it and don't even feel the horrors." That, decides Mr. Mundstock, is the kind of reassurance Mrs. Stern and her family desire from him, that is the reason they want to see him; but Mon angrily interjects: "That's not why! . . . It's because he doesn't tell them that, just because he tells them the exact opposite. Because he'll tell them there aren't any transports going to Lodz and aren't going to be any, that's why they ask him round. Because he'll say it's all imagination, expecting the summons."

Trapped between illusion and truth, Mr. Mundstock gradually enacts the abortive tragedy of man on the stage of that unique theater of atrocity called the Holocaust: although he slowly acknowledges the claims of "truth," ceasing to lie that others may "live" (and as he does so Mon disappears from the pages of the novel, much as Lear's Fool vanishes from the play), his partial insight produces no real change, either in himself or in the affairs of others, no moral dignity compensates for the grim death that awaits him, and his "heroic" attempts to prepare for his fate with the

8. Ladislav Fuks, *Mr. Theodore Mundstock*, trans. Iris Unwin (New York: The Orion Press, 1968), p. 2.

resolution of an intelligent human creature merely reveal that the possibility of doing so is the ultimate illusion in a universe whose reality inflexibly rejects the expectations of the tragic vision—an insight, incidentally, accorded the reader but denied Mr. Mundstock. "To lose hope is the worst that can happen to anyone," Mr. Mundstock observes before he visits the Sterns; "Do you know what the grave is, chicky?" (pp. 8–9). Man's fate at the entrance to the gas chambers of what Böll in another context had called this "new reality of death," must have been illuminated in the instant before extinction by the glare of a statement and question such as these; and as Fuks alternates Mr. Mundstock's fate between hope and the grave, he creates a fable which makes of this "new reality" the very nucleus of existence.

This existence has turned negative at its core: Mr. Mundstock seeks not an affirmation of life in the face of potential disaster, but simply "a way out of the horror" that has become a fait accompli. He alludes nostalgically to "before the war" as if it were a distant ancestral past, but this simply reinforces our sense of the sharp rupture that exists between then and now; and as if to confirm the discontinuity, Fuks assembles a series of traditional literary images which earlier would have represented for the writer symbolic avenues of insight. Wishing for an escape from the threatening terror, Mr. Mundstock turns to his books, "collected over thirty years" but containing no wisdom relevant to *l'univers concentrationnaire;* to his sofa, "turned into a bed at night so I can lie there and sleep," though sleep brings no solace or comforting dreams, only nightmares that intensify his fears; to a door, but "you can't escape from the concentration camp that way"; to a lamp, which in an earlier century lighted the way for romantic transcendentalists into a heaven of unity, but for Mr. Mundstock contains only a painting of Columbus's ship on its shade, sailing round and round on an endless sea, a mockery of the spirit of discovery (and escape from persecution), since you can't "hop on board and sail away, on a lamp shade"; a mirror, again in traditional metaphorical language a challenge to the visionary imagination to invent worlds liberating to the spirit, "but all I can see in that is myself"; and finally, the light from the window, but even this, as he observes drily, "comes in through it only as long as it isn't blacked out" (p. 9).

All these images, which in a more familiar literary world might offer him comfort, and Fuks the opportunity of extending Mr. Mundstock's experiences into a complex realm of alternative possibilities, are recorded to emphasize their futility and the total alienation of Mr. Mundstock from an order of reality—literary and actual—that we, like him, have grown accustomed to. Divided against himself, Mr. Mundstock retires that night desperately searching for some principle that might enable him to reunite his personality and revitalize the impotent images of his past life, thus affording him some defense against his impending doom—but the "night" of the approaching *univers concentrationnaire* seems total, as it did for Elie Wiesel:

> he stared into the darkness as though he wanted to catch sight of him, he desperately wanted to catch sight of Mon, at least his outline, at least the shadow he cast, but it was hopeless and in vain. All around him hung the thick darkness no light could penetrate. Outside in the street everything was plunged in the safe darkness of air-raid precautions and the window of his little room was carefully blacked out. [p. 16]

The duel between Mr. Mundstock and Mon, between his former self and the reality introduced into his life by the menace of deportation, is clarified by the confession that he hadn't known Mon before the war: "it was only since the first days of the German occupation that they'd been together." The reluctance to abandon earlier aspirations ("Truly, though, it was not too late! There was still time to make up for it! No, no police boot was going to kick his happiness to pieces," p. 32) coexists with the melancholy awareness that they have already been sacrificed ("as he scurried along he felt his uneasiness growing even worse . . . fear of time past that cannot be thought out of existence, and then fear because he was hurrying, a hunted animal, alone, alone, alone," p. 27).

Mr. Mundstock (again the parallel with Ivan Karamazov is illuminating) is trapped by twin longings, irreconcilable yet both asserting their primacy in his puzzled, distraught mind; unable to accept "no exit" as a principle of human existence, he first chooses a number of diversionary tactics, each designed to elude the unbearable "unreal reality" which is the necessary condition of the opposition between himself and Mon, between a man whose past leads naturally to the future and a creature whose present is circumscribed by the iron manacle of a gruesome and only dimly conceivable death. Indeed, the nightmare of having to be *both* simultaneously, once drives Mr. Mundstock to a terrifying moment when he wills his own depersonalization, as if withdrawal from the legions of the living were the only solution to his situation. Walking by the park in the twilight of a misty evening, he envies the bushes, which are fixed in one place, not suspected of anything, not threatened with deportation:

> How much better off they are than people who have to be watched and investigated, how much better to be a bush than to be a person called Mundstock. . . .

But his other voice quickly redresses the imbalance: "if I was a bush I wouldn't be on my way to the Sternses'. And I couldn't even feel hope. It's better to be a man, after all" (p. 33).

But at the Sternses', who hang on Mr. Mundstock's every word of encouragement for sustenance, the weird contest between illusion and doubt intensifies, until he begins to submit to the blandishments of his own lies, and to see in his predictions of an early termination to the war and his fortune-telling with a pack of cards about imminent good fortune for the Sterns, a possible role for himself in the midst of confusion and despair: he would be a seer, a consoler of others, an apostle of hope, his mission would be to deny despair and in so doing to recreate a world of possibility; and as this sudden vision spread through his soul, he "felt something green beginning to sprout inside him, as if he, the Mr. Theodore Mundstock that was, was rising from the dead" (p. 47). Only after he leaves the Sterns and hurries home in the fearful twilight does he begin to recognize how terrifying is the prospect of turning Messiah before the Holocaust, whose dimensions are as yet barely discernible to him, though fiercely clear to us—a contrast which itself intensifies unbearably the futility of his confidence in ancient premises, however adapted to the needs of the historical moment.

In a remarkable epiphany that in its language and imagery appears to mock his humanity and strip him of his sanity, while its intention seems to confirm his newly discovered role as savior, Mr. Mundstock struggles to preserve an identity in a world that has simply abandoned him:

> He felt his panting breath and the heat of his body throughout his own limbs. He felt it in his thoughts and it beat at the temples of his

mind. In his brain he could hear Mon's voice explaining and expounding, but he resisted his words as a horse resists the bit when his rider is plunging into an abyss. The darkness round him grew redder and redder and at the same time more sparse. It was a wild attack on his reason, with horror and physical pain wrought in with it until it became unbearable. When it overstepped the limits of reason and reached regions where there seemed to be nothing in human guise, his poor tormented reason surrendered.

A flood drowned his consciousness, carrying with it all that linked him to reality. All that floated on the surface were scraps of himself, transformed into the strangest creatures, and he realized what was hidden in all this.

The others were to be saved through him. In the hour that was to come he would be—the savior. [p. 58]

Mr. Mundstock's little room becomes a modern Garden of Gethsemane, his anguish the agony of a twentieth-century Messiah who is called to his "mission" not by a divine voice, but by the suffering of a helpless humanity. But whereas once the painful road to Calvary was a clear and undeviating path, now it is overgrown with the brambles of an incomprehensible horror, and Mr. Mundstock stumbles searching for the way: "the actual method, the way in which he was to put his vocation into practice, was still hidden in his mind" (p. 60). The spiritual channels joining the concept of Messiah to *l'univers concentrationnaire* are clogged, and finally we wonder whether the attempt to unite them was valid from the beginning; during his night of torment a "dreadful message" forces its way through his head "as the whirlpool of his thoughts raged" (p. 60), and the next morning he awakens to the knowledge that the "future was a compact of horror" (p. 64), and that for all his powers as a seer, he could not describe it or discover how he might save his people from it.

The paradox for Mr. Mundstock and for the world he inhabits is that "seer" and "salvation" belong to the vocabulary of a period that did not prepare humanity for a dictionary of behavior which included euphemisms like "resettlement"; Mr. Mundstock's noble ambitions suffocate from a presentiment of futility and impotence:

Yes, he was horrified at the thought of being a seer, horrified. It was wiser not to know what that horror was. It was enough to knock against the letter box and his nerves gave way a bit, and he could not

> bear it if they were to give way altogether. Man is a weak creature, and especially if he is called Mr. Theodore Mundstock and lives in the Nazi hell. [pp. 64–65]

Ironically, the flames from this "hell" finally blind Mr. Mundstock's gaze toward his "heaven" of some obscure salvation for his people and turn his eyes toward himself, and one is tempted to believe that he is at last about to enter into a quest for the self-knowledge which will, if not redeem, at least mitigate, the tragedy of man caught in the fatal noose of the Holocaust.

Arriving home one day, he discovers a postcard from an old friend and former business colleague, who announces his deportation with the melancholy words: "I am leaving tomorrow," and Mr. Mundstock searches vainly for an invisible message describing his destination in greater detail; reviewing the fate of those who were still "left," he is overwhelmed by a sudden access of horror and confronts Mon, his alter ego, hiding behind the door, "waiting, because it could be his turn next, Mr. Theodore Mundstock." The disfiguration of reality that has prevented the transfiguration of Mr. Mundstock into a savior commensurate with that reality is dramatically suggested by the spectacle of the hapless Jew

> sitting there on the sofa with his shoes untied, counting up who had gone and who was left, a man with a graying face and scraggy neck, who could not sleep at night and had aged a hundred years in those three since the Nazis came and spread their brown darkness over everything. [pp. 66–67]

On this same sofa Mr. Mundstock experiences another crisis, as the brown darkness which obliterates his future now seeps backwards in time to illuminate his past with an unholy glow, while simultaneously forcing him to revisit psychologically that moment when reality had been rent and his fate determined: he recalls the day when he arrived in his office to find a uniformed German insultingly announcing that he was "fired." Returning home, he had sunk on the same sofa, weeping, and at that instant "something inside him *split in two*." It was the birth of the shadow Mon, the offspring of the "brown darkness" that had cleft his life; and with a sudden clarity, the mist shrouding and fusing past and present dissolved and Mr. Mundstock, "tormented, afflicted . . . knew it was the end" (p. 75). If the future was a compact of horror, as he had earlier reflected, the only escape, neither salvation nor triumph, was to submit to the ultimate form of that horror, the death that lingered on the periphery of consciousness for all potential victims of the Holocaust and introduced such an uncanny imbalance into their existence.

Failing as a savior, bringer of life and soothing lies to others, Mr. Mundstock next responds to the challenge of the universe by choosing the option that Camus refused: suicide. But death mocks him even here, as if Fuks wished to emphasize the futility of self-destruction itself in the illogical and nightmarish *univers concentrationnaire*, which denied all principles of causality. Because behind Mr. Mundstock's attempt to take his own life lies the premise that a connection still exists in human experience between what a man does and what he suffers, the premise that if a man has no power to affect his life, he at least may be the instrument of his own death. In Fuks's fictional universe such a possibility is ruthlessly eliminated when Mr. Mundstock's homemade noose breaks and he is left an "unhappy man with a rough reddened mark on his neck" (p. 77).

The rhythm of the novel at this point has carried Mr. Mundstock through one full cycle of experience, from the apex of illusion to the nadir of despair. After his frustrated suicide a new cycle begins, as he searches for a new role to sustain him in his daily activities while he awaits the unavoidable confrontation with the fearful summons. During a mysterious visit to a "terrifying" house with "Gothic windows and gargoyle-like heads with long undulating necks" (p. 77), he hears from a shadowy figure (presumably the Rabbi of the Jewish community) the "wisdom" that will determine his future conduct: "Mr. Mundstock thought he could be a seer and a messiah, and take his own life, when he used to be a sensible, practical, logical man with a method of dealing with everything?" The words fall on fertile soil, and shortly will bear ironic fruit, as Mr. Mundstock develops an obsession with finding a personal "method," sensible, practical, and logical, for facing his own impending deportation and the fate that awaits him in the concentration camp. The consoler himself receives "consolation" which purges him of all longings to be a seer: "Our life cannot pass without suffering. Suffering is our vocation. In our suffering we are eternal" (p. 83).

The *pathos* of Mr. Mundstock, though he never perceives this himself, is that he takes seriously the "conventional" definition of human (and Jewish) destiny offered him by a voice out of the gloom; perhaps his deepest *tragedy* is that all other options, given his situation, are equally futile. Hence Fuks describes the place of this interview, which is to have such a decisive influence on the career of Mr. Mundstock, as a "house that looked like a nightmare castle." The modern Delphic oracle who inhabits it gravely tenders orphic advice that had sustained a people through generations of its ordeal with history—"Mr. Mundstock must remember that he is a Jew, and not try to flee suffering and avoid his grave responsibility" (p. 84)—but the context of the novel illustrates that the Holocaust, as Fuks dramatizes its implications, has undermined the strength of our fundamental moral and philosophical vocabulary itself; for the subsequent events in the life of Mr. Mundstock suggest that terms like "suffering" and "responsibility" belong to an order of reality that mankind has outlived. Or perhaps, as the image of the "nightmare castle" would confirm, such concepts of a world where the Lord might "turn his countenance upon thee and grant thee peace" belong to an order of unreality that has lost its relevance to the present, although human creatures like Mr. Mundstock, in the absence of any other orientation, cling to this solace in the vacuum of their despair.

"The damp chill of the evening before had turned to bitter frost" begins the chapter following the encounter between Mr. Mundstock and the Rabbi, and this simple modulation in nature reinforces the aesthetic counterpoint which exists betweenMr. Mundstock's efforts to endure disaster and the reader's peculiar "retrospective prevision" of the "compact of horror" that awaits him in gas chamber and crematorium. This particular kind of tension is unique to the literature of atrocity, since the "bitter frost" of the opening sentence (together with other images and episodes built into the novel) evokes a literal sense of the sinister in the consciousness of the reader which adds a significant dimension to the less complex awareness of the character. For as Mr. Mundstock, armed with a feeling for his religious heritage, begins to muse on a "way out of the Jewish history of suffering" (p. 104), he turns his imagination to the specific future that threatens him, and imposes layers of invention on reality until we ourselves have difficulty distinguishing fantasy from truth. Or rather, what he often prefigures as fantasy we ratify retrospectively as truth, until the action of the novel begins to operate for us, as well as for Mr. Mundstock, on two levels, what actually happens and what his mind contrives. *L'univers concentrationnaire*, with all its accompanying uncertainties and horrors, displaces the everyday and distorts its features, like the arrested agony in a Francis Bacon portrait, behind whose grotesque visage we detect, perhaps through nostalgia, the face of a man, but search for concrete evidence in vain.

Mr. Mundstock's experience is not so grotesque, but grim enough. His delegated task during the occupation is to sweep the refuse daily in a particular street of his town, and when one day he discovers that the accumulated litter exceeds the capacity of his little cart, he concludes that the challenge is a test of his humanity, a threat to his ability to survive the hostility of the Holocaust:

> he seemed to notice queer people in the street, people he had never seen there before; they seemed to be watching him furtively as if they wanted to see how he was going to set about his job, and it occurred to him that this was a trap that had been set for him, this street. So that he wouldn't be able to sweep it clean and they could accuse him of disobedience, of refusal to obey orders, and even of sabotage. [p. 106]

Mr. Mundstock stands before the public as in a dream exposed, yet none of the passersby has an idea of what is going on in the mind of "this man in his worn black coat with the yellow star" whose "very existence was at stake" (pp. 106–07). But to him it is the happiest day of his life, the one in which "his destiny began to be fulfilled"; and although Mr. Mundstock has no conception of how accurately, as a trash collector, he anticipates his destiny, his assault on the rubbish of others offers us an important clue to the true value of this last step in his supposed progress toward the recognition and acceptance of his fate under the Holocaust.

For the careful planning and methodical piling which finally enable Mr. Mundstock to transport in one trip all the refuse from the lane to the city ash dump—who can hush the portentous echoes rising from this new valley of ashes?—inaugurate a second and more far-ranging ambition than that of seer: "That if he thought the same way as he had done that afternoon in Armorers Lane, method and a practical approach could save him. He would be *saved!*"

(p. 111). Who could survive the concentration camp, Mr. Mund-stock explicitly inquires?—and replies: "The man who went about things sensibly, with a logical method" (p. 112). Infatuation with his new program obscures and finally excludes from the realm of consciousness and, for a time, from literary possibility, the funda-mental illogicality of history (also the basic fictional premise of the novel)—that a summons in the letter box could lead to the extermination of a man who has done absolutely nothing to merit such a punishment.

Mr. Mundstock's acceptance of this premise, and his determina-tion to fight the consequences rather than resist the cause, marks his final unwitting submission to the principle of death that has haunted his world since that day three years before, when the Nazis arrived and "something inside him *split in two*." In his earlier epiphany, announcing his mission as savior of others, the very language—"A flood drowned his consciousness, carrying with it all that linked him to reality. All that floated on the surface were scraps of himself, transformed into the strangest creatures." (p. 58)—in this passage, the very language recreates the distress and passionate apprehen-sions that overwhelmed Mr. Mundstock when he accepted his role as self-proclaimed savior; now, as he decides to be merely an example to others by saving *himself*, he experiences a different kind of epiphany, whose language is totally devoid of feeling in its description of the method he adopted to "survive" the threat of the concentration camp:

> In the colossal investigation of every possible situation, the working out of a method of action in each of these situations, down to the last minute detail, including all possible eventualities, and fantastic perseverance in practical training for them all. In the understanding and thorough comprehension of reality, at the same time stripping it of all fantasy, illusion and invention. [p. 116]

Rejoicing, Mr. Mundstock feels "as though he had been born again"; and indeed, as a victim of the official diction in whose name millions were slaughtered, the contours of his personality and the mode of his behavior, to say nothing of its milieu, have perceptibly shifted. If one cannot prepare for the encounter with death by pretending that it can be postponed, that indeed the concentration camp may be simply rumor, or at best a temporary measure to be

halted as the German military situation worsens—his argument with
the Sterns—one can "prepare" for the encounter (in Mr. Mundstock's case this means for deportation and some form of violent
end) by applying the powers of reason to the sequence of events
linking the "summons" to all its possible consequences.

"Outside of that single fatality of death," writes Camus near the
end of *The Myth of Sisyphus*, "everything, joy or happiness, is
liberty. A world remains of which man is the sole master. What
bound him was the illusion of another world. The outcome of his
thought, ceasing to be renunciatory, flowers in images." [9] As if in
deliberate contradiction to Camus's assumptions, Ladislav Fuks
creates in Mr. Mundstock a man who eventually grows so obsessed
with outwitting "that single fatality of death" that he becomes its
victim, pursuing with a delusive pleasure a course that draws him
ever closer to its grasp. So long as he clung to the "illusion of
another world" (though not the afterlife to which Camus presumably alludes), Mr. Mundstock's thoughts flowered in images; but as
soon as he dedicates his energies to an understanding of all "possible
eventualities," as we see in the passage from the novel just quoted,
his thoughts are drained of metaphorical content and his mind (and
subsequently, his actions) reflects a kind of lucidity Camus never
intended; for if some "crushing truths perish from being acknowledged" (p. 90), as Camus would have it, other crushing truths, like
the concentration camp which summons Mr. Mundstock, *crush*
from being acknowledged. Mr. Mundstock's desire for a "thorough
comprehension of reality," stripped "of all fantasy, illusion, and
invention" may seem equivalent to Camus's "lucidity," and may
even, as Camus insists, "make of fate a human matter, which must
be settled among men" (p. 91); but as Sisyphus, abandoning
together with his creator the metaphysical world located on that
other hill called Calvary, struggles toward the peak of his solitary,
secular insight—"the wholly human origin of all that is human"
(p. 91)—he overlooks the possibility that, for the inhabitant of
l'univers concentrationnaire, whose journey is not upward but as
level as the railway tracks leading to Auschwitz, this insight may be
a grave source of terror, not a secret cause for joy.

"There is no sun without shadow, and it is essential to know the

9. Camus, *The Myth of Sisyphus*, p. 87.

night" is the austere tragic principle with which Camus concludes his essay, and it seems as if Fuks would test this conviction too, the possibility of tragic insight in the atmosphere of the Holocaust, as his Mr. Mundstock applies the faculty of human intelligence to the "night" that threatens him with extinction. At first his efforts in this direction are invested with a nearly comic futility, as he plans to ease the burden of carrying a suitcase to the point of deportation by practicing with one filled with stones, and notes the "important" detail that a piece of flannel wrapped around the handle, together with a careful shifting of the load from one hand to the other every five paces, considerably reduces the physical strain. The account of these preparations constitutes a kind of fictional palimpsest, as Mr. Mundstock actually sits in his room and simultaneously, by the power of imagination, accompanies his deported friend and former business colleague to the station, boards the train with him, and makes the journey to the frightful destination—all in an attempt to anticipate the difficulties he will encounter when his own summons arrives. Mr. Mundstock replaces his daily routine (sitting in his room) with his conception of the journey to the concentration camp; and we measure his conception against our own knowledge of such journeys, although his imagined experience assumes an authenticity that forces both him and the reader to relive its details.

But Fuks has complicated the episode, and added to its dramatic tension, by limiting Mr. Mundstock's ability to "foresee" his own destiny: the abyss between the imagination of disaster and the disaster itself is deep and wide, and perhaps for the first time in history, as mentioned earlier, reality exceeded the capacities of this imagination. Indeed, the inability of the imagination to conjure or anticipate the realities of *l'univers concentrationnaire* is a central theme of Fuks's novel, as Mr. Mundstock, in an incident that would be humorous were it not laden with terror, is compelled to "discover":

> The train slowed down beneath his feet and came to a stop. It was standing by the sort of raised siding they use for freight trains. Crowds of uniforms were rushing about under the windows in jackboots and yelling. Probably: All out, please, *bitte aussteigen*. Mr. Mundstock strained his ears.
>
> "*Heraus, Schweine, heraus!* Get out, you swine, get out!"

The thought crossed his mind that perhaps there was a wagon of pork attached to their train. . . .[10]

Horror ousts humor, a horror born less of the events themselves than of the naturalness, not to say naïveté, with which Mr. Mundstock seeks to sort out misconception from "truth," and especially, a horror born of his ill-placed confidence that such knowledge will make a difference in his fate. As his assurance grows—he simply records his error and "observes" for future use that on arrival at the camp the guards will be brutal, not friendly—our certainty of his helplessness, of man's helplessness in a universe where no *human* rules prevail (yet *in*human rules are manmade too, a paradox Camus chooses to avoid), increases too, until the very notion of preparing a primer for the deportee (which in a sense is what Mr. Mundstock is doing), a handbook on how to endure the concentration camp experience, so reasonable from his point of view, appalls our sense of reality. Logic and organization are the weapons of the persecutors, and in employing them Mr. Mundstock unconsciously succumbs to the effects of their strategy.

But for Fuks himself, logic and organization were "fantasies" which both victims and persecutors invented to conceal the even more inconceivable consequences of deportation—humans exterminated by humans. After spending his first imagined night in the camp, where he "discovers" that inmates sleep on wooden planks and thus decides to sleep in the future on his ironing board instead of his comfortable sofa, Mr. Mundstock reflects on his "ordeal":

he thought that after all, that couldn't be everything. There must be worse things, the real thing that you had to go to the concentration camp for; but never mind. Those things would come to him in time. [p. 134]

One revelation leads to another, as the veils shrouding the "real thing" from Mr. Mundstock's imagination slowly fall away, disclosing a series of increasingly severe trials, that intensify in horror for us as he searches for reasonable ways of meeting them. Under ordinary circumstances, one admires the human intelligence for the qualities that enable it to meet with courage and prowess the challenges of fate; but under the extraordinary circumstances in Fuks's novel—and this is perhaps the most fearful feature of

10. Fuks, *Mr. Theodore Mundstock*, pp. 126–27.

l'univers concentrationnaire—one is virtually compelled to con-
demn such efforts of the intelligence, since they pay homage,
through a kind of acquiescence, to an order of reality that mocks
and ultimately reduces to impotence man as a creature of reason.

Madness—and Jakov Lind will build a world of fiction around
this paradox—may be the only "reasonable" response to the
experience which Mr. Mundstock tries to manipulate through
method. When it suddenly occurs to him that the camp will require
strenuous physical labor, perhaps in a stone quarry, he promptly
devises a way of "preparing" for it that makes one wonder whether
he is, indeed, not mad; but the fictional palimpsest that Fuks has
devised to permit his protagonist to shift from one layer of reality to
another assures us that he is sane and in deadly earnest:

> He threw off his jacket and shirt and found himself faced with a really
> enormous block of stone. At first he couldn't do a thing with it. He
> struck again and again, until the lamp nearly fell from the table, but
> nothing but splinters of stone flew off. He strained himself to the
> utmost and struck again and again, until the pick was red-hot and the
> wall was shaking, there were sparks behind his eyes, and then he felt
> he was beginning to get into his stride, and he realized why. [p. 135]

The recollection of Holocaust experience, the darkening influence
of the past on the present, as illustrated in the recurrent dream of
Primo Levi recounted in chapter 2, is a common theme of the
literature of atrocity; its anticipation, the shadow of the future cast
backward in time until it merges indistinguishably with the events
of the present, is a more unique conception, vividly dramatized by
Fuks in a passage such as this. For Mr. Mundstock is actually
beating at the table in his room with an old poker that probably
belonged to his grandmother; but simultaneously he is pleased that
his training with a suitcase filled with stones has enabled him to
endure the "coming" test of the quarry, the next physical challenge
that will confront him in the concentration camp.

But his weird jubilation is momentarily arrested by the vision
which lies behind the next veil: the possibility of future violence
committed against his own person. One of Fuks's most significant
achievements in this novel is his ability to make the *prospect* of
atrocity more terrifying than the act itself; and in an age of hovering
mushroom clouds and the threat of fatal nuclear fallout, this offers a

profound insight into the destiny of the human race in the twentieth century: to "prevent" extermination, Mr. Mundstock is engaged in the futile activity of building fallout shelters in the mind. The equanimity with which he contemplates the prospect of future violence only emphasizes the widening gulf between the possible fulfillment of that prospect and the mind's ability to envision it:

> It was no easy matter to receive a crashing blow and immediately think of how to loosen your teeth and not clench them and not bite your lip and not look the beast in the eye but at his tie, and the Lord only knew what else. That would be no trifle at such a moment.
>
> How could he prepare for this possibility? [p. 137]

Mr. Mundstock's plan is to provoke the local butcher, non-Jewish but always friendly and sympathetic to his plight, into striking him in the face; but the best he can do, after insulting the tradesman's competence as well as his wares, is to elicit a few shakes of the shoulder, whereupon: "Two of his front teeth fell out on the counter in front of the enraged purple face. His mouth half open, he fixed his eyes on the thief's throat, at the spot where a brown tie would be" (p. 144). The teeth are not real, Mr. Mundstock has a collection of them at home; but by now he is thoroughly convinced that playing at brutality is the only certain way of insuring oneself against its onslaughts, just as he believes that an intelligent cooperation between mind and body in the face of any destiny assures a causal connection between man and the reality that surrounds him. But the reality that awaits him is literally unimaginable, and although in the absence of empirical evidence Mr. Mundstock cannot be expected to know this, the reader himself gradually recognizes the subversion of a traditional consolation which men draw on to confirm their intuition that life at its heart is not chaotic.

The confusion—one is tempted to say perversion—of values which prompts Mr. Mundstock to regard the abnormality of what threatens him as a normal consequence of his existence, testifies to the enduring power of such traditional consolations and the inability—even the steadfast refusal—of the human imagination to accept the fragility of its position in *l'univers concentrationnaire*. Lacking a heritage that would permit him to evaluate so grotesque an abnormality, Mr. Mundstock is left with no alternative, in order to preserve his sanity, but to contest it on his, rather than "its" terms—for he has no way of discovering its terms.

The dilemma sears the reader with a stunning clarity when Mr. Mundstock asks his friend the baker to allow him to help carry the heavy baskets of bread, in order to strengthen his physical stature and thus to improve his chances of surviving the concentration camp. "I might watch the oven for you," he pleads, "and take the loaves out, that's the sort of thing I was thinking of." Out of the question, replies the baker with innocent scruple, "the oven would kill you, it's terribly hot work, the heat simply roars out at you. I couldn't ask you to do anything like that, and you looking so well now" (p. 149). An ominous avocation, baker's helper, for Mr. Mundstock, whose inarticulate affinity for ovens was simply intended to support his "method," though the seemingly harmless episode floats in the pool of the reader's terror and threatens to drown him with the horror of implication.

Unperturbed by his temporary setback at the baker's, Mr. Mundstock rushes home and eagerly searches the letter box to see if his summons has arrived: "The letter box was empty. There was not even a postcard in it" (p. 150). And Mr. Mundstock is disappointed! The most insidious effect of *l'univers concentrationnaire*, suggests Fuks, is that it reduces man to the awful irony of—voluntarily, if not wholly consciously—accelerating his own extinction by failing to comprehend the true nature of the inhumanity introduced into history by the crematorium and gas chamber. In training for his survival, man actually rushes toward his doom, which—such is the incomprehensible nature of this "new" reality, or "irreality"—cannot be anticipated. The vain "heroic" endeavors of Mr. Mundstock to reckon with an indifferent destructive power beyond the reaches of his imagination can be read as a sinister parable for our time; while Camus's optimistic prophecy that for the modern era fate will be "a human matter, which must be settled among men," could turn out to be an ironical epitaph that he never intended.

The utter futility of the situation is emphasized by Mr. Mundstock's second visit to the Sterns, whose distress as they helplessly await their summons is no longer concealed by pretense. "Is it any wonder my nerves are going to pieces?" exclaims the matriarchal Mrs. Stern. "Where can you turn for strength? I don't blame people for escaping into dreams, I certainly don't. You've got to find a refuge somewhere. How can we just go on holding out?" (p. 153). But "No refuge" is precisely the motto standing above the gates leading to *l'univers concentrationnaire*, a human condition far more unendurable than the "Abandon hope" of Dante's theological scheme. Mr. Mundstock's advice may sound like the wisdom of a Virgil, but its assured tone cannot hide its roots in the rhetoric of illusion, even less consoling than his optimism of the earlier visit: ". . . take all the eventualities into account. Take all the facts one by one, step by step, methodically, and prepare yourself for them all" (p. 162).

But one of the most terrible effects of the atmosphere of fear and uncertainty that surrounds the characters in Fuks's novel is the solitude which alienates them from each other. Mr. Mundstock's friendly gesture—"The whole secret, you see, is not to have any illusions. If you go about with your eyes open there's nothing to be afraid of."—falls on deaf ears ("The expressions on their faces were just what they had been when he came to join them just before five," p. 162), whatever its value for himself, because it is no longer possible for the Sterns to behave as if hope were possible. They would welcome an illusion that would serve *them*, but Mr. Mundstock can only offer them his own; thus the procedure of his first visit has been completely reversed, and this time the Sterns commiserate with *him*, in their glances if not their words. This time the "deceitful images" of his fortune-telling pack of cards, announcing joy, luck, love, good news, and good health, fool no one, as the human values that normally cement a family crumble and disappear, leaving a void in which they passively await their fate. "No illusion" thus qualifies the behavior of both Mr. Mundstock and the Sterns, though they recognize their helplessness, while his illusion that one can face *l'univers concentrationnaire* without illusion and remain calm is perhaps the greatest delusion of all.

At the Sterns, Mr. Mundstock learns of the condition of another old friend, Mr. Haus, who has devised his own "method" of confronting his destiny under the constant threat of deportation. "I don't blame people for escaping into dreams," Mrs. Stern had announced, and shortly afterward described Haus's theory, which is especially relevant because he was employed at the Jewish Community Office and thus had access to the most reliable news about the "realities" in the concentration camps. Ordinarily, Mr. Haus's

theory would brand him immediately as a madman; but as Mr.
Mundstock visits his old friend to obtain the latest information on
the status of the deportations, reality seems to dissolve, and together
with Mr. Mundstock we experience a sense of total disorientation.
According to Mrs. Stern, this is Mr. Haus's theory:

> there wasn't really any war on at all, and we were all living on a star,
> I've forgotten the name of it, now, it's just billions of miles away. . . .
> the war and living here on the earth is all something we've dreamed.
> Up there on the star there's plenty of everything, nobody wants for
> anything, but when we go to sleep at night, up there on the star,
> dreams come to us, and that's what we are doing down here. The best
> thing is to take sleeping pills and then we don't have these awful
> dreams. To take sleeping pills at night, up there on the star, of course.
> Do you make sense of that? [p. 155]

"It's his fantasy," responds Mr. Mundstock glibly, not realizing that
the "fantasy" of the concentration camp, to which the mind cannot
assent as a fait accompli but which it cannot expunge from the
future either, breeds fantasies in the potential victims until the lines
of demarcation between fantasy and reality vanish in the fruitless
search for a meaningful orientation to an incomprehensible experience, one that violates any prior sense of human expectations.

Mr. Haus's notion bears a remarkable resemblance to Mark
Twain's speculations, at the end of *The Mysterious Stranger*, about
the relationship between dream and reality, speculations growing
out of his own inability to reconcile the moral horror of the human
scene with his private conception of what civilization might have
been. Mr. Haus's retreat into the privacy of his dream world rests on
an illogic—"he thinks the evening is the morning and the day's the
night and the earth's a star. Only the pills are right." (p. 156)—that
reflects a similar inversion of values in his world, where Jews are
swine and men are exterminated like insects. For Mr. Haus, life is
the nightmare from which he escapes via sleeping pills to his
reassuring dream-fantasy; and given the "nightmare" for which Mr.
Mundstock seems to be preparing himself, one is tempted, together
with Mark Twain, to approve the desirability (if not the plausibility)
of Mr. Haus's path.

But as the reader wanders through this maze of irreality, Fuks
brings him abruptly—if temporarily—back to that sordid, inescapa-

ble instant in the present when man during the Holocaust
surrendered to the power of death and lost his struggle to maintain
his dignity as a human being; for as Mr. Mundstock enters the
"terribly ramshackle" house of his old friend, we are suffused with
the imagery of degradation that leaves an unmistakable impression
of the actual fate awaiting all the victims, whatever their strategy of
illusion:

> An incredibly filthy passage led into it, with cobwebs hanging from
> the ceiling and rubbish caked in the dried mud underfoot. The only
> living creature about was a mouse. . . . In the yard the ash cans were
> on their sides by a pile of rubbish, and a rusty old bucket lay there.
> . . . The upper windows were broken and stopped up with planks
> and straw, and nobody seemed to be living there. . . . It is light for a
> long time in May, especially in Summer Time, he thought, but it's as
> dark as the grave inside there . . . [p. 165]

Mr. Mundstock's "visit" confirms what was suggested earlier—that
the fact of death was less important in the literature of atrocity (and
in the historical events that inspired it) than the shadow cast over
the imagination and the milieu of the prospective victims, who
found themselves plunged into a world of incomprehensible reasons
and incredible methods that mocked every effort at "intelligent"
response. Thus, the inside of Mr. Haus's wretched dwelling
contradicts its exterior, as if one were moving insensibly from
nightmare to tolerable dream without being able to perceive the
transition. Mr. Mundstock wants to speak to Mr. Haus about
"what's going on in the Jewish Community Office" (p. 168), but the
young girl who cares for him, and announces first that he is "not
there" and then "asleep in the next room" (p. 169), confuses Mr.
Mundstock, who finally realizes that she is out of her mind; and
suddenly Mr. Mundstock finds himself in a situation he cannot
contend with:

> He touched his forehead. It was wet. No, not from fear; it was a
> strange and unaccustomed feeling of anxiety. He tried not to show it.
> He ran his eyes round the room, and felt as though a shadow had
> started to hover round him. [p. 169]

This is an unacknowledged prelude to the future, as the premise of
sanity is immersed in an atmosphere of madness, like the human
creature in the sealed gas chamber wondering what logic of

existence has led to this absurd, unfathomable, monstrous death. And in another moment, in a scene that wavers between fairy tale and mystic ritual, Mr. Mundstock enters into the secret of Mr. Haus's fate—and his own:

> There was a door in the wall which he had not noticed before.
> She opened it.
> "You can see him now, can't you? I'll give you a light."
> She took a candlestick and carried it toward the open door.
> "But you mustn't speak to him in here, sir," she said firmly; "this is where he sleeps."
> He looked into the tiny place.
> In a long wooden washtub lay Mr. Moyshe Haus.
> "Eloi!" Mr. Mundstock cried out and the flame of the candle flickered. "He's dead." [pp. 172–73]

Mr. Mundstock is shaken, but he awakens the following morning unmoved by the revelation, fortified by his own ironic determination: "That was not the way out, it really was not. . . . Poor old Haus, who had chosen to commune with the spirits instead of facing reality" (p. 173).

Thus Fuks has created a situation where "facing reality," once an essential quality of the reasonable man, has become a fetish rather than a means of insight, an invented enactment of a ritual on an imagined stage that pretends to duplicate the drama of life. Between language and action, the conception of an eventuality and the event itself, an enormous gulf of silent implication intervenes, and as Mr. Mundstock mentally verbalizes the last steps in his carefully formulated program for anticipating (and thus hopefully defeating) the future, one feels the singular force of Wolfgang Borchert's conviction that the ultimate cannot be put into words: "Today he was faced with the most terrible thing fate had forced on him, the final stage of his strictly systematic preparations. All he had to do was decide which time of the day would suit this last horror of all" (p. 175). Having forgotten his failure at actual suicide, Mr. Mundstock retains his belief in the unity of self that persuades a man he still pulls some of the strings at the puppet show of his life, even if that show should end in personal disaster. The notion that he can imagine the various visages of "this last horror" is the final refuge of his tottering human dignity, and he clings to it like a man who fears that reality itself will shatter into fragments of chaos if he should once abandon his hold.

But reality has already loosened his grasp, and as Mr. Mundstock "plays" at being executed, in an attempt to envision or experience the feelings of the condemned as they impotently await their awful doom, he unwittingly joins the conspiracy that is plotting his extermination. He has already abandoned the living for the condition of nonbeing his persecutors seek to impose on him even before his death; and the supreme irony of his existence is that his attempts to face *in advance* "the most terrible thing fate had forced on him" exactly fulfills the plans of his persecutors, not his own. Mr. Mundstock's efforts to conceptualize his destiny represent not faulty but irrelevant logic, just as the language in which he "expresses" himself indicates not excessive but inadequate rhetoric, circling around a reality for which the human imagination has not yet discovered appropriate terminology, while that reality itself spills, undefined but threatening, over the circumference:

> The last step, today, would be terrible and a chill would shudder down his spine; he thought it over, concealing nothing, pretending nothing, looking at it objectively, but all the time he felt there was a degree of conflict in his mind. If his practical method proved its worth, as his preparatory exercises ought to show, then this last step would never happen and his preparations for it were unnecessary. On the other hand, if he were properly prepared for it, there would be not the shadow of a doubt in his mind even if it appeared to be a threat. It was very well thought out and it could not be avoided. Even the single crack disappeared, although it was self-contradictory. [p. 184]

The drama going on in Mr. Mundstock's imagination is not supported by any concrete details based on personal experience— the singular absence of imagery in the quoted passage reinforces this feeling—whereas the drama going on about him, of which he is scarcely aware, offers the reader an opportunity to evaluate the unique role that actual history plays in the *content* of the literature of atrocity.

For while Mr. Mundstock prepares for his major "scene," in which he imagines his own death, an SS officer is assassinated in the vicinity, and although Fuks never specifies his name, it is evident to the informed reader that he is Reinhard Heydrich, Gestapo chief, whose death led to unimaginable atrocities, including the destruction of the town and the entire male population of the city of Lidice. The reader thus has "concrete details" in abundance to experience the threat and horror such an episode will inspire, and the intricate tensions between Mr. Mundstock's obliviousness to the significance of this "actuality" and the reader's vivid sense of its implications, based on his retrospective familiarity with the situation (a "foreknowledge" which Mr. Mundstock vainly strives to achieve)—such tensions lie at the heart of the aesthetic effect of the literature of atrocity.

The deepest horror of the Holocaust may have been man's inability to recognize it for what it was, or the desperation with which he suppressed the darkest portents about its true purpose: this is indeed the compassionate theme of Fuks's novel. Immediately after the assassination, Mr. Mundstock's neighbor confronts him with an unadorned fact—"They're beginning to shoot people" (including, perhaps, her own husband)—but his response only confirms how far the reality of his private fantasy has insulated him from this fantastic reality: "It was so unexpected he could not think of his excuses" (p. 186).

The "unexpected" plays a peripheral role in a civilization that believes in the power of the human intelligence and imagination to synthesize the fragments of reality into a unified whole; and so long as Mr. Mundstock continues to believe in this power, and the system of causality it implies, he is untroubled by the possible difficulty of accommodating the unexpected into his conception of reality. But the more persistently he pursues his stubborn defense of an outmoded conception, the more persuaded are we that the disintegration of a way of life has already begun, and that the process is irreversible—a sense of finality resembling our inarticulate despair at the spectacle of old Lear searching vainly for a breath of life in the corpse of Cordelia.

As Mr. Mundstock stands against the blank wall of his own room, blindfolded, hands self-tied behind his back, a toy metal frog between his teeth to enable him to imitate the clicking of rifles at the crucial moment, the past and all its cherished values lie behind him like a vast desert and the chaotic future rushes to meet him with unacknowledged but triumphant glee; and still the unseeing victim struggles to attribute *meaning* to his fate. The consolations of philosophy that run through his mind—"If we exist, there is no death; if death exists, we do not" (p. 188)—mock him with their irrelevance, and even his private attempts to formulate a coherent interpretation of his imagined experience—"Death is a landmark at which people come to a stop" (p. 189)—though bleaker than the philosopher's paradox, grope vainly for a mirage of solace where only barren desert prevails.

Reflecting on the clichés about Jews which the Nazis spread before the world on their posters, Mr. Mundstock concedes that life is always more complicated than one supposes—"To discover the difference between the posters and the truth the world had to sink deep into the darkness, and even so people did not see it" (p. 189) —but the darkness of the impending *univers concentrationnaire* is impenetrable, especially to the "eyes" of Mr. Mundstock, which lead him finally to the conclusion that if a man cannot defeat his fate, he can at least achieve the dignity of surrendering to it gracefully: "any suggestion that he could do anything about it was nonsensical. He was an elderly, worn-out man" (p. 190). But even as he crumples to the ground at his "practice" execution, the rules of his fantastic game called "facing reality" reassert themselves, and he undertakes one final maneuver to incorporate the "unexpected" into his method:

> he quickly got to his feet, for he knew this death was not enough. There could be another death, a far stranger one. Could there really be? He hesitated for a moment, as though in horror of something, then his old determination was restored. It would be so, he confirmed his own thoughts, and I must not give in. I am almost at my goal! Beasts like the Nazis would find incredible things to do. He had heard that in concentration camps people were shut up in cells without windows and left to die of suffocation.
>
> Yet there could certainly be even worse things than suffocation for want of air. They could turn gas on in cells like that, for they were indeed beasts who would think of things no normal person would do. [pp. 190–91]

Thus Mr. Mundstock imagines the ultimate horror, which cannot be put into words, turns on the gas, and just before he lapses into unconsciousness, shuts it off and opens the window. Gradually, imperceptibly, only half-aware of the direction of his endeavors, he has ended his attempts to prepare for, and thus to defeat his fate, by pretending to succumb to its most fearful symbol.

Ionesco speaks of one of his dramas as "a realistic play into which fantastic elements have been introduced, a contrast intended at one and the same time to banish and recall the 'realism.'" Although much more pertinent as a literary technique to Ilse Aichinger's *Herod's Children* and the stories and novels of Jakov Lind, this principle is also employed in a limited way by Fuks, who creates for his protagonist fantasies of atrocity which simultaneously banish the "realism" of the assumptions that generate the fantasies, and recall (for the reader) the far more grotesque "realism" of the common doom Mr. Mundstock tries so desperately to imagine. As Mr. Mundstock lies on the floor of his room unconscious but not fatally overcome by the real gas that he has liberated in "play" (banishing the significance of suicide in *l'univers concentrationnaire* while recalling for us the terror of Zyklon B), he retreats into the supreme delusion of his life, which implies the very reverse of what it says and presses the intelligence of the reader to acknowledge another dramatic axiom of Ionesco's, that "the real must be in a way dislocated, before it can be reintegrated." [11] For round Mr. Mundstock's mouth "a happy smile was playing,"

> the smile of a man who has put his earthly life behind him and reached his last goal. The last reality, the real thing waiting for him in the concentration camp, had been experienced too. The most terrible fate in store for him had been fulfilled. Death had revealed its simplicity to him.[12]

If one ever doubted it, one is here persuaded that the work of the imagination—Fuks's novel, in this instance—can coordinate dislocated realities as no single mind in real life (or as here, the fictional mind of Mr. Mundstock) could ever do; for at the very instant when Mr. Mundstock celebrates his blissful discovery—a bliss that would be comic were its object less gruesome—the Gestapo breaks into his room, searching for evidence about the recent assassination, and the naked brutality of their behavior, firmly rooted in physical fact, rudely shatters the serenity of Mr. Mundstock's "dream-death,"

11. Eugene Ionesco, *Notes & Counternotes: Writings on the Theatre*, trans. Donald Watson (New York: Grove Press, 1964), pp. 26, 28.

12. Fuks, *Mr. Theodore Mundstock*, p. 192.

although his failure to perceive this only intensifies our own efforts to reintegrate our dissociated feelings, floating between the imagined and the real. His apparent indifference—"I've finished my epilogue. This is mere playing around compared to what I've just been through" (p. 193)—challenges the reader's imagination to create its own epilogue, since the "last reality, the real thing waiting for him in the concentration camp" conceals secrets that Mr. Mundstock has not begun to penetrate; in a sense, he has already passed from life into death, insofar as his inner vision has alienated him from the actual events of his life. The prospect of his awful fate has drawn a shroud across his eyes that has destroyed his ability to distinguish between fact and illusion, and his remaining efforts to do so merely testify to the victory of *l'univers concentrationnaire* over a world-view which affirms the existence of moral order at the heart of the universe, and which conceives of death as an imaginable and at least aesthetically viable reality.

Illusion had begun to play a momentous role in Mr. Mundstock's life when he had received his first "summons" from Mrs. Stern, asking him to bring some words of reassurance to her troubled family. His traffic with illusion, first on their behalf, then on his own, is qualified by a second and final letter, in which she announces that their "death warrant" has arrived—deportation to Terezín. (Another striking example of the way history collaborates with invention in the literature of atrocity; for Terezín, or Theresienstadt, is sufficient to set up vibrations of horror that a fictional place-name could never inaugurate.) With the exception of the youngest son, who is to go with "the next lot," they are to leave immediately, and the prospect paralyzes Mrs. Stern with fear and confusion, since unlike Mr. Mundstock she knows that no past experience will help her unlock the mysteries of their fate, which remains a giant, grim question mark, printed on the blank tablet of reality:

> The idea of it is sending me out of my mind. Has it happened to other people? Has it ever happened to parents, Mr. Mundstock, to have their children torn from them and then to be driven to their deaths, each on his own? Has what is happening to us ever happened to anyone in the world before . . . ? [p. 195]

Perhaps the greatest "tragedy" of the Holocaust was that it wrenched its victims from any recognizable cycle of human destiny and thrust them into an anonymous and "meaningless" suffering that precluded the possibility of tragedy as we commonly understand it. The anguish of the tragic figure—and again, Lear may be the sole exception—is usually mitigated by a recognition of some pattern in the events leading to his ordeal, an insight which in turn is transmitted to the reader (or audience), who can then verify their common humanity, as well as their common doom. But the questions raised by Mrs. Stern introduce the possibility of a unique dislocation of reality which—notwithstanding Ionesco's literary theories—no one can reintegrate, because no one has yet pieced together the shattered vision of *l'univers concentrationnaire* enough to permit a pattern to emerge.

Thus, the literature of atrocity, by design and of its very nature, frustrates any attempt to discover a moral reality behind the events it narrates; its questions compel not "answers," but a reliving of the nightmare that inspired them. And part of the nightmare is the impulse to reject the nightmare: hence Mr. Mundstock's responses to Mrs. Stern's letter reflect man's last, desperate, necessarily inadequate efforts to affirm what Camus calls the absurdity of his existence, and conquer anonymity. For the absurd, Camus argued, was born of a "confrontation between the human need [for happiness and for reason] and the unreasonable silence of the world." [13] Mr. Mundstock in his determination may be a caricature of the absurd man: for his illusions are his weakness, not his strength, and when, despite everything, he concludes, with Sisyphus and Oedipus, that "all is well," he submits in total defeat to a universe he neither understands nor is able to negate.

For in seeking a satisfactory human response to the "fundamental fact at the bottom of it all" [14]—that the Sterns were being deported—Mr. Mundstock assembles a gamut of possibilities, ranging from insight to delusion, which only confirm the bleak fact that, for the unique reality of the Holocaust, none is sufficient. First he acknowledges the "crushing truth" that Mrs. Stern had never believed any of his words or promises about a better future; then he confesses with "immeasurable horror" that for the young boy left behind "he had done nothing of any use all his life"; he further

13. Camus, *The Myth of Sisyphus*, p. 21.
14. Fuks, *Mr. Theodore Mundstock*, p. 198.

realizes for the first time in weeks that "his life had been wasted, useless and vain"; but these recognitions, representing if not tragic knowledge of human limitation at least an approach by Mr. Mundstock to his own past inadequacies, furnish no weapons against his impending deportation, so he dismisses them with abrupt irony as "his grim dream, his dark, nonsensical fantasy" (p. 199). In his world of inverted values, reality forces him to repudiate even the seeds of tragedy, and in a parody of Camus's stern optimism Mr. Mundstock unconsciously denies his own prescribed method of preparing for the worst:

> Don't I know we're not going to die? Who said the transport was a misfortune that had to end in death? What ever made me think that? It's not too late at all. There's still time to do everything. [p. 199]

In dedicating his energy henceforth to the son the Sterns have left behind, Mr. Mundstock asserts a tradition of education—one more component of moral order—against the prospect of extinction; but by now his resolution is so irrelevant to the impending threat that it reveals the total exhaustion of the tradition on which he relies:

> I shall teach you my methods and my way of doing things. I shall teach you to look the facts in the face so as to be able to stand up to them. . . . And then, when we come back from the concentration camp. . . . [p. 199]

Incorrigible hope at this point seems as fabulous as Mr. Haus's distant star: nor does it ever occur to Mr. Mundstock that survival itself might be meaningless under certain conditions of existence. When the long-awaited summons finally arrives, he greets it serenely, prepares his suitcase, and helps the young boy do the same. On the way to the assembly point he compliments himself for having suppressed his shadow Mon, "the shadow of his own self, of that sorry, hounded, exhausted, torn individual" (p. 211), and for a moment we wonder whether his greatest error—paradoxically—has not been his attempt to banish fear and disunity from his life. Yet when he arrives and gazes with misguided satisfaction at the crowds of "poor creatures" waiting in "despair, helplessness and terror" (p. 212), without knowing what to expect, we are forced to admit with a sense of paralyzed shock that in *l'univers concentrationnaire*, perhaps for the first time in history, man found himself in a human situation where he was totally without refuge or consolation.

For even as Mr. Mundstock strives to establish his individuality when confronted with this undifferentiated mass of deportees—"he had been through it all, and nothing could take him by surprise, he reassured himself" (p. 212)—we are convinced that, like his fellow Jews, all wearing the same yellow star, he is simply a victim, nothing more, a victim without recourse, whose efforts to link the present with the future through will and intelligence reflected an order of reality that is no longer relevant to his life. Like the others, he was "given over to death" by the fact of his being, not in the general sense of all human tragedy, but in the restricted context of his Jewish identity; and this irrational principle, which defined his universe and determined his behavior and inspired his queer, nightmarish communions with death even while he was still alive, so confined the range of his imaginative existence between the expected summons in his letter box and the concentration camp to which it inevitably led, that the time and manner of his death—to such a state of awful nonbeing is the victim in *l'univers concentrationnaire* reduced—seem superfluous and almost irrelevant.

The supposed salvation of self called "facing reality," which Mr. Haus had abandoned at the cost of his sanity (and ultimately, of his life), proves just as ineffectual for Mr. Mundstock, who approaches deportation at the last instant wondering whether after all there is any value in his "method" for the young son of the Sterns; and this momentary doubt provokes in turn another faint glimmer of perception, one of the most devastating truths of the Holocaust, which trembles on the brink of Mr. Mundstock's imagination: "perhaps there were things you could not prepare for" (p. 212). It is enough to seal his destiny, which comes roaring down at him as he crosses the street to the assembly point in the form of "an enormous military truck," crushing out his life even as his last shriek of justification fills his mind, the appalling epitaph of the millions who entered the gas chambers he had only imagined: "what were we doing, just practicing, we couldn't prepare ourselves for everything, it was all some terrible mistake I made, I must have made an awful mistake" (p. 213). Mere arrival at the point of deportation, for one who has spent his days and nights anticipating the "last horror of all," is a sufficient death warrant; thus it seems both ironic and fitting that the end should come from such unexpected quarters, since the strategy of liquidation was designed to allay or divert suspicions until the victim could no longer resist.

Mr. Mundstock's last cry is for his shadow Mon, long absent, that mocking, contradictory part of his nature whose abandonment had certified his life of illusion, and whose return—in a tragic admission of past error or oversimplification—would at least restore a semblance of unity to his character in death. But as if to verify the impossibility of tragedy in *l'univers concentrationnaire*, Fuks denies this ultimate dignity to man as victim, instead transferring the remnants of Mr. Mundstock's inadequate vision to "the little shadow trembling terrified on the paved street by the dead man" (p. 214), the boy Simon, the last member of the Stern family, abandoned now and about to enter into the only legitimate bequest his prospective teacher can offer him—the heritage of death.

The spectacle of a young boy about to embark on a journey toward life and a future full of creative possibilities is a traditional conclusion of the *Bildungsroman* in our time, but the prospect of a child about to undertake a voyage that will culminate in his extinction, under circumstances so fantastic that even a willing suspension of disbelief cannot envision their enormities, yet so terribly real that the power of recollection alone is sufficient to evoke their concrete details—on a paradoxical note such as this Fuks concludes his novel, deliberately leaving the epilogue to the reader's imagination, and thus forcing him to relive the role of Mr. Mundstock himself, immersing him in a painful, frustrating quest for a reality whose exact definition neither mind nor language can encompass completely, but which remains permanently suspended between the two in the energizing balance of art.

*And if the sufferings of children go
to swell the sum of sufferings that
was necessary to pay for truth, then
I protest that the truth is not worth
such a price.*

Ivan Karamazov

*Once upon a time there were gas
chambers and crematoria; and no
one lived happily ever after.*

A Modern Fairy Tale

"How could it be possible for them to burn people, children, and for the world to keep silent? No, none of this could be true. It was a nightmare." History has been unable to answer Elie Wiesel's fearful question, and art would not presume to try; yet the extermination of children during the Holocaust remains a unique atrocity, one which more than any other offends the sensibilities and the imagination of men who consider themselves civilized. If man's fate in war is to die, and woman's to mourn, a child's fate—as always—is to live and rejoice in his youth and innocence while they last; and the mind has special difficulty adjusting to any situation that reverses this "normal" trend.

Shakespeare drew on this expectation in his audience in his profoundest drama: the supreme moment of horror in *King Lear* occurs when the aged father enters with his daughter (not quite a child, but the extreme contrast in their ages makes her seem so) dead in his arms. The inarticulate cry, half pain, half despair, which Shakespeare transliterated as a repeated "Howl," leaves the spectator feeling the kind of emotion that must have led to Wiesel's question; such an injustice, so far beyond the explanation of "mere" human malice, paralyzes the imagination and turns the tongue almost mute—Albany's terse "Fall and cease," whether an appeal to the intolerably persecuted Lear or to the entire universe, seems the only appropriate one. Whether "the promised end" or "image of that horror," the spectacle of the dead Cordelia makes survival seem superfluous, and the restoration of tranquillity after the expenditure of evil, so characteristic of Shakespeare's other trage- dies, virtually impossible here.

Cordelia's meaningless, almost gratuitous death stretches our sense of justice beyond its ability to rebound, and pushes tragedy past tolerable frontiers into the terrain of moral anarchy and nihilism. In such a nightmare world, reunion between father and daughter, age and youth, the past and the future, the contrite and the forgiving, would appear sentimental; after a point—and by now this should have a familiar ring—atrocity so transforms reality with its abuses (the hanging of Cordelia awakens quiet echoes of the hanging of the boy recorded by Wiesel in *Night*) that one no longer recognizes its contours. Of all the minds antecedent to the Holocaust, the author of *King Lear* would, perhaps, have under- stood Auschwitz best.

Yet *King Lear* in no sense is a play seriously concerned with the suffering of little children; the literary imagination after Shake- speare was far more explicitly immersed in this problem. Dos- toevsky, for example, whose faith always balanced the nihilism espoused by some of his characters, made the question a central moral and religious issue of *The Brothers Karamazov*. The unity of his world-view depends on a satisfactory "solution" to this riddle, just as the agony of his great "Nay-sayer," Ivan, resulted from *his* failure to find one. If *Lear*, in its implications, nevertheless appears closer to *l'univers concentrationnaire* than *The Brothers Karamazov*, it is chiefly because Dostoevsky was unwilling or unable to postulate a world absolutely beyond moral reason, one so governed by animal impulses (as in *Lear* with its bestial imagery) and an atmosphere of brutality, that the reader would be shaken to the roots of his emotional and spiritual being.

The question is stylistic and formal as well as intellectual; it may be that Ivan's prolonged monologues and schizophrenic dialogues best suited the uncertainties and tensions which beset the questing nineteenth-century mind. For Dostoevsky, at any rate, the crisis of faith and doubt, though perhaps to be "solved" experientially, could be represented in fiction only through a logical progression of ideas; ironically, they were self-defeating, these ideas, since an exclusively intellectual approach to reality stifled the possibility of active love, which for Dostoevsky was the supreme virtue. Yet he knew of no other way to introduce the theoretical dilemma of the suffering of little children: the most powerful indictment of a divine universe to appear anywhere in his novels falls from the lips of Ivan Karamazov, whose orientation to reality is strictly intellectual, and whose objections, paradoxically, are logical deductions from the illogic of the suffering which he condemns. Even the "Legend of the Grand Inquisitor," his supreme intellectual achievement, is not a myth that immerses us (like the "snow-episode" in Thomas Mann's *Magic Mountain*) in a contradictory world of impulses simultaneously within and beyond reality, but the cerebral tour de force of a man who is unable to love life more than the meaning of it. Since Dostoevsky did not himself believe that these contradictions accurately reflected spiritual reality, but only the confused mind of his character, Ivan's rebellion, for all its powerful appeal to the intellect, is *in the context of the novel* a literary formulation, verbally horrifying, but emotionally undercut by its experiential equivalent in the action, the fate of little Ilyusha Snegiryov, who dies pathetically and is mourned, but whose memory among the boys surrounding Alyosha at the end of the novel is a cause for rejoicing rather than despair.

Ivan's ambiguity about the nature of reality turns inward upon himself rather than outward on his world, thus fundamentally distinguishing Dostoevsky's concern with the problem of children's suffering from the interest of the authors of atrocity—Ilse Aichinger's *Herod's Children* (1948),[1] for example—where the fantastic world of terror that unaccountably threatens innocent children becomes the stylistic as well as the intellectual substance of the work, transforming setting, characterization, dialogue—everything. No careful reader of *The Brothers Karamazov*, on the other hand, could fail to distinguish between Dostoevsky's religious premises (with all their limitations for the modern mind), dramatized in the figures of Alyosha and Father Zossima, and Ivan's deviation from them. As a result of this distinction, consistently maintained throughout the novel by Dostoevsky, our total imaginative involve-

---

1. *Die Grössere Hoffnung (Herod's Children)* was first issued in 1948 by Bermann Fischer Verlag, Amsterdam. According to Miss Aichinger (in a letter to the author), a second, revised version with numerous stylistic alterations was published in 1960 by S. Fischer in Germany. The translation by Cornelia Schaeffer (New York: Atheneum, 1963) used in this chapter is of the second, revised edition.

ment in the kind of injustice Ivan describes is diminished: he seems
to protest less against the suffering of little children than the
implications (for him personally) of living in a universe where such
suffering is possible. This is not to say that Dostoevsky has failed to
create a rhetorically persuasive argument for Ivan's point of view,
one which temporarily crushes even his devout brother. But Ivan
remains an "arguer," an exponent, the victim of a dialectical
struggle within his own divided consciousness, searching for concrete evidence to support his conception of a nihilistic and
anarchistic world, though limited in his efforts by his creator, who
himself offered evidence to the contrary. Curiously, the events of
the Holocaust cast an even more theoretical shadow over Ivan's
attempts to penetrate the mystery of theodicy, and especially the
dilemma of the suffering of innocent children.

Retrospectively, one is tempted to argue, Dostoevsky planted in
his chapter on "Rebellion" in *The Brothers Karamazov* seeds for an
art of atrocity which only history could fertilize: the fact of
Auschwitz, and everything it came to symbolize for the modern era,
gave tangible substance to Ivan's desperate objections to a universe
in which unavenged suffering, especially of little children, could
exist. Yet Dostoevsky went about his work of gardening for the
future unconsciously; for him, Ivan's image of man and his world is
the distorted and perverse product of a sick mind, which offers
information about atrocities in the form of second-hand testimony—
Ivan has read or heard his stories of crimes against children, but
experienced none of them himself. For some authors in the tradition
of atrocity, however, Ivan's "sick" vision becomes the "healthy"
insight of the twentieth-century creative imagination, "inventing"
nightmares of reality undreamt of in Ivan's philosophy.

Ivan, in short, is a rebel before his time—as Albert Camus clearly
recognized; he is afflicted with a Euclidean sensibility in a world
where theorems and formulae no longer respond to the assaults of
logic, but which offers the mind no other terms than those of logic,
so long as it continues to seek answers to its questions, and to
believe (or at least to espouse belief in), as Ivan does, traditional
categories like order and harmony and justice: "I must have
justice," he cries, "or I will destroy myself." [2] The literature of

2. Fyodor Dostoevsky, *The Brothers Karamazov*, trans. Constance Garnett (New York:
Modern Library, College Edition, 1950), p. 289.

atrocity compresses Ivan's disillusionment and anguish into a single inquiry, more aesthetic than philosophical, and transforms the response into the immediate substance of its art; it asks: "What is a world like in which the *categories* that make Ivan's arguments meaningful—including his obsession with the suffering of little children—disappear in the smoke of the crematorium?"

Yet Ivan (and hence Dostoevsky) is not entirely unaware of the implications of his position—a flash from the twentieth century illuminates his conversation with his brother and provides Camus with material for his more contemporary treatment of related problems in *The Myth of Sisyphus*, *The Plague*, and *The Rebel*. After reciting the last in a series of atrocities, about a general who set his hounds on a child and permitted them to tear the boy to pieces before his mother's eyes (Ivan had just read about it "in some collection of Russian antiquities") Ivan asks Alyosha what punishment the general deserves: "To be shot?" "To be shot," his brother murmurs, then adds: "What I said was absurd, but——."

A germ, just a germ of the atmosphere of *l'univers concentration-naire* intrudes at this instant, as Alyosha momentarily succumbs to the "logic" of vengeance, then recognizes the illogicality of its coming from the lips of a Christian novice, then lapses into silence as he retreats from the implications of the situation in which he finds himself trapped. Ivan gleefully seizes on his brother's confusion as confirmation of a view of reality that he himself has difficulty expressing:

> "That's just the point that 'but'!" cried Ivan. "Let me tell you, novice, that the absurd is only too necessary on earth. The world stands on absurdities, and perhaps nothing would have come to pass in it without them. We know what we know!"
>
> "What do you know?"
>
> "I understand nothing," Ivan went on, as though in delirium. "I don't want to understand anything now. I want to stick to the fact. I made up my mind long ago not to understand. If I try to understand anything, I shall be false to the fact, and I have determined to stick to the fact." [3]

Ivan fails to recognize the contradictions implicit in his own words, so obsessed is he with the contradictions in his apprehension of

3. Ibid., pp. 288–89.

reality; actually, the need to understand is the basic drive of his nature, and the dissonance between the fact of atrocity and the principle of justice ultimately drives him to the brink of madness. Yet, out of his solitary "but," and the notion that the "world stands on absurdities" will sprout not only Camus's philosophy of absurdity, but the attitude implicit in much literature of atrocity, which is founded on a literary "irrealism" virtually defined by the phrase "the absurdity of fact," and which absorbs Ivan's potential madness into the nucleus of its vision.

Ivan and his creator, however, lacked the critical vocabulary and the literary will to develop this intuition into a *Weltanschauung*, or into a principle for reshaping the realistic atmosphere of fiction. Dostoevsky's main intuitions, like those of his "hero" Alyosha, were sent out like threads into the universe, to bind together the disparate impulses that so disturbed Ivan and to create a spiritually coherent pattern in human experience. The existence and example of an archetypal Sufferer minimized (without totally vanquishing) Ivan's vigorous dissent against a universe that permits the torture of little children, diminished, too, the force of Ivan's chafing question: "What good can hell do, since these children have already been tortured?" But the literature of atrocity, confronted with desolate evidence that makes Ivan's isolated instances seem almost trivial, does not even consider Dostoevsky's "easy" acquiescence, using Ivan's interrogative instead as an unanswerable ingredient of its nightmare vision.

If we eliminate from our apprehension of reality the stabilizing figure of an archetypal Sufferer (and the religious impulses and values that accompany him), and transform Ivan's negative revolt (leading, in Dostoevsky, to mental collapse) into an affirmative, humanistic rebellion against an indifferent universe, we enter the literary and philosophical realm of Albert Camus, whose sensibility was far more attuned to *l'univers concentrationnaire* than his progenitor's. Yet even Camus, notwithstanding his symbolic approach to the atrocity of the war and its decimation of victims, is more concerned with the substance of experience than with altering the mode of perceiving or the manner of expressing reality by artistic means. In *The Plague* he employs conventional literary devices—the monologue, the dialogue, the journal entry—to convey the implications of the absurdist situation in which the people of the

The logical subsequent step, aesthetically, would be to eliminate the dialectic and dialogue entirely and to incorporate the very terms of the tension—the suffering of children and the injustice of their situation—into the style of the work of art, to cease to ask "why" or to measure the agony of the sufferers against a preconceived religious or humanistic notion of man's dignity, but to draw the reader into an imaginative world where the supremacy of such a tension has altered the nature of reality. The result would be a fictional response to Elie Wiesel's question that began this chapter, not in any sense an attempt to formulate an answer intellectually, but to render the nightmare that generated his incredulous, palpitating inquiry. And the inspiration would be, not the literary researches of an Ivan Karamazov, or a single representative instance of the universe's injustice leading to the rebellion of a Dr. Rieux in the name of a lower justice, but a historical circumstance without precedent, and therefore capable of disorienting the reader and making him acquiescent to the literary experience of the absurd—submerging him in the terrors of alienation to a degree that the philosophical implications of Camus's attitude never achieved.

The death of M. Othon's son in *The Plague* seems a relatively simplified approach to the problem when compared with the challenge to the literary imagination represented by the following testimony, taken from the trial of about twenty Auschwitz guards and medical officials that ended in 1965:

> "the witness saw how Scherpe [a defendant] 'personally' administered injections in Block 20 [the 'hospital' barracks]. It happened during the murder of children from the vicinity of Zamosc. There were so many of them that they had to line them up between the barracks. Some of the children were led into the area of Block 20, where Scherpe killed them while the others were still playing outside. There were more than 100."

> He remembers this case so well because Scherpe had suddenly paused. "We thought he was conscience-stricken and that was the reason he broke off in the middle of murdering the children. I clearly remember him stopping. He left, and we never saw him again after that. Hantl [another defendant] took over. Hantl finished the murder of the children."

The words are pale and dispassionate. And yet they conjure up the terrible moment when the children of Zamosc put their thin arms

across their mouths, the poison needle jabbed between their skinny
ribs, and they fell down like cut blades of grass and were dragged out
to the other victims, to make room for those who were still playing
outside.[8]

That "terrible moment" stretched interminably across a facade of
"playing outside," of the familiar world of childhood; an atmosphere of threat and fear commingled with childlike innocence; the
inoculation of the sensibilities of children, accustomed to trust the
world of adults, with a serum of insecurity dissolved in terror, so
that they are forced to retreat into protective fantasies that mirror
their fears without obscuring them—these are the contradictions
that assault the imagination of the writer who ponders the
monstrous evidence just quoted.

"There is no need of determining whether art must flee reality or
defer to it," says Camus, "but rather what precise dose of reality the
work must take on as ballast to keep from floating up among the
clouds or from dragging along the ground with weighted boots." [9]
In its sordid aspect, the murder of the children of Zamosc drags
along the ground; in its inconceivability, it floats among the clouds;
the delicate task of recreating something of each requires a vision of
experience virtually unique, a kind of art for history's sake which is
not historical art or fiction, but conceals the features of history
behind an imaginative mask pierced, one might say, with explicitly
allusive eyes.

In Dostoevsky and Camus, the suffering of innocent children is
dramatized from the point of view of adult vision: we look on with
pain and horror at the ordeals of Ivan's examples and M. Othon's
son. Neither Dostoevsky nor Camus has attempted to recreate the
universe of their suffering, however, from the perspective of the
children's confused and tormented eyes; the resulting concentration
and intensity of outlook and action would have imposed limitations
too restrictive to the artistic designs of their works. Nor was either
author, the Christian Dostoevsky or the humanist Camus, prepared
to admit some of the nightmare implications which such a literary
strategy might have endorsed, especially those conveyed by an
experience like the extermination of the children of Zamosc. Such

8. Bernd Naumann, *Auschwitz*, p. 138.
9. Albert Camus, "Create Dangerously," in *Resistance, Rebellion, and Death*, trans. Justin
O'Brien (New York: Modern Library, 1960), pp. 202–03.

an event in history must either be disregarded by the artist as nutriment too bizarre and melodramatic for the literary imagination, or embraced with a determination to invent a form and a language commensurate with a world where children's destiny is to fall down "like cut blades of grass," and to be "dragged out to the other victims, to make room for those who were still playing outside."

Almost a decade after *The Plague*, and only a few years before his death, Camus summarized his feeling about such a world. Speaking in "Reflections on the Guillotine" (1957) of what the condemned man must feel at the moment of his execution, he wrote: "No, what man experiences at such times is beyond all morality. Not virtue, nor courage, nor intelligence, nor even innocence has anything to do with it. Society is suddenly reduced to a state of primitive terrors where nothing can be judged. All equity and all dignity have disappeared." [10] Of course, the "central intelligence" of a child, even one of Henry James's precocious little protagonists, could not be expected to absorb the mature insight expressed by Camus. But this in itself would add to the dramatic power and literary fascination of a work that filtered the experience of the Holocaust through the sensibilities of a child, itself not totally aware of the implications of the dark fate which history was preparing for it. The distortion to be achieved by excluding the adult vision from a central place in the narrative, while still focusing on terrors that only adults could fully "understand," would result in the new imaginative world which Camus anticipated when he called on the artists of his time to create dangerously: "an equilibrium between reality and man's rejection of that reality . . . different from the everyday world and yet the same, particular but universal, full of innocent insecurity." [11]

Such a world, given the special emphases required by a specific concern with the atmosphere of *l'univers concentrationnaire* (to which Camus was not restricting his remarks), appears in Ilse Aichinger's *Herod's Children* (*Die Grössere Hoffnung*, 1948), a novel whose singular tensions prompt one to describe it as a fairy tale enveloped in a nightmare. These terms coalesce in Camus's precise

10. Camus, "Reflections on the Guillotine," in *Resistance, Rebellion, and Death*, p. 155.
11. Camus, "Create Dangerously," in *Resistance, Rebellion, and Death*, p. 203.

formulation "innocent insecurity," as they do in the novel itself, which narrates the attempts of a band of children in an unspecified wartime city (clearly Vienna) controlled by the Third Reich to escape a threatening tyranny and gain freedom. Though it, too, is never named, it does not take long to guess the nature of the monster from which they are fleeing; the children are so uncertain of their status or identity because they are from Jewish or part-Jewish families.

But such information *appears* peripheral to the central drama of the novel, intruding only intermittently through the mask of language that insulates the fantasies enacted by the children from authentic reality. The vagueness of the enemy in their own consciousness is played off against our awareness of their hopeless situation, and the endurable—their fantasies—merges with the intolerable—the "real" world that will destroy them. Thus desperation and hope unite in the very structure of the work, not as intellectual attitudes espoused by various characters (as in *The Plague*), but as the emotional nucleus of civilization in which children feel themselves trapped and exempted or expelled from humanity, and are forced to invent situations which reassure them that they still inhabit a world of the possible. The possible, however, like the fruit of Tantalus, is ever just beyond their reach, beckoning with the elusive appeal of desirable images in a wish-fulfillment dream that vanish upon waking—leaving in their stead, as in a Kafka narrative, not the humdrum world of daily routine but a threatening environment that drives the imagination to recreate, while awake, the protective atmosphere of the dream.

To be young in *Herod's Children* is to be a victim not only of one's religious heritage and of the Nazi tyranny, but of all those who are older: "Our grandparents don't vouch for us. Our grandparents have become our fault." [12] The situation of the children is partly a consequence of circumstance, partly a result of their refusal to surrender to a fate that has paralyzed the will of their elders or driven them into an exile where children cannot follow; whatever the reasons, their figurative orphanhood leaves them only the realm of fantasy, of children's "games," to secure their identity and verify their humanity. Reality no longer offers the opportunity for such

12. Aichinger, *Herod's Children*, p. 44.

discoveries; in fact, in *l'univers concentrationnaire* as Ilse Aichinger conceives of it, life seems to have discarded the notion of individual identity, so that in self-defense, paradoxically, the child searches in fantasy for its meaning and destiny.

Accordingly, what the children experience in this fantasy world cannot be casually dismissed, because for them it is equivalent to reality, an expression of the longings and fears introduced into their existence by the peripheral presence of the "secret police" and the possibility of deportation. Among the characteristic recurrent dreams reported by Charlotte Beradt in *The Third Reich of Dreams* were those of people whose wishes could not be fulfilled in reality, "due to insurmountable external, not internal, obstacles—people whose problem was not some 'wrong' political outlook but rather perhaps a 'wrong' grandmother; in short, people whose objective situation was such that they could fulfill their wishes only in their sleep." [13] In the totally frustrating fictional milieu created by Ilse Aichinger in *Herod's Children*, the imagination invents a substitute for an intolerable "normality," not as an escape—and this is the singular source of its impact—but in an attempt to *assert* life and wrench some coherence from an existence that has been reduced by "reality" to the illogic of nightmare.

Like so much of the literature of atrocity, the novel begins with a dream and an awakening, but the line of demarcation dividing the two is deliberately obscured by a veil of stylistic incertitude, an elusive diction that permeates the descriptions and the dialogue, so that the action repeatedly trembles on the edge of dissolution and the attentive reader must struggle perpetually to reorient his confused sensibilities to these alien but coexistent worlds. The dreamer is a little girl named Ellen, whose literal situation as the daughter of an aryan father (a German soldier) and a Jewish mother (who presumably has emigrated to America) has rent the security of her childhood; the substance of her dream is a projection of her explicit anxieties, so that any impulse toward surrealistic distortion is drawn back to earth by the substantial hand of history. Ellen dreams of a ship carrying children "that had something wrong," children "with the wrong grandparents, children without a passport or visa, children for whom nobody could vouch, now." [14]

13. Beradt, *The Third Reich of Dreams*, p. 127.
14. Aichinger, *Herod's Children*, p. 4.

In the midst of an oppressive present, Charlotte Beradt had also proposed in her study, dreams anticipated "both the great and the small difficulties to come. Although in those days many Jews' dreams were full of the problems of where to go and what to do . . . they unavoidably appear pale by contrast to the horrors that later actually occurred. These people had the most fantastic dream-experiences with passports, documents, and visas. They are not permitted to cross borders or go ashore, or the ship they are on sails aimlessly through the ocean. And when they do reach their destination, they are unwanted guests of strangers." [15] With remarkable intuition, Ilse Aichinger has translated into fictional terms the atmosphere of mingled yearning and apprehension that was later confirmed by the researches of psychology, one of the many instances in which art could evoke complex levels of experience that the social scientist, with his necessarily more precise formulations, could not approach. In her novel she employs a language of paradox to simultaneously conceal and reveal the terrifying uncertainty that hovered over her adolescent characters, an ambiguity that intrudes into Ellen's dream itself, where the children are trapped by a dilemma that defines the limits of their existence: "None of them had permission to stay and none had permission to go" (p. 4).

In a normal world such conditions are meaningless, yet existence by permission is a stark reality in theirs, and like Kafka's Joseph K., Ellen seeks some assurance of her right to survive in it, some confirmation of her desire to be free. The locale of her initial dream reflects the geographical vagueness that must have characterized the forbidden or impossible voyages haunting the imagination of many a potential victim:

> Round about the Cape of Good Hope the sea grew dark. The ship lanes lighted up one more time and then died away. The airlines stopped short, as though caught in an excess of daring. Groups of islands huddled together. The sea flooded all latitudes and longitudes. It laughed away knowledge of the world and clung like heavy silk to the bright land, leaving only the southernmost tip of Africa like a foreboding in the twilight. It robbed the coastlines of their consequence, and softened their raggedness.
>
> Darkness landed and moved slowly northward. It traveled up the

15. Beradt, *The Third Reich of Dreams*, pp. 140–41.

desert like a huge caravan, wide and irresistible. Ellen pushed her
sailor cap up off her face and wrinkled her brow. Suddenly she laid a
small, hot hand over the Mediterranean. But it was no use. Darkness
had settled on the ports of Europe. [p. 3]

The sea and accompanying darkness not only rob coastlines of their
consequence, but also the reader of his sense of order, as the
familiar outlines of continents seem to fade under the "groping"
hand of the sleeping child.

To Ellen and the unvouched-for children in the dream, the flight
by ship from an unspecified fear toward an unknown destination
occurs in Camus's atmosphere of innocent insecurity; but the
sinister implications of the language—"A shark swam along beside
them. It had conferred on itself the right to protect them from
people"—and the episodes—"A U-boat surfaced in front of them,
but when the sailors saw that some of the children were wearing
sailor caps, they threw them oranges and didn't hurt them"—implications that the child's intelligence is not expected to fathom,
undermine the "innocence" and apparent playfulness of the vision
for the reader and introduce presentiments of horror that intensify
steadily as the certainty of the children's fate is measured against
their inability to comprehend fully the nature of the corruption that
is infecting their games. "Huge, bright and unattainable," dreams
Ellen, "the Statue of Liberty loomed out of their fright. For the first
and last time" (pp. 4–5)—but the only alternative for the children to
the futile game called "sailing to America," is to seek assistance and
advice from an adult world itself impotent to resist the evil of
history or to offer refuge to those too young to understand the
"logic" of its crimes—an endeavor equally committed to failure.
They are trapped between the limits of their longings.

Ellen is asleep on the floor of the consul's office, though how she
remained there unnoticed after closing hours is never considered,
any more than Kafka explains how the warders gained entrance to
Joseph K.'s bedroom: in a world bound by the logic of reasonable
causality, such questions may have sensible explanations, but this is
not such a world. Ilse Aichinger (again like Kafka) persistently
affronts our sense of the credible, provoking repeated inquiries of
"How is this possible?" even though we perceive in advance that
her fiction will leave such confusions suspended in a void of

uncertainty—the same void which her characters inhabit, and which in turn reproduces the atmosphere of baffled apprehension that so often distinguished *l'univers concentrationnaire*. From the consul, Ellen hopes to secure a visa that will permit her to follow her mother into a safe exile, but their conversation runs at cross-purposes, as he pursues the premises of his official position and she talks a kind of sense that he is unable to translate into adult terms:

"What have you done with the map?"

"What map?" asked the Consul in confusion. He straightened his tie and rubbed his eyes. "Who are you?"

"Where's the map?" repeated Ellen threateningly.

"I don't know," said the Consul angrily. "Do you think I've hidden it?"

"Maybe," muttered Ellen.

"How can you think that?" asked the Consul, stretching. "Who would want to hide the whole world?"

"It's clear you don't know much about grownups!" Ellen replied indulgently. "Are you the Consul?" [p. 8]

Only our perception of the genuine menace of death lifts this dialogue out of the humorously exaggerated universe of Alice in Wonderland, where from the child's-eye point of view fantasy is also a necessary refuge in a world where those in "control" of reality have either exploited it for their own benefit or have permitted themselves to be victimized by it. The consul, himself a helpless representative of a bureaucratic system which has surrendered its power to be governed by human principles, describes the older victims as "all those people with white, hopeful faces who wanted to go away because they were afraid and because they still thought the world was round. Impossible to explain to them that the rule was an exception and the exception no rule" (p. 6). Less a piece of Alice's impish whimsy than the kind of message Kafka's K. might have received from the Castle, this indecipherable but enticingly suggestive formula of illogic defines the "new" reality which Ellen has inherited, one in which a round world is no guarantee that all will be permitted to travel its curved surface. Those who exhaust their energy in seeking to do so will succeed no better than Ellen in liberating themselves from the vague terror that threatens.

Indeed, Ellen and her friends inhabit a kind of Anne Frank attic from which all the adults have vanished, so that the children are free to imagine their situation, and to alter it at will. In most of the episodes of the novel at least one adult intrudes, uninvited but representing a reality that creates for us a perspective of human despair and suffering of which the children are never totally aware. The analogy with the Frank family offers an interesting contrast, for when the Gestapo battered down the door of their supposed haven they shattered an innocent *security* that is the very reverse of the atmosphere with which Ilse Aichinger informs her narrative. Normally, children depend on adults for help and protection—so Ellen instinctively goes to the consul. But in the disordered world of *Herod's Children* this bond must be broken, and the perplexities that ensue as the young like Ellen reluctantly realize that they are *condemned* to be independent, cast off by the cruel necessities of history—these perplexities represent innocence entering alone into a heritage of terror: as if, to vary the literary analogy, there were no adults gathered about the bed of M. Othon's little son in *The Plague* to "interpret" the agony of his dying.

Thus, when the consul finally exclaims with impatience to Ellen: "Shall we talk like grownups?" (p. 9), he unconsciously expresses one of the consequences of the Holocaust that Ellen and her friends enact rather than understand: the sacrificing of that period of innocence we identify with childhood, which is disrupted, orphaned, and finally destroyed by an adult vision that is unequipped to absorb it into the realities of impending liquidation. Less an enemy than a spokesman for an extinguished tradition, the consul offers comfort that is irrelevant and even misleading (though familiar), given Ellen's circumscribed possibilities: "You know, in the end everyone's his own consul. And whether or not the wide world really is wide is everyone's own affair"; and when he adds, "whatever happens, you'll keep believing that there's someplace where things are blue. Whatever happens!" (p. 13), we are dismayed by the distance that separates this combination of sentimental optimism and Emersonian individualism from the stern exigencies of *l'univers concentrationnaire*.

In a sense, Ellen tests this "wisdom" in the remainder of the novel, though its antithesis has already infected her dreams in the subsequent episode:

The half-moon caught her up, tipped treacherously like all cradles, and slung her out again. It wasn't true that clouds were feather beds and the sky a blue vault. The sky was open, deadly open, and as she fell it became clear to Ellen that up and down had stopped. Why didn't they know? Poor grownups, why didn't they know, when they called falling downward jumping and falling upward flying? When would they understand? [p. 15]

Or more exactly, her dreams, and the fantastic "games" she plays with the other children, project insights that cast grim shadows over their imaginative escapades, all of which focus on the goals of freedom, identity, and flight. The behavior of children as children (unlike the situation in Anne Frank's diary) is consistently framed by *fear*, as their inner desire to retain the securities of their youth impinges on the oppression that disrupts the normalcy of their lives. The tension is woven into the fabric of the novel; for example, awaking from the dream just cited, Ellen refuses to believe that her mother, though unable to secure a visa for her daughter, has really left for abroad:

The walls were inimical. Ellen played a note on the piano. It echoed. She played a second and a third. None stayed. None led to another. None comforted her. It was as though they rang out reluctantly, wanting silence; as though they were keeping something from her.

If my mother knew, her heart would burst in her breast. Those were the words in the fairy tale.

"You just wait. I'll tell my mother!"

Ellen threatened the silence, but the silence remained silent. . . .

As David had fought Goliath, she fought against the dread of abandonment, fought against a new, terrible knowledge that lifted its head out of a flood of dreams, like a specter. [p. 18]

But Ellen lives in the age of Goliath, when legends like David's victory no longer come true, and her stubborn efforts to "prove the contrary, stuff the wide-open gullet of reality, find her mother" are useless; her anguished protest, "Nowhere—that was impossible! Nowhere?" (p. 18), faces the "new, terrible knowledge" of a reality where mothers are compelled to desert their children to insure their own survival. Thus, Ellen is confronted with the mute truth that "nowhere" cannot become "somewhere" in a world where "let's pretend" only intensifies fright, a truth that is painfully confirmed when she transforms her quest for her mother into a game of tag, then tries to restore the past by invoking the principle of children's play that the "rules" can be abrogated at will: "It doesn't count, Mother, it doesn't count!" (p. 19). Like "the words in the fairy tale" and the legendary prowess of David, such hopes have been permanently extinguished in a universe whose grim premises are yet to be discovered: on the table in her room Ellen finds only the unofficial "visa" that she had drawn up and signed herself at the consul's suggestion, a passport to nowhere, a fraud further nullified by experience.

Hence, when Ellen is seen in the final episode of the first chapter leading a blind man across the street and vainly seeking directions from him for finding the consul again (whose location unaccountably seems as elusive as the Law Court Offices for Joseph K. in *The Trial*), the futility of her efforts at legal avoidance of her inexplicable fate is figuratively confirmed; for the young guiding the old is as much an inversion of normal reality as the sightless instructing the seeing, and Ellen is helplessly left to discover that she must accept the responsibility for her own future at an age when it is virtually certain she will succeed no better than the adults who have previously misled or forsaken her.

Ilse Aichinger carries the atmosphere of uncertainty a step beyond Kafka by removing even the ambiguous warnings and reassurances from · an impersonal bureaucracy that alternately encourage and exasperate his junior bank official and land-surveyor. Wandering into a church, Ellen encounters no parable of the man before the door of the law, like Joseph K. in the cathedral episode of *The Trial*, but only a painting of St. Francis Xavier, staring at her in silent amazement. Her request of the saint is pathetic, desperate, and frightening, no ordinary prayer but a cry from the heart of one who is unwilling to surrender her premise that an individual, even a child, has some control over her destiny, if only in the form of a forlorn hope: "couldn't you suggest to someone that he might vouch for me?" St. Francis persists in his silence, and Ellen reformulates her plea in more general terms, a spokesman for suffering humanity bemused by the sudden and incomprehensible expropriation of its most precious and meaningful possession: "I meant—I meant—I don't know what I have to do to be free" (p. 24).

In Kafka the "voucher," in the form of a lawyer, a Titorelli, a Klamm (or some other spokesman or messenger from the Castle) plays a crucial if unspecified role, adding a complex though admittedly vague qualification to the situation of the alienated hero-victim—to our conception of him, and his attitude toward himself. But Ilse Aichinger introduces no Godot-figure into the imaginative cosmos of her novel, and if Ellen's final petition to a mute St. Francis seems to denote otherwise, this only stresses—together with the irony of her half-Jewish heritage—the anguish of suffering from an undefined status. "Please—please," she exclaims, "whatever happens, help me to believe that there is someplace where things will be blue. Help me across the sea, even if I must stay here!" [p. 25]. During the years of the Holocaust, "inner emigration" of this and other sorts proved to be a futile refuge for more than helpless children, a fact dramatically illustrated by the unequal struggle between Ellen's appeal to the "greater hope" of the novel's original title *(Die Grössere Hoffnung)* and the nightmare conditions of her actual existence.

This tension finally produced what we now recognize as a kind of reality in transition, at least for those artists who truly believed that one form of civilization disappeared in the ashes of Auschwitz to be replaced by an as yet unspecified but wholly different sort of universe. Ilse Aichinger was one of the first to create a language that might sketch in the landscape of this transition and the schizophrenic emotions it generated, together with an illogical logic of narration commensurate with the theme, that in its unexpected stylistic and intellectual effects resembles the *discordia concors*, or yoking together of heterogeneous ideas, which Dr. Johnson attributed to the imagery of the metaphysical poets. Combining the sinister with the simple, attributing to expressions that under normal circumstances might appear harmless and even senseless a portentous significance, she redesigns and ultimately redefines the foundations of an unfamiliar but compelling world, much as John Donne, exploiting the discoveries of the new science and mathematics, helped to shatter the complacencies of the Elizabethan world picture.

For example, as some of the children in her novel are "introduced," the threat of the Holocaust undermines and gradually displaces the universe of innocence and hope it has permanently corrupted: "That's Bibi. She's got four wrong grandparents and a lipstick she's very proud of," or "that's Kurt. . . . He's got three wrong grandparents and he plays goalie," or Herbert, who has "three and a half wrong grandparents he loves very much and a red water ball he sometimes lends us," or their spokesman, who has "four wrong grandparents and a butterfly collection" (pp. 28–29). The children are "playing" a serious game called "waiting for a child to drown," and the ensuing dialogue illustrates the horrible logic of its absurdity, anticipating, too, with remarkable clarity the futile (if more self-conscious) verbal encounters of Beckett's Gogo and Didi, who play at their own suicide with a comic despair beyond tragedy:

> "What are you doing?"
> "We're waiting."
> "For what?"
> "We're waiting for a child to drown."
> "Why?"
> "We're going to save it."
> "And then?"
> "Then we'll have made good."
> "Have you done something bad?"
> "Our grandparents. It's our grandparents' fault."
> "Oh. Have you been waiting long?"
> "Seven weeks."
> "Do a lot of children drown here?"
> "No."
> "And you want to wait till a baby comes floating down the canal?"
> "Why not? We'll dry it off and bring it to the Mayor. And the Mayor'll say: Good, very good! Beginning tomorrow you may sit on any benches you want. We won't mention that matter about your grandparents any more. And we'll say, thank you, Mr. Mayor."
> "Not at all [says Ellen, entering into the role of the Mayor], nice to have seen you. My regards to your grandparents."
> "Oh, you said that well! If you like, you can play the Mayor from now on" [replies one of the children, who has been explaining the "game" to Ellen].
> "Again!"
> "Here's a child, Mr. Mayor!"
> "What about this child?"
> "We've saved it."

"How did this happen?"

"We were sitting on the bank waiting for it——"

"No! You can't say that!"

"Well, then: We just happened to be sitting on the bank, and splash—in it fell!"

"And then what happened?"

"Well, it was all so fast, Mr. Mayor. But we did it all gladly, you know. Now may we sit on the benches again?"

"Yes. And you can play in the park again. We'll forget about your grandparents."

"Oh, thank you, Mr. Mayor!"

"Wait a minute! What shall I do with the child?"

"Oh, it's yours to keep."

"But I don't want to keep it!" Ellen shouted desperately. "It's an awful child! Its mother has emigrated and its father is in the service. When it meets its father, it's not allowed to talk about its mother. And wait a minute . . . there's something the matter with its grandparents: two are all right, but two are all wrong. Undetermined, no, that's the worst—that's too much!" [pp. 26–27]

As in Beckett, here the usual distinctions between "role" and "reality" break down, and a confused audience must watch them merge and recombine until one is no longer sure whether ideas like "the right to sit on benches" and "wrong grandparents" belong to the invented fantasies of the fictional "stage" or reflect authentic images of human experience. Dialogue creates disorientation even as it attempts to "explain" the rules of Ilse Aichinger's conception of *l'univers concentrationnaire;* and the effect is as unsettling as the spectacle of an "old" inmate of Auschwitz explaining to a new arrival the "rules" that will enable him to stay alive as long as possible. The premises leading to Auschwitz or to the "wrong grandparents" of *Herod's Children* have already been incorporated into reality, and the reader, like the inmate and Ellen in the quoted passage, is repeatedly forced to face with desperate fear the inevitable consequence of such "roles" or "rules"—the undetermined and fundamentally helpless status of the victim, whose faith in the generosity of imagined mayors ill conceals the fact that the values supporting it have long since been discarded by history. In an epiphany worthy of Joyce, Ilse Aichinger evokes the principle of personality, and the paradoxical attitude behind it, that make the adoption of roles seem a more natural approach to reality than the outmoded habit once called "discovery of self":

> A man was walking along the canal [where the children are waiting to "save" a child]. The flowing water dissolved his mirrored image, folded it, pulled it apart and then left it for an instant itself.
> The man looked down and laughed. "Life," he said, "is full of benign cruelty." And he spat wide across the dirty mirror. [p. 31]

The children still assume that benignity can be divorced from cruelty, though the man recognizes that the very terminology can be inverted in its implications: To his inquiry about where she lives, Ellen replies, "With my wrong grandmother. . . . But she's all right," to which the cynical philologist responds, "Wait till you find out how wrong right is!" (p. 32).

The inability of the children to penetrate the implications of this sinister paradox is a major source of the despair and apparent madness that darken the atmosphere of Ilse Aichinger's novel. When primitive men failed to understand the natural catastrophes and other phenomena that threatened their survival, they designed rituals to pacify the anonymous hostile forces with which they identified their misery and apprehensions, in an effort to rehabilitate the future for their own benefit. In *Herod's Children*, a voice representing the collective anguish of the children makes a similar appeal, though it echoes in a silence that the primitive mind overcame by populating its voids with spirits and demons—a voice floating off into desolation amidst a world that has already determined the nonbeing of creatures with a "wrong" heritage. "If you can't show an identity card," says the voice, "you are lost. . . . Where shall we go? Who will find us our real identity? Who will help us to ourselves?" (p. 44). One is tempted to conclude that these are the wrong questions, framed as they are in the familiar rhetoric of "self-discovery" that has characterized literature (and so much of life) since the beginning of the nineteenth century; yet assumptions about reality, like traditional literary forms, die hard, if only because the human imagination finds it virtually impossible to conceive of a situation in which "no refuge" would be a perfectly accurate reflection of the human condition. Thus, the further questions of this collective children's voice—"Where will it end, the path of this sin? . . . Where does the scornful laughter stop?" (p. 44) presume a continuity in time and a validity to the idea of temporal expectation that—retrospectively, at least—the experience of the Holocaust seems to have canceled.

Elsewhere we shall have to examine in detail the influence of *l'univers concentrationnaire* on the usual relationships between past, present, and future; here it is sufficient to suggest the ironic and deceptive role which "possibility" plays in the literature of atrocity, since it is an especially vigorous force in the life of Ilse Aichinger's children. The ritual of defiance and apparent hope which they invent and finally enact remind one of the arrested tragedy of Beckett's pair, whose repeated avowals of departure are contradicted by their failure to move from the spot. The children appear to be governed by an admirable determination, a mutiny of the spirit against intolerable oppression, yet the direction and locality of their rebellion displaces courage with an ominous fear, more akin to primitive intimidation than romantic revolt:

> Since you have forbidden us to play in the parks, we will play in the graveyards. Since you have forbidden us to rest on benches, we will rest on gravestones. You have forbidden us to expect a future—but we do it still. [p. 45]

The scene of their diversion, which has grown far more grisly, shifts to the "last" remaining graveyard (for the Jews?) in the city, where they play a desperate game of "hide-and-seek" among the gravestones, searching for life in the habitat of death. One recalls Wolfgang Borchert's description of the grass amidst the rubble of Hamburg, alive "like the hair of the dead," or the setting for Pierre Gascar's *Season of the Dead*, an improvised cemetery in which the only life-sustaining labor is the burial of one's comrades; here, death has so permeated the landscape of atrocity that the distinctions between the living and the dead vanish and the collective voice calls upon the corpses to justify the existence of the children:

> One, two, three; on your mark, hide-and-seek. When you find yourself, you'll be safe. Over there, the white rock! There space becomes sanctuary. . . . The dead will play with us. Did you hear that? Testify for us, stand up, lift your hands and swear that you're alive and that you'll vouch for us. Swear that we're alive and that we are like all the others. [p. 45]

But one of the participants introduces a counterpoint to this appeal, repeating in gruesome incantation the "rules" of this peculiar ritual while unwittingly expressing the fate that has already figuratively overwhelmed them: "Be careful, so we'll find each other again. . . . Be careful so we won't be buried by mistake. . . . Be careful so we won't get mixed up with the dead!" (p. 46). Yet even this urgent warning to maintain the separation reflects a forlorn and discarded reality, since unlike the "living dead" in Eliot's "Hollow Men," who are the agents of their own spiritual destruction, Ilse Aichinger's children are the victims of an external agency, which has "buried" them by intention, not by mistake, though an elusive narrative point of view, deliberately inconsistent, provides them with only an obscure awareness of this fact. Their encounter with death in the cemetery is a weird *danse macabre* illuminated by occasional flashes of insight that offset but do not extinguish hope; still, even these "reasonable" alternatives between illusion and despair are mocked by the concrete situation of the children, who in their frantic game of hide-and-seek among the gravestones take on a spectral quality, like disembodied ghosts searching vainly for a home. On the one hand they acknowledge nonbeing: "The path grows black. To the left and right there are graves, graves without names. The graves of children. We don't exist anymore. We're dead, and no one has identified us. . . . Who knows whether we're here at all?" (pp. 46–47); and on the other, they indulge in a painful parody of possibility, which in its earnest desperation reverberates with yearning for release from persecution even as the imagery of the passage stifles their cry:

"It would seem as though our dead weren't dead," said Leon.
The children took each other's hands and started to circle around an unmarked grave.
"That's what it is! That's what it is! Our dead aren't dead!"
Like a rain of sparks, their shouts sprang into the gray sky. Into a sky that hung over them like a face, like the pity of a stranger, like light that sinks to disappear. The sky sank heavily over them, like wings that are too big.
"Our dead aren't dead."
"They're just in hiding."
"They're playing hide-and-seek with us."
"Let's go look for them," said Leon.

The others let their arms fall and suddenly they stood still.
"Where shall we go?" [p. 48]

Again the anticipation of Beckett is unmistakable, for the fundamental illogic of their environment, predicated on unreasonable premises (the threat of deportation because of "wrong grandparents") forbids them from rejoining the ordered world they dimly recall. Looking for the dead, like waiting for Godot, is a vain endeavor, and the lyrical narrative voice of *Herod's Children* records the attrition and ultimate paralysis of longing implicit in the reality of the Holocaust even as the children cling to it as a last vestige of self-identification.

But the moment one speaks of "the reality of the Holocaust," one is compelled to include its "unreality," since the two coexist as a fundamental principle of creation, in Ilse Aichinger's novel and in most literature of atrocity. The unreality—the presence of children in graveyards, their obsession with death, the indefinite atmosphere which surrounds and threatens them—causes the aesthetic ground to shift continually, so that the reader is forced to grope for new footholds, and to alter his own interpretive point of view along with the narrative, until uncertainty becomes part of his experience of the narrative vision too. "The style of the [modern] novel," says Alain Robbe-Grillet, "does not seek to inform, as does the chronicle, the testimony offered in evidence, or the scientific report, it *constitutes* reality. It never knows what it is seeking, it is ignorant of what it has to say; it is invention, invention of the world and of man, constant invention and perpetual interrogation." [16]

Although the notion that style constitutes reality sounds like a commonplace, in its most literal application, of the language itself and not merely the idea behind the language reshaping and modifying a reader's sense of reality, it is exemplified by a comparatively small number of modern writers: but Ilse Aichinger is clearly one of them. In her unorthodox style—"A thick twilight fog muffled the shape of things, as though everything were a mistake" [17]—image collides with concept instead of reinforcing it, like the arrivals at Auschwitz who saw flames and smoke assaulting

16. Alain Robbe-Grillet, *For a New Novel: Essays on Fiction*, trans. Richard Howard (New York: Grove Press, 1965), p. 26.
17. Aichinger, *Herod's Children*, p. 53.

the evening sky and assumed they were bread-ovens instead of death, because the inconsistency of ovens with death introduced a dissonance into the reality with which they were familiar. If they gradually grew accustomed to the notion that this dissonance *constituted* their reality, they merely became a foil for the artist of atrocity like Ilse Aichinger, who knew that literary art could never succumb to custom but would have to incorporate Robbe-Grillet's "constant invention and perpetual interrogation" into the marrow of its substance, if it were to recreate an atmosphere in which the reader himself could experience the absurd collision of oven with death or fog with mistake.

The finest works of our contemporaries, Robbe-Grillet also suggests—and though they are not, his remarks seem directed specifically at the literature under consideration—leave us empty, out of countenance:

> Not only do they claim no other reality than that of the reading, or of the performance, but further they always seem to be in the process of contesting, of jeopardizing themselves in proportion as they create themselves. Here space destroys time, and time sabotages space. Description makes no headway, contradicts itself, turns in circles. Moment denies continuity.[18]

Where, if not in the unpredictable world of *l'univers concentrationnaire*, with the disappearance of a system of moral causality, did space destroy time, time annul space, and moment deny continuity? Out of the indefinable atmosphere of historical actuality, Ilse Aichinger distills a fictional strategy that permits not only herself but also the children of her novel to resort to "constant invention and perpetual interrogation" as a principle of art and existence, as a means of "jeopardizing themselves in proportion as they create themselves." And the result reverses the habitual course of history and fiction, for each inquiry further shrinks the range of human possibility, and every new "game" confirms the failure of imagination to pacify time and conquer space within the circumference of the Holocaust experience.

In a gruesome parody of their fate, the children join the mourners in a small funeral procession, following the coffin to the awaiting grave, which appears to beckon with tempting solace: "It suddenly

18. Robbe-Grillet, *For a New Novel*, p. 155.

seemed to them as though this was the last way out, ending here, the last way to get over the border, the last way to be identified" (p. 57), and for a moment one is captivated by this brief insight into the tragic course of human destiny, like Hamlet reading his future in the skull of Yorick, followed closely by the interment of Ophelia. But death in *l'univers concentrationnaire* withholds the consolations of tragedy—this is one of the axiomatic revelations of the vision that surrounds it. The coffin itself betrays a deceptive sense of liberation: "Dependent on the motion of the bearers, its sway made it appear free. It seemed anxious to prove that in this last silent swaying dependency there lay a kind of final independence" (p. 54)—and it is perhaps appropriate that the inverted logic of the desperate children should cause them to regard its unknown occupant as "the only one who might protect them now, give them reason and foundation" (p. 55).

The last refuge of a life gone mad may indeed be the "sane" culmination of death, but this presumes a sequence in human experience which is nonexistent in the imaginative world of *Herod's Children*. There, in Robbe-Grillet's phrase, moment persistently denies continuity, resulting in an anti-Proustian, anti-Faulknerian fictional atmosphere in which behavior and event offer no temporal referent and everything returns, both recollection and hope, to an instant and terrible "now." Are there moments in history when terror dissolves time and death represents not a conclusion to existence but merely reflects the condition of the living? This sounds like a description of some of Robbe-Grillet's own novels, with the important qualification that the context of the Holocaust enlarges the dimension of association in Ilse Aichinger's work by introducing an inescapable historical allusion that is absent in Robbe-Grillet. A mysterious coachman, apparently driver of the hearse, makes an appointment with the children to meet them the "day after tomorrow" to drive them (for a sum) over the nearby border, and though the venture is patently absurd and impossible in their "real" situation, it is perfectly consistent with the logic of their hopeless fantasy. The reader assents and dissents simultaneously—precisely the response desired by the author's strategy—and then is confronted with the paradox of an appointment that is irrelevant to time because the events of history have transformed expectation— at least for some—into a permanent illusion:

> The day after tomorrow. No mistake? To live and die for the day after tomorrow. Isn't it a false rendez-vous? Isn't it always like an agreement with an unknown driver? Like a meeting beside the wall of a graveyard? Expecting the day after tomorrow—fearing the day after tomorrow?
>
> The day after tomorrow was the day they would be expelled from their present quarters. "Chased like dogs," said Ellen's grandmother.
>
> And tomorrow, that was the day before. [pp. 58–59]

Few passages could more accurately reflect the mood of temporal confusion that prevails in *Herod's Children*, where nothing changes in the midst of desires to alter everything until the *wish* becomes a more vital necessity for existence than actual events. Imagination begins by contending with reality, then displaces it, until we are no longer certain what is happening and what is not—and when.

On the weird carriage ride, which gets nowhere because the driver goes in a circle (though the journey probably does not even take place in the world of reality), the children are joined by a number of legendary heroes, whose accomplishments history has insulated with a tradition of acclaim, and fairy tale merges with reality until the two are indistinguishably cemented together. In turn, the fleeing company is joined by Lieber Augustin, who "many hundreds of years ago, had gone on singing his songs in the face of the plague, and, it is said, went on singing even as he died" (p. 64); Christopher Columbus, whose philosophy—"dreams are more watchful than events or achievements; dreams watch over the world and keep it from ending" (p. 65)—has a singular if ironic relevance to the exploratory spirit that informs the novel; and a stranger with dark and kinky hair who identifies himself as King David and also offers some paradoxical advice that helps to define the alienated universe of the children: "He who hates is stranger than he who is hated, and strangest of all are those who feel entirely at home" (p. 66).

But these heroes of the imagination, with their jumbled words of wisdom and consolation, now assault the fantasies of the children with attitudes that belong to an exhausted tradition of faith and optimism; and though the children respond to their inquiries—"Are you ready to sing your song in the place of plague?" asks Lieber Augustin; "Are you ready to kill Goliath in your hearts?" asks King David; "And are you ready to discover Jerusalem for yourselves?"

(p. 70) asks Columbus—with affirmative determination, they are roused from their dreamlike journey into the nightmare of their present by the coachman, who announces that it was "all in vain. All is lost. We won't get over the border." But even then, it seems for an instant as if this fantastic escapade has successfully rescued them from the threat that afflicts their spirit, as they shout back at the driver "But we're over!" and run, "without once looking behind them, back into the dark" (p. 70). Only our recognition that their discontinuous moment has ended, without consequence in their lives or the fiction that creates them, exposes the delusion of their supposed imaginative triumph. Subsequent chapters—virtually all new beginnings, with only the vaguest of narrative links to the preceding ones—recount further attempts to overwhelm reality and counteract the bleakness of their future with games of increasingly sinister import; but all fail to conceal the single inescapable fact in the midst of their fantasies that finally seems absorbed (though not avoided) by them: their "wrong heritage," leading to eventual deportation.

This is illustrated in an extraordinarily complex interweaving of motives when the scene unaccountably shifts to a dark room where the children literally enact a play, the search for the King of Peace, which is cast into a lurid, ironic setting by the part-Jewish identity of the performers. In the cast are Joseph and Mary, an angel and three kings dressed as tramps, and an additional character not found in the original "text"—War. Play, says the narrative voice, "was their only chance left to stand proudly before the inscrutable, to keep their grace in the presence of dark secrets" (p. 120), but even this voice is soon to be contradicted by events, in line with Ilse Aichinger's practice of undermining the reliability of a perspective soon after she establishes it—a natural extension of the children's own situation. Fearfully assuming their roles in the dusk, "they had to bear the old terrible uncertainty as to whether we are kings or nothing" (p. 111), even as history depletes the cast of its actors. Throughout the scene the doorbell rings insistently, a sound of impending peril, and the children fear to answer because despite their assumed roles they know that for them the secret police have canceled the meaning of the Saviour whom they seek. When they finally answer, Ellen is at the door, who brings with her a tiny fragment of reality, enough to taint their insulating fantasy even as she joins it:

> "Let me play with you."
> "You don't belong to us." [Two wrong grandparents, apparently, are not enough.]
> "Why not?"
> "They won't come for you."
> "I promise you," said Ellen, "they'll come for me."
>
> . . . .
>
> "We don't have a part for you."
> "Let me play the World."
> "That's a dangerous part," said Leon.
> "I know that," said Ellen impatiently.
> "And besides, Hannah plays the World," muttered Kurt.
> "No," Ellen said softly. "They came for her last night." [p. 119]

Thus fate interrupts their game, and though they continue their futile drama, the "real" dénouement in store for them continues to prepare itself on the other side of the door: the bell begins to ring shrilly again, and this time it is not a fellow "actor." "Let's play" becomes a refrain of the children, but the ominous counterrefrain— "Our play, or what's played with us?" (p. 131)—reveals how tenuous is the veil separating actual threat from the children's attempts to protect themselves from it: once more, the language itself evokes the strange terror which contradicts the rules of the world-stage man believed he understood: "He who has missed his entrance is lost, and he who has missed his exit is doubly lost" (p. 131).

Perhaps only such suggestive verbal paradoxes—more apparent than real—can force one to literally rethink the premises of a civilization which for generations, whether Christian or not, has presumed to live by the values implicit in the drama the children are reenacting—peace and love, good will and human community. As Mary and the World struggle over a veil each wants as part of her costume, it disengages itself and floats "like some enormously forgiving thing between day and dream—like the stillness of the Annunciation," and finally sinks to the ground, "something intangible" (p. 124). With it sink and vanish the contours of the past, of civilized life, as history in the form of a shrilling bell, in the form of *Herod's Children* itself, introduces a new annunciation, and one of the child-performers suddenly recognizes the "veil" as a curtain Hannah had sewn just before she was "taken away," while another identifies its symbolic role in a universe more akin to nightmare than "day and dream": "A shroud for a bier . . . when children die" (p. 125).

A divine and demonic apocalypse abruptly coalesce, then part, until we are uncertain whether the drama we call life is performed at the behest of God or the Devil; a transfiguration occurs, but we grope through the mist of language and image to define its nature:

> what is played with us only changes through pain into what we play. They found themselves in the midst of the transformation, feeling distinctly the rags on their bodies, but at the same time the hidden gleam of the tinsel ropes around their necks and waists. The two games now began to merge together and weave inextricably into something new. The backstage disappeared, and the four walls of the tangible broke down. Triumphant as falling water, the unnamable appeared. Thou shalt play before My countenance! [pp. 131–32]

Before *whose* countenance life in *l'univers concentrationnaire* is played we are not told, nor is the "unnamable" delivered from its ambiguity; but the alternative apocalypses emerge from their obscurity as the children's drama draws to its conclusion, and the unspoken epilogue raises visions of unmistakable horror:

> Mary drew the bundle closer. War, leering, pounced out of the shadows. He sprang out of one corner and yet out of all at the same time, and with the shrilly ringing bell seemed to ooze out of an untold number of trap doors in the floor and the ceiling. [p. 132]

This time the bell-ringer is the man from across the hall, who unaccountably—but the unaccountable is a principle of existence in the literature of atrocity and the world it recreates—is an informer, with orders "to detain these children in this apartment until the truck came" (p. 139), as if the children had no families, no homes, no link whatsoever to "ordinary" society. To the children's innocent request that he join their play, the stranger replies, "Is this the rehearsal or the performance?" (p. 137), another example of language breaking down the security, the substantiality of imaginative truth; for we suddenly realize that the question is as remote as the choice it offers, yet seems to refer to a specific reality. As the bell rings for the third and last time, announcing their betrayal and not their "mission," Mary gives her child to the fleeing World, and amidst shattering glass they run toward the door, not to peace but to a fate enshrined in the grim image that concludes the episode: "Their play closed over them like a huge dancing flame" (p. 140). Silence is the most eloquent epilogue to their supposed doom.

But one of the most bewitching paradoxes of the art of atrocity is that, like music, it depends on sounds, not stillness, for its aesthetic effect, even though the theme it chooses, in certain of its features, may seem inexpressible. Ilse Aichinger's method of composition reverses the principle of the Wagnerian leitmotif: she introduces a harmony, rouses the "ear's" expectation, fills the mind with familiar association—then adds a dissonance that abruptly undercuts the continuity and produces an intellectual shock which in turn seems exactly to fulfill Wolfgang Borchert's request for new laws of harmony that would discard the well-tempered clavichords of prewar German prose and thought. "From a half-open window came the sobs of a child trying not to go to sleep" (p. 144) illustrates this principle, and also serves as a prelude to a chapter in which everything else violates expectation, as if this itself had become the controlling premise of reality.

The emotional security (not to speak of the aesthetic gratification) one receives from recognizing a leitmotif, whether in music or life, and thus gaining an insight into the connection between separate experiences, is deliberately traduced in *Herod's Children*, in an attempt to reflect a universe without pattern, one in which nostalgia and memory are the only slight impediments to total chaos. Because she has only two wrong grandparents (hence two "right" ones), Ellen does not qualify for whatever fate lies in store for the other children: she is sent back to "the freedom of the damned. . . . thrown back into the imprisonment of her own heart; out of the very last into the next to last; out of endless silence into the hell of little agonizing questions" (p. 146). These questions, provoked by the world of the "next to last," evoke without describing the world of the "very last," like a missing dissonant theme lacking verbal equivalent that resounds from the silence through its absence. The two worlds again collide in the unspoken dialogue prowling beneath the surface of this spoken one, in which the child Ellen seeks reassurance from an "adult" grandmother whose existence has

already been undermined by fear and apprehension; the result is a
terrifying example of the fairy tale wrapped up in a nightmare that
is a signature of Ilse Aichinger's art:

> "Grandmother," Ellen said softly, "I wish you would sit down
> beside me now and tell me a story. A completely new story, one I've
> never heard. It can be a fairy story."
> "They might come for me tonight!" said her grandmother. . . .
> "Tell me a story now, Grandmother!"
> "Then again, maybe they won't come tonight."
> "A story, Grandmother, a new story!"
> "And do you know whether they cover the truck with a tarpaulin?
> Somebody told me the other day——"
> "That's no story!"
> "I don't know any."
> "That's not true, Grandmother!"
> . . . "Once upon a time, Grandmother, once upon a time!
> Sometime once, something must have been, something nobody knows
> about but you, Grandmother. You always used to know what the
> Turkish coffee cups talk about in the dark and what the fat dog in the
> courtyard tells the pigeons."
> "I made it all up."
> "Why?"
> "Because you were still very small."
> "No, because you were still very grown up, Grandmother."
> "At that time we weren't in danger. Nobody could have come to
> take us away."
> "But you always said that when it gets dark there are robbers."
> "Unfortunately, I was right."
> "Stay being right, Grandmother!" said Ellen. [pp. 148–49]

In the now vanished world of normality, fairy stories used to
begin "Once upon a time," but in *l'univers concentrationnaire* both
past and future have been gathered into a continuous present, like
Primo Levi's timeless dawn command of Auschwitz, and the
grandmother's life is concentrated in the single fearful question of
whether or not "they" will come for her tonight. The myths
invented by adults to frighten children—"when it gets dark there
are robbers"—were originally employed to create opportunities for
exposing the insubstantiality of such myths, for replacing them with
the "real" world of security interposed by the stable figure of the
adult. But when we are forced to admit, together with Hermann

Kasack in his account of the writing of his novel *The City Beyond the River*, that reality has not only caught up with but has actually confirmed the most uncanny terrors conjured up by the imagination—"Unfortunately, I was right," the grandmother tersely observes—then the plea of the distraught child that she "stay being right" only reveals Ellen's inability to acknowledge the total alteration in the foundations of reality that has taken place, the dispossession of the fairy tale by another kind of fable that looms before them in the form of a literal and figurative deportation from the fixed abode of the past. But the mind of the child clings to its intuitive faith in the power of elders to modify the inevitable, to dispatch the robbers, to control time and the future: "Ellen demanded a story; she demanded of her grandmother, in the middle of a black, dangerous night, the readiness to live" (p. 153).

The fairy tale allusion produces extraordinary reverberations, since in many respects it epitomizes the continuity in experience which characterized the imagination's attitude toward life prior to the advent of *l'univers concentrationnaire*. "Once upon a time," the traditional refuge for children, always ended "and they lived happily ever after," assuring an uninterrupted adventure from past to future—what the narrative voice calls a "readiness to live." But beneath the surface of Ellen's childlike desires a grim melodrama is taking place: her grandmother has obtained poison as a final security against deportation, Ellen has hidden it, and the two are engaged in a dreadful struggle over the prize: death. The readiness to live is confronted by the determination to die, not in a tragic acceptance of fate but in deference to the fear of an unimaginable —and hence all the more terrifying—oppression. Finally, in a gruesome bargain, Ellen agrees to exchange the poison for a story, as if she were testing invention's ability to allay her own fright, as if Ilse Aichinger herself were creating a parable for our times of the supreme rivalry between the potency of art and the imagination, and the impulse toward extinction. And in this crucial test the truth which reality would convey seems to conquer through its essential horror the mind's capacity to invent: "Silence ebbed into every cranny of the room, a strenuous, thoughtful silence that waited for the truth in this very last story, waited for the prompter's whisper" (p. 152). The grandmother searches helplessly for words, stammers "once upon a time," but gets no further, and at last—falls asleep.

Perhaps *Herod's Children* is the story she never told, the "last story," the "ultimate" of Wolfgang Borchert, that paradoxically communicates most through the silences of its characters. Searching vainly through the corridors of memory for the fund of tales that had once spilled over into speech, the old woman thinks: "Some secret police had come and taken them from her, and they had disappeared into the dark" (p. 153).

Ellen in the end is compelled to tell her own story, with only the night for audience, and if "Little Red Riding Hood" seems an appropriate choice, the variations she introduces illustrate in a macabre way how the literature of atrocity, by merging history with fiction, transforms the fairy tale of imaginative perception into the existential nightmare of a hideous and imperishable threat:

> "So Little Red Ridinghood said: But, Grandmother, what big ears you have! The better to hear you with! But, Grandmother, what long teeth you have! The better to bite you with. But, Grandmother, what thick lips you have! The better to swallow it. The poison? Do you mean the poison, Grandmother?" [p. 157]

In a series of ironic reversals, consistent with the inversion of expectation that undermines the durability of Ilse Aichinger's fictional universe, the young lull the old to sleep with stories that cannot console, and then lapse themselves into a restless, troubled slumber, though no nightmare could be worse than the one Ellen falls asleep to escape:

> Ellen jumped down from the bed. She stood barefooted in the middle of the room, trembling with cold and fright. The old woman slept and never moved. The poison gleamed on the table, but Ellen let it lie. With one leap she got into her bed. She pulled the covers over her, buried her head in her arms, and searched for the last question. "Grandmother, why do you have such cold hands?" But there was no answer. [p. 157]

The answer was vague terror, the cause a betrayal of expectations that left humanity bereft of weapons, unprepared to encounter an indefinable reality that forbad the dying even the dignity of death. Ellen does indeed dream, of a young soldier fleeing a pursuer he can neither see nor describe, and his plight mirrors precisely the vision of the human condition offered by the literature of atrocity: "Somebody's following me—no, no one's following me—no one, that most dangerous of followers—no one—no one—the emptiness of the world."

But actual dreams, as we have seen, in *Herod's Children* cease to influence reality, itself the most terrible dream; Ellen awakes, and promptly forgets her nocturnal vision, "immediately and completely, as though it had never wrung her heart" (p. 159). She must contend not with huntsmen come to save her and rescue her grandmother from the wolf, but with the secret police, come to arrest her grandmother and leave her totally abandoned—or at least this is the content of her apprehensions. The prospect, as with Mr. Theodore Mundstock, is enough to shatter the equanimity of her world and populate the darkness with threats that are even more vivid than their probable consequences; the possibility of being drawn into the whirlpool of persecution generated by *l'univers concentrationnaire* animates that shadowy realm before its agents appear, and Ellen finally consents to be her grandmother's "executioner" because she thinks she hears the footsteps of their oppressors on the stairs—she gives her grandmother the poison.

The fairy tales of childhood, with their naïve and avoidable terrors, are vanquished by an environment that taunts the imagination with an equivalent atmosphere of unreality but offers no asylum from itself, not even the seeming sanctuary of a self-determined suicide. For the grandmother's death has come too "soon"; ironically "they" have not yet come for her, only the united fear of the old lady and the child have fancied their arrival: the real murderer has been the ominous silence, "that most dangerous of followers" of Ellen's dream—"the emptiness of the world." And this survives beyond the grandmother's death, reducing to a painfully ironic ritual of futility Ellen's attempt to baptize the departing spirit of her grandmother—"in the name of the Father, and the Son and the Holy Ghost. Amen." (p. 166)—by pouring the remaining liquid from the half-empty glass of poison over her bony white forehead. The peace that passeth understanding does not conquer but is absorbed by the imagined milieu of dread encompassing human experience in the novel, and makes Ellen's vain appeal all the more irrelevant—and appalling.

In the unreal reality of an empty world, where act has little to do with sequence, we are not surprised to find Ellen shortly in the hands of the police, captured while trying to board an armaments train destined for the front, in the hope of finding and joining her friends in the camp to which they have been deported. An angry captain conducts a frustrating interrogation, and the ensuing confrontation, in which answers dissolve into paradox and ambiguity, furnishes a microcosmic glimpse of the vision that limits Ilse Aichinger's narrative universe:

> Ellen stood under the dim lamp, silent and frightened. The captain covered the door with his back. "You all have the possibility of going to the front." He wiped the sweat from his brow. "Death is open to us all."
>
> "No!" shouted Ellen. "Life is open to us all. You mustn't die before you've been born."
>
> "This is too much," said the captain.
>
> He couldn't understand how it had come to this. A quick and extraordinary conversation took its course, contrary to all expectation, in a quick and extraordinary fashion. A feverish policeman pushed a strange child through the door and everything previously well established turned out to be false. [p. 188]

Once again, death and life vie with each other as principles of existence, but the incertitude that governs the struggle reduces the engagement to the level of rhetoric, and the charge which the captain hurls at Ellen—"You're guilty of sabotage by direct questions and undesired answers" (p. 189)—recapitulates the initial, frustrating debate between the girl and the consul. The reasonable longing for freedom, for a "life open to us all," expresses an inherited desire rather than the actual condition of reality; identity as a conception of character is obliterated by the events of the Holocaust, whose tormenting bequest—even today—remains an enormous, hovering interrogation point.

Thus, as Ellen races into the night, escaping—again unaccountably—from the police station, she glimpses a page of the calendar, and we discover that it is the night before St. Nicholas: "So it became clear that this evening was the eve of something" (p. 190). St. Nicholas or Santa Claus—the securities of Christmas Day, even more than fairy tales, confirm the identity of children and the freedom of childhood to stuff the stockings of the future with cheerful expectation. Religion and tradition coincide at this moment in time to celebrate the resurrection of hope. But when these previously well-established truths turn out to be false—as they do for Ellen, who on the next day is trapped in a cellar by an air raid and finally emerges into a landscape of horror "among cannons and ruins and corpses, among noise and disorder and all that is Godforsaken,"—her strength fails, and she is "consumed by expectation, burned out and gone" (pp. 216, 219). Her quest for identity, humanity's attempt to find meaning in the Holocaust and thus to preserve and perhaps justify convictions about reality and a conception of character which the events themselves appeared to contradict, suffers defeat at the hands of the paradox of unanswered questions, which nevertheless urgently had to be asked; they assume symbolic dimensions, and one is reminded of the frustrated inquiries of Elie Wiesel, which were greeted only by the silence of an awful doom:

> Why had she left the cellar? Why hadn't she listened to the distinguished lawyer, to the neighbors and the janitor, to all those who never stopped valuing caution and convenience above all else? Why had she heeded an urgency driving her to discover the undiscoverable? [p. 219]

She asks these questions in a dark garden by a dried-up river, pursued by the drone of tanks and a shrill loud voice calling "Ellen! Where are the children?"—another haunting query to which history alone supplies the answer, because Ellen "was no longer among the children. She had run after the star, urged on by the last breath of her childhood" (p. 219). The unmistakable imagery of suffering and salvation, the agony in the garden and the star of hope, merge with exploding shells and other adjuncts of battle to create a convulsion in nature that betokens a new and grisly revelation for mankind, a ghastly apocalypse that momentarily extinguishes the star and offers the imagination in its stead the element which originally gave the Holocaust its name, and is literally embodied here:

> A flash lit up the dark garden. The earth reared up, the hanged man began to dance, and the dead rolled restlessly in their fresh graves. Fire tore open the sky. A fire is all flames conjoined—those that billow out of windows, those that live in lamps, those that light up towers. And all flames are fire; those that warm your hands, as well as those that shoot out of cannon muzzles. [pp. 219–20]

All flames are fire—the literature of atrocity possesses the singular advantage of not having to be any more specific than this to reach its dénouement or bring its action to a dramatic conclusion. Nor could it be any more specific, since the very nature of the reality it seeks to apprehend repudiates the mind's attempts to organize its insights into a comprehensive pattern, or to suggest an interpretation of the events of the fiction consistent with the expectations of reason or tradition.

Ellen's fragmentary perceptions never fuse into a lucid whole, as contending forces cause her city—and the values that gave it life—to collapse about her. Her fate is settled, without motive or warning—after a brief encounter with an enemy soldier, for whom she carries a message to a bridge—by an exploding grenade, which blows her to bits. Like Mr. Mundstock, she dies without preparation, only half-suspecting at the end the futility of expectation, and perhaps—the supremest irony—not at all; for in a final hallucination she regresses to the optimism of childhood and the pre-Holocaust view of reality, as she "converses" with one of the children swallowed up by the camps:

> "George, the bridge isn't standing any more!"
> "We'll build another."
> "What shall we call it?"
> "The Bridge of Good Hope—our hope!"
> "George—George, I see the star!"

Only the gloom of the narrative voice can balance the desperate pathos of the children-as-victims, as the following epiphany places the imagery of expectation in its proper perspective:

> Blinking, [Ellen] noticed a great many figures running back and forth; beams and guns and gray-green muddied water. A chaos for which no solution could be found. [p. 238]

One searches in vain through the muddy waters of this chaos for a unity of impact, a culmination, some explanation which, however grimly, might relate consequence to an implicit cause. But reality, like Ellen, has been shattered into a million tiny fragments; disintegration of "everything previously well established," including conventional notions of character, is an aesthetic premise of the literature of atrocity, and one is left with the helpless feeling of contemplating what has been wrought, without being able to understand how or why.

Perhaps speechlessness, with a dry silence of the brain and a paralysis of the emotions, rather than empathy, is what the literature of atrocity substitutes for Aristotle's idea of purgation. Not the grave relief of having shared the tragic destiny of a heroic if fallible human creature, but a kind of stupefied uncertainty as to whether or not the events we have encountered have actually occurred, and if so, as fantasy or reflection of authentic experience —this is the response which *Herod's Children* evokes. Lacking heroes *and* culprits, such literature incarnates a prototype whose fictional ancestors were created by Dostoevsky and Kafka—the victim. No Iago or Goneril treads the stage to garner our hatred or antagonism; no imagined cause to rouse the moral indignation of an Ivan Karamazov appears; as often in Kafka, the effects of fear and despair seem to lack sufficient, and certainly sufficiently concrete, stimulus—nevertheless, the effects remain. Nor can a heroic protagonist, an Ahab, endow a neutral reality with malignant power, and thus invent a worthy antagonist in the fictional drama.

In most literature of atrocity, the specific forces behind the suffering of the victims are as anonymous as they themselves are destined to become; and the choice of children as victims compounds the anonymity (because of the even more limited comprehension of the children) and intensifies the atmosphere of intimidation. No ponderous, menacing Moby Dick looms on the children's horizon, nor is any effort made to conceptualize the danger threatening them, beyond the mere verbalizations of "secret police" and "camp." Their very obscurity—in art as it was in history—is the primary source of their terror; Ilse Aichinger has put to excellent use Ishmael's ominous conjecture in *Moby Dick* that though "in many of its aspects this visible world seems formed in love, the invisible spheres were formed in fright." [19] In *Herod's Children*, this world of love is part of the nostalgia of the modern imagination which the mind clings to through habit, even as contrary emotions

19. Herman Melville, *Moby Dick* (New York: New American Library, 1961), p. 196.

engendered by the spheres of fright eat into its substance, until one is compelled to acknowledge the new reality rushing into the void and to rewrite the Little Red Ridinghoods of our youth and past, granting to an amorphous wolf the triumphant role that fairy tales may deny but the history of the Holocaust confirms.

5: MEN INTO BEASTS

"Why should a dog, a horse, a rat have life
And thou no breath at all?"

King Lear

At any moment, the beast's nature
can change: we are at the frontier.
The horse can be mad, the sheep
rabid, the rat cunning, the bear ruth-
less: secondary states which give us a
glimpse into an animal hell, and in
which we recognize, with an astonished
sense of kinship, our own tortured like-
ness, as in a scratched mirror.

Pierre Gascar

The urge to circumvent the literal realities of *l'univers concentra-tionnaire*, to discover legitimate metaphors that might suggest without actually describing or even mentioning its world, has borne dramatic fruit for several authors in the tradition of atrocity. Friedrich Dürrenmatt spoke for many of them when he observed, in reference to the representation of Auschwitz on the stage, that there are terrible things, in the face of which art is always weaker than reality; yet Dürrenmatt knew that there are ways of bringing Auschwitz to the audience without bringing Auschwitz directly to the audience, not by ignoring the horrors of the gas chamber and the crematorium but by inventing situations equally gruesome, reported with remorseless exactitude, but only peripherally—if at all—identifiable with the events of the Holocaust. Ortega y Gasset, prophesying better than he knew when the literature of atrocity was still in its period of gestation, once called metaphor the most radical instrument of dehumanization in modern art; and though he had no particular writing in mind, it appears as if his remarks on the subject were specifically designed to illuminate the work of the authors to be considered in this chapter.

Perhaps nowhere in modern fiction—certainly not in the litera-ture of atrocity—is Ortega's conception of metaphor as an instrument of dehumanization more effectively exploited than in Jerzy Kosinski's *The Painted Bird*. One wanders through its pages with sensations ranging from awe to revulsion, much as Dante must have felt when introduced by Virgil to the bizarre horrors of Hell, though unlike the pilgrim Dante the reader plunges into an abyss of moral chaos devoid of reason, a landscape not systematically sculptured according to the sins of the sufferers but ripe with terrors that seem the offspring of human creatures who are prey only to superstition and a latent bestiality. Dante's Inferno is a model of pattern and causality, with each torture a logical extension of the victim's sin, and the total panorama of Hell the supreme expression of a divine justice; with the exception of a few sensitive souls like Stephen Dedalus, its terrors rouse for the modern reader only an aesthetic passion. Perhaps one reason for this is that for the twentieth-century mind the grand metaphorical purpose underlying the poetic achievement of the *Commedia* is the *humanization* of art, in the name of the sanctification of life, and not the reverse.

But Auschwitz was built on unhallowed ground, and Kosinski seeks to transform its legacy into primary truths more basic and universal in our time than the single Primary Truth which is the culmination of Dante's vision. Humanity's inescapable complicity in evil is his theme; Dante's cosmic love is not only absent from the universe he creates, but an unknown, an undiscovered, rather than a forgotten force. In Kosinski's hands metaphor is an instrument of desecration, a tool of the imagination shaping a world populated by creatures whose values coincide with those of Auschwitz, as if no other had ever existed. In such a world man appears as a fugitive from all but his animal origins, a heritage reinforced by the ironic epigraph to the novel, taken from Mayakovsky: "and only God, omnipotent indeed, knew they were mammals of a different breed."

"There was an age," says Ortega, "when fear formed the strongest incentive of man, an age ruled by cosmic terror. At that time a compulsion was felt to keep clear of certain realities which, on the other hand, could not be entirely avoided." If the Holocaust was not such a time, it at least reproduced part of its atmosphere; and chief among its features was the disappearance of so-called civilized values and the ascendancy of an instinct for survival which primitive man expressed through ritual and for which a modern artist like Kosinski seeks metaphorical equivalents: what Ortega called "a primordial metaphor preceding verbal imagery and prompted by a desire to get around a reality" [1]—a reality which the primitive mind could not understand, and which the modern mentality, as we have heard so often, finds inexpressible.

Since the power of discourse is one of the distinguishing features of the civilized human being, Kosinski banishes it from his fictional scene: *The Painted Bird* is literally a speechless novel, totally lacking in dialogue and containing less than half a dozen fragments of language presented through direct quotation. Its setting is a series of peasant villages in an unidentified area of Eastern Europe, already overrun by the Germans; and although the death-camp trains which traverse the landscape occasionally disgorge a wounded or dying victim (whom the peasants regard with animal curiosity or superstitious dread), these iron agents from an alien world do not disturb the vast silences behind the reality that govern the behavior of the inhabitants. Kosinski's characters communicate with their environment through rituals far purer than the macabre games of Ilse Aichinger's children; while the machinery of extermination grinds on at the edge of the imagination, they enact in the foreground, in an unconscious conspiracy with beasts and nature, the violence and passions, the rage and desire, the fear and superstition which precede verbal imagery and permit, not only themselves, but Kosinski and his audience, to "get around a reality" like *l'univers concentrationnaire* while simultaneously exposing the naked horrors of its profoundest universal implications.

In a brief but pertinent exposition of artistic intentions in *The Painted Bird*, prompted in part by the accusations of Polish critics that he was defaming the national character (though no country is mentioned in the book), and by others who confused the difference between literal reality and the uses to which the creative imagination puts it (one is reminded of Tolstoy's naïve charge that in *King Lear* Shakespeare makes his characters do and suffer what it is not in man's nature to do and suffer)—in this exposition, Kosinski offers a number of striking theoretical contributions to what one day may add up to an aesthetics of atrocity, and which certainly are consistent with Ortega's views on the dehumanization of art (and

1. José Ortega y Gasset, "The Dehumanization of Art," in *The Dehumanization of Art and Other Writings on Art and Culture* (New York: Doubleday Anchor Books, 1956), p. 31.

perhaps of man?) in our time. The modern literary use of language, suggests Kosinski,

> is contrapuntal, employed to lay bare the significant area which exists between language and action, and to highlight the gulf between them. This gulf also seems to be the focal point of modern art. But in *The Painted Bird* the situation is taken further; in the attempt to recall the primitive, the symbols are sought more pertinently and immediately than through the superficial process of speech and dialogue. In addition, the sense of alienation is heightened by depriving the characters of the ability to communicate freely. Observation is a silent process; without the means of participation, the silent one must observe. Perhaps this silence is also a metaphor for dissociation from the community and from something greater. This feeling of alienation floats on the surface of the work and manifests the author's awareness, perhaps unconscious, of his break with the wholeness of self.[2]

A primary source of unity, both of world-view and of character, in Dante's *Commedia*, was the power of discourse, Virgil's ability to comment on and interpret for his "pupil" the significance of his journey; and even in the *Paradiso* Beatrice and St. Bernard translate the insights of religious intuition into speech, leading the spiritual voyager to the radiant if ineffable mystery of incarnation, the summit of Christian truth. But for Kosinski modern history has forced language to abdicate its ancient role as a medium of coherence—best illustrated, perhaps, by the figure of Socrates—in favor of elemental and often uncanny modes of behavior that are too concrete to appear visionary but at the same time too dissociated from familiar patterns of action to encourage anything but the most painful groping for meaning on the part of the reader. And since the reader in turn depends on the dazed and frightened intercession of the young boy through whose sensibilities the events of this first-person narrative are filtered, he is faced with the challenge of inventing or discovering for himself some form of orientation to a community or universe into which he has been drawn, one he has been condemned to witness, like Wiesel on his first night in Auschwitz, by his very sense of alienation: "without the means of participation, the silent one must observe."

What Kosinski compels us to observe is the unique feature of his

2. Jerzy Kosinski, *Notes of the Author on The Painted Bird* (New York: Scientia-Factum, Inc., 1965), p. 17.

achievement, for by the time we have completed the grotesque and semi-picaresque adventures of his narrator, we wonder along with Mayakovsky how one is to tell the mammals that are men from those that are not. Although it would probably be an error to identify too closely the episodes in his novel with the circumstances of the Holocaust, Kosinski himself confirms the existence of a bond between them in his commentary. The appearance of the fugitive boy, he admits, coincides with the arrival of the Germans who, unlike the boy, are "a very real threat of annihilation. . . . The peasants, caught in the midst of this process, already aroused by the war, are worked up, compelled to violent action by the pressures of these many tensions rising to the surface." [3] It is as if the Auschwitz implicit in the modern imagination is unleashed in the behavior of the peasants and confirmed by the boxcars that run intermittently through their forests, a perpetual reminder that the extermination camp reflects deeply embedded human—or perhaps primitive— attitudes, not exceptional aberrations confined to a few particular localities. Kosinski scrutinizes most of the premises that cause man to conceive of himself as a distinct—and superior—species (ostensibly distinguished above all by his propensities toward love and reason) and incorporates his conclusions in *The Painted Bird*; and if one novel is insufficient to convince an audience that the post-Holocaust era has witnessed the exhaustion of such values, it dramatically indicts the dangerous narrowness of a vision that continues to affirm them with an easy acceptance.

Love and reason, and the other "civilized" values we identify with them, disappear before the inception of the novel's action, together with the parents of the six-year-old narrator, who have been forced by the exigencies of war and their anti-Nazi past to flee for their lives. To facilitate their escape, they leave their son in the hands of a man who promises to find foster care for him in a "safely" distant village among the peasants. Like the newly arrived deportees dragging their useless relics from the boxcars almost into the shadows of the gas chamber, as desperate testaments to some link with a more familiar past, so the boy begins his narrative with the conviction that the two realities could still be connected: "I lived in Marta's hut, expecting my parents to come for me any day,

3. Ibid., p. 24.

any hour." [4] But unlike the children in *Herod's Children*, who collectively draw on various myths of hope—Columbus, King David, the King of Peace—to give substance to their expectations, and unlike Elie Wiesel in *Night*, whose devotion to his father at least until his death furnishes a minimal stabilizing contact with human community, the boy in *The Painted Bird* is totally alone, isolated not only by his suddenly irrelevant childhood but also by his inability at first to speak or understand the local dialect, and—perhaps chiefly—by his appearance, for his swarthy skin and dark eyes and hair mark him as a child of gypsy or Jewish origin (we are never told, nor does it matter), conspicuously dangerous signs to the fair, blond peasants who ever more grudgingly shelter him.

Thus, temporally and spatially, physically and spiritually, the boy is abruptly sundered from civilization and the roots that nourished him there, until like Conrad's Marlow on his journey into the heart of darkness he is immersed in primary emotions that gradually awaken similar feelings in himself, in his elementary struggle for survival. His extreme youth offers Kosinski an opportunity to trace the evolution of a still unformed human creature's response to atrocity, with an immediacy not available—because of fundamental differences in the imaginative universes they project—to authors like Wiesel, Fuks, and Ilse Aichinger. Like Gulliver returned disillusioned from the land of the Houyhnhnms, or Marlow from the Congo, their tales still exist—intellectually—within the boundaries of civilization, and a contrapuntal effect is part of their aesthetic strategy. Perhaps one should say that *The Painted Bird* completes the dissociation between two worlds implicit in their works, as if the electrified barbed-wire barricades around Auschwitz were not enough, but dark curtains were drawn across the outside, excluding from view and finally from memory that other existence we call "normal reality." Human life, man's expectation, is inverted, and he becomes a creature, in Kosinski's words, who "fears more than welcomes each new day, who sees not the promise of the sun, but feels the threat of storm." [5]

According to the research of a psychologist, reports Ortega y Gasset, one of the roots of metaphor lies in the spirit of the taboo.

---

4. Jerzy Kosinski, *The Painted Bird* (New York: The Modern Library [1965], 1970), p. 4.
5. Kosinski, *Notes*, pp. 15–16.

Certain objects and beings—the ancient Jahweh comes to mind—are too awful to name; but since they exist and cannot be avoided, they must somehow be approached, through symbolic action as well as through language. "Such an object," says Ortega, "has to be alluded to by a word denoting something else and thus appears in speech vicariously and surreptitiously." [6] The rulers of the Third Reich, especially the framers of the "final solution," put this principle to viciously cynical use (explaining in part why critics like George Steiner felt so strongly that language had been corrupted for an artistic expression of the theme). Kosinski employed the principle with more honorable aims, combining the idea of metaphor as a means of expressing the inexpressible with actions that themselves invariably were related to a fear of superstition growing out of a taboo. This is not an unexceptionable practice in the novel, but occurs often enough to justify the conviction that it constitutes a major device for evoking the atmosphere of terror in *l'univers concentrationnaire*.

For the peasants are surrounded by the menace of the unknown, and the rituals they engage in to propitiate it, together with the crude or brutal methods they use, bare reality to its most natural layers and present vicariously, as if in a dream, though with the concretest of imagery, the unimaginable cruelties of the Holocaust translated into universally potent metaphors. Thus we approach the taboo, the awful truths of Auschwitz, by circling about them, contemplating the "distinctive elementary symbols," in Kosinski's terms, as "simple keys to the European culture of the mid-twentieth century." [7] Rather than diminishing the evil or horror of the real atrocities, they make them seem less strange, less unique, less alien to recognizable human experience: a common universe of suffering, though set in a preliterate and almost preconscious milieu, is paradoxically more terrible *and* more tolerable than a private and artificial corner of hell from which all but the immediate victims are exempt.

One of the numerous items to which a taboo is attached in the novel is the eyes. They are among the most remarkable features of the Marta mentioned on the opening page, who because of her poor

6. Ortega y Gasset, "Dehumanization of Art," p. 32.
7. Kosinski, *Notes*, pp. 19–20.

sight "peered at the light through tiny slits embedded under thick eyebrows. Her lids were like furrows in deeply plowed soil. Tears were always spilling from the corners of her eyes." When she dies, the confused and frightened boy stares at her watery eyes and reflects that he had seen such only once before: "when the stream threw up the bodies of dead fish." His next mistress, a kind of peasant witch-doctor, warns him that his black eyes are bewitched, that he might stare at other people and "unknowingly cast a spell over them," or with his mysterious glance cause a healthy child to waste away, a calf to drop dead of a sudden disease, hay to rot after harvest.[8] The eyes thus early become an object of fascination, a source of danger as well as an inspiration of fearful reverence, a focus for a kind of primary tribal energy that threatens momentarily to erupt into a ritual of self-protective vengeance and outlandish physical cruelty.

Perhaps the most horrifying scene in the novel, the most brutal episode in a narrative compounded of bestialities, involves the destruction of eyes, as if Kosinski had deliberately sought an aesthetic equivalent for atrocity that would of its very nature set up reverberations beyond the specific malevolence of the Holocaust: a miller, with whom the boy is now living, brings to the evening meal his plowboy, whom he suspects of lusting after his wife. Finally drunk, he seizes his iron spoon, shoves the terrified plowboy against a wall, and exacts his revenge with a cruelty fusing metaphor and act and bringing the literal and symbolic so close to each other that from the confrontation, as Kosinski points out in another context, arises the meaning:

> With a single kick the miller got [his wife] out of his way. And with a rapid movement such as women use to gouge out the rotten spots while peeling potatoes, he plunged the spoon into one of the boy's eyes and twisted it.
>
> The eye sprang out of his face like a yolk from a broken egg and rolled down the miller's hand onto the floor. The plowboy howled and shrieked, but the miller's hold kept him pinned against the wall. Then the blood-covered spoon plunged into the other eye, which sprang out even faster. For a moment the eye rested on the boy's cheek as if uncertain what to do next; then it finally tumbled down his shirt onto the floor. . . .

8. Kosinski, *The Painted Bird*, pp. 5, 11, 20.

The eyeballs lay on the floor. I walked around them, catching their steady stare. The cats timidly moved out into the middle of the room and began to play with the eyes as if they were balls of thread. Their own pupils narrowed to slits from the light of the oil lamp. The cats rolled the eyes around, sniffed them, licked them, and passed them to one another gently with their padded paws. . . .

The miller, evidently annoyed by the cats' play, kicked the animals away and squashed the eyeballs with his heavy boots. Something popped under his thick sole. A marvelous mirror, which could reflect the whole world, was broken. There remained on the floor only a crushed bit of jelly.[9]

The literary precedents for this episode in Sophocles and Shakespeare are clear enough, but the self-inflicted blinding of Oedipus is offset by the tragedy of insight which it symbolizes (thus, oddly enough, *separating* the literal from the symbolic and minimizing the physical immediacy of the episode), while the blinding of Gloucester, much closer in effect to Kosinski, is so succinct that the spectator is scarcely afforded the leisure to experience his own complicity in the event. Taking a hint from the imagery of the Shakespearean passage—prodded by Regan and Cornwall to explain why he sent Lear to Dover, the faithful Gloucester replies: "Because I would not see thy cruel nails / Pluck out his poor old eyes; nor thy fierce sister / In his anointed flesh stick boarish fangs," to which Cornwall responds as he stomps out Gloucester's remaining eye: "Lest it see more, prevent it. Out, vile jelly! / Where is thy lustre now?"—Kosinski translates the loss (or the destruction) of human vision into a traumatic experience of family life in which "common" passions like suspicion and jealousy, and not an elaborate political program of racial extermination, lead to scenes of unutterable horror.

The thinking behind this adroit transformation of "transitory" historical impulses into the permanent and universal tensions of art is illuminated by some spontaneous remarks of Kosinski's in an interview in 1968, remarks which incidentally offer a significant insight into the variety of options open to the literary imagination engaged with the problem of atrocity in the modern era:

I remember a woman who told me that she couldn't read the book; she reached this particular episode and couldn't go through it. When I

9. Ibid., pp. 37–39.

said why, she said, the eyes are being gouged out. And I said well, there are worse things, there were worse things, there have been worse things in our reality. Have you heard of the concentration camps? Or gas chambers? And she said, gas chambers? Certainly, this I understand very well, but gouging out someone's eyes, how can you explain something like this? And this is my point. The concentration camp as such is a symbol you can live with very well. We do. It doesn't really perform any specific function. It's not as close to us as the eyesight is. When you describe the atrocity of the concentration camp you are immediately reminding the reader that this is not his reality. It happened, you say, it happened in such and such a place. . . . But when you describe the eyes being gouged out, you don't make it easier for the reader, he cannot help feeling his own eyes disappearing somehow, becoming blind.

The tendency to reject the eye-gouging passage in *The Painted Bird*, to find it and others in the novel "too horrible to be real," suggests Kosinski, has nothing to do with the literary experience but reflects the philosophy of the reader, who sees himself as a potential victim and flees from the consequences of this possibility. As a result, he continues,

you make yourself even more vulnerable. The tragedy, for instance, of East European Jewry was when they were, well—collected—perhaps I should say, by the Germans and transported to the concentration camps; until the last second they did not believe that they would perish in the gas chamber. They heard of it, but they didn't believe it. They said, it's simply incredible. Why would a civilized nation do something of that sort? The inability to see the trauma of daily life as such breeds future victims.[10]

Though *The Painted Bird* is hardly a tract designed to reduce the number of such potential victims, it is very much concerned with dramatizing the "trauma of daily life" so as to produce a shock of recognition quite other than the one Melville had in mind. Episodes like the gouging out of the eyes seek to induce a sense of complicity with the extremity of cruelty and suffering in modern experience, from which history (with its customary distinctions between "then" and "now"), conspiring with the reader's reluctance to acknowledge such possibilities, unconsciously insulates us. The art of atrocity is

10. Transcribed interview with the author, 4 July 1968.

the incarnation of such possibilities through language and metaphor.

Kosinski carries much further than his predecessors the break-down of the "integration of self" that once constituted the goal of characterization in much fiction, and especially in literary tragedy. The fugitive boy of the novel is subjected in his wanderings less to the moral and spiritual incertitudes that fragment the perceptions of a Kafkan anti-hero, than to repeated assaults on his physical being, a far more concrete and immediate threat to the unity of the individual, and certainly a more effective means of stripping man of the perspectives of civilization from which he traditionally views himself. Shortly after his arrival at the "medicine-woman" Olga's, the boy seems to fall victim to a plague epidemic that is decimating the neighborhood, and his superstitious mistress seeks to cure him by burying him up to the neck in earth and leaving him exposed in a field overnight. The boy thus undergoes the first of a series of "immersions" in a natural element, a process which accelerates his alienation from his civilized heritage and identifies him with those primitive creatures who crawled from the ooze at the birth of time and painstakingly accommodated themselves to reality, and we are made to feel as if history had completed one cycle and returned to the beginning, when the mind had scarcely begun to evolve and the instinct for survival made men equal to beasts in the struggle for existence. The human legacy of the boy is distributed between vegetable and animal impulses, in an ironic inversion of the usual development of the young protagonist in the novel of education; "planted in the cold earth," thinks the boy,

> my body cooled completely in a few moments, like the root of a wilting weed. I lost all awareness. Like an abandoned head of cabbage, I became part of the great field. [p. 23]

And when a flock of ravens, taking advantage of his helpless position, literally attack his body and begin pecking at his head, he seems to surrender his human identity entirely and in his imagination transforms himself into the image of his tormentors (a tantalizing metaphorical extension of the familiar psychology of the camp victim identifying himself with the attitudes of his persecutors):

> I gave up. I was myself now a bird. I was trying to free my chilled wings from the earth. Stretching my limbs, I joined the flock of

ravens. Borne abruptly up on a gust of fresh, reviving wind, I soared straight into a ray of sunshine that lay taut on the horizon like a drawn bowstring, and my joyous cawing was mimicked by my winged companions. [p. 25]

The projected metamorphosis of human into animal creature (or victim into persecutor) in a vain attempt to be accepted by a "community," culminates in the central symbol of the novel, the painted bird itself, which, its feathers daubed with brilliant colors by its keeper, was released among a flock of its own species, only to meet a fate that reflects the intrinsic importance of natural analogy in the strategy of the novel: for while the painted bird circled about struggling to convince its kin that it was one of them, they forced it away until finally "one bird after another would peel off in a fierce attack." The passages involving the buried boy longing to be free and the beleaguered painted bird, though separated in the novel, are linked imaginatively by the destiny of a feathered changeling who is a raven: its fellows attack it until it plummets, fatally stricken, to the earth: "Its eyes had been pecked out, and fresh blood streamed over its painted feathers" (p. 51). The complex interweaving of natural and animal imagery that threads through the novel enforces a revision of the values that conventionally distinguish man from beast: rejection becomes a premise of existence in such a world, fear displaces love, and metaphysics is merely a matter of contending with the elemental.

Earth, air, fire, and water once constituted all of physical reality for primitive (and even classical) man, and though the modern mind rests on the comfortable assumption that they exist for man to exploit in support of his life, in the universe of *The Painted Bird* they represent, together with the beasts and spirits and demons that inhabit them, a primary obstacle to survival. Man is not in tune with his environment, any more than the painted birds harmonize with the flocks they seek to join; only cunning and violence and an irrepressible will to endure facilitate—without insuring—the continuation of life. The boy in the earth and the birds in the air form a prelude to an alternating rhythm of up and down, immersion and flight, that emphasizes the tentative relationship of man to elements and reduces the individual's struggle for liberation from restraint, which has characterized human destiny since the romantic era, to more urgent, more fundamental, perhaps even more authentic terms. But even this "freedom" is not a philosophical or political concept, a personal value carefully nurtured through centuries by the conscious mind, but is an instinct embodied in the unconscious to resist the assaults on the self—here, as mentioned, confined to the physical self—inaugurated by the very condition of being alive. Each new day for the boy, as for the camp inmate, is a threat, not a promise: any values beyond the physical have no opportunity to develop, as all his energies are exhausted by the mere effort to keep the body in existence.

The obvious humiliation of such a condition may not flatter the devotée of culture and progress, to say nothing of the religious image of man, but it accurately reflects the state—and the psychology—of the victim in *l'univers concentrationnaire*. The central (and longest) episode in *The Painted Bird* dramatizes this un-Darwinian descent of man from the pedestal of civilization into the mire of brutish endurance, for at its end the boy has lost his last link with his human heritage—the power of speech. For Darwin, biology and man's capacity to adapt to his environment gradually differentiated him from his animal ancestors; in Kosinski, history, as an expression of the ambitions of the Third Reich, sanctions cruelties that are as generic to human nature as the charity which once was idealized into its fundamental attribute. "Throughout this war," says Kosinski in his commentary, "the peasants of Eastern Europe were not relics of the past, an underdeveloped society missed by the progress of civilization. On the contrary, the peasants in *The Painted Bird* symbolize and personify the level to which the so-called European Civilization was forced down by World War II. These peasants became part of the great holocaust of violence, murder, lawlessness and destruction which the war had been preparing for them." [11] Although the central episode (and others) in *The Painted Bird* may appear to be indebted to the spirit of naturalism that infiltrated European and American literature shortly before the turn of the nineteenth century, the context of the novel as well as Kosinski's own remarks make it clear that his conception of human nature and the imagery into which he translates it owe their most powerful impetus to the events of the war, and particularly to the supreme horror of its atrocities.

11. Kosinski, *Notes*, p. 22.

In this episode, the boy has come to live with a solitary peasant whose unprovoked beatings seem to make him an agent of gratuitous evil. The household consists of the farmer Garbos "who had a dead, unsmiling face and half-open mouth; the dog, Judas, with sly glowering eyes" (p. 116); and the victim of their perpetual if inexplicable animosity, the boy. Nothing in the boy's behavior— his industry, his attempts at conciliation, his flight from their presence—can shield him from their joint malice: they seek him out, they persecute him. Like all those outraged or frustrated by Hannah Arendt's conclusion that the evil caused by an Eichmann might be rooted in a banality of temperament, the boy at first seeks a "serious" cause for the animosity of master and dog—though the constant coupling of the two suggests that the reader should search for "motive" in the sheer, unmotivated pleasure in predatory destruction that we ordinarily (and incorrectly) associate with certain beasts.

The boy's quest for motive is a parody of humanity's dilemma in trying to account for the unaccountable, and the lengths to which we will go rather than accept the possibility of the pure will to torture and destruction (not to be identified with sadistic perversion) as a valid expression of human instinct under certain historical and psychological circumstances:

> I came to the conclusion that Garbos's seemingly unmotivated fits of rage must have some mysterious cause. . . . I decided to observe all the circumstances accompanying Garbos's attacks of fury. Once or twice I thought I had detected a clue. On two consecutive occasions I was beaten immediately after scratching my head. Who knows, perhaps there was some connection between the lice on my head, which were undoubtedly disturbed in their normal routine by my searching fingers, and Garbos's behavior. I immediately stopped scratching, even though the itching was unbearable. After two days of leaving the lice alone I was beaten again. I had to speculate anew. [p. 122]

Under the influence of the faith in magic of Marta and Olga, the boy virtually reenacts primitive man's attempts to explain and pacify the forces in his external environment hostile to his well-being; but all efforts naturally prove vain, and when the boy finally seizes on prayers for indulgence to allay his situation—an idea he overhears from the local priest—the inclination of man to discover order in his universe by asserting some control over his fate is simultaneously reasserted and undermined, as the irrelevance of what the boy suffers to his efforts to minimize that suffering is exposed with ruthless irony. Such quests for control only divert attention from the primary focus of action in a situation of atrocity, revealing the individual's reluctance to confront the immediacy of what is happening to him: to enforce such confrontations is a major thrust of Kosinski's art.

Thus, all intellectual and moral considerations suddenly appear trivial when Garbos suspends the boy from leather straps attached to two large hooks embedded in the ceiling of a small room, and locks him in with the ferocious dog Judas. Man faces beast, mirror images of each other, as life is transformed into a contest between physical cruelty and physical endurance; and if the boy survives, it is not a triumph of the human spirit over bestial will, but a simple conditioning of the muscles of the boy's arms and legs (which he withdraws from the dog's reach whenever it snaps), so that he can sustain the stretched position for many hours without falling. In a painful parody of the crucifixion, the human creature comes to resemble the side of beef in the Francis Bacon painting, a figure that may once have been a man but which no previous training in humanistic values can help us now to identify.

The victim is temporarily rescued from his daily torment when he is chosen by the local priest to replace an ill altar-boy at services on Corpus Christi Day; and in a sequel to the parodic episode just described, the symbolic reversal of self-discovery is completed, as the boy stands face to face with the literal image of his Savior and fails the ritual "test" that might confirm his spiritual identity. The "challenge" is to carry the missal on a heavy wooden tray from one side of the altar to the other, and though the boy had been able to resist the assaults of the aptly named dog Judas on his body—his exertions, indeed, seem to have destroyed any supplementary resources—he cannot endure the strain of bearing the burden of Christianity: "The book itself was too heavy, even without the tray" (p. 138). As the peasant congregation, already hostile to his gypsy appearance, watches in suspicious stillness, modern man as victim, in the figure of the trembling boy, is desanctified in the presence of the archetypal Victim—humanity's last hope in *l'univers concentra-tionnaire* is defeated by the inexplicable silence of God:

> I stood on the altar platform, the lean flames of the candles flickering in my eyes. Their uncertain flutter made the agony-racked body of the crucified Jesus seem almost lifelike. But when I examined His face, it did not seem to be gazing; the eyes of Jesus were fixed somewhere downward, below the altar, below us all. [p. 138]

From the congregation behind him the hesitating boy hears an impatient—and ominous—hiss; he steps backward, slips, falls, and drops the missal, thus failing to execute the private, ritual act which would have prevented the communal gesture of vengeance that follows.

The peasants' superstitious rage at this defilement of the temple exudes primitive fear more than divine love, as if Kosinski would reduce even Christianity merely to a source of cultural forms that provide a precarious insulation against the violence at the heart of their lives. The degradation of the boy reaches a nadir of humiliation when they hurl him into a steaming manure pit near the church, a baptism in filth which divests him of the last semblance of human purity; and as he crawls from the pit, "barely able to see through my slime-obscured eyes" (p. 140—an image almost more loathsome than the eyeballs of the blinded plowboy), it is like a vision of man emerging from excremental origins, a disgusting but bitterly effective variation (given the experience of the "human form divine" during the Holocaust) on the scriptural account of man's physical beginning and end in something as innocuous as dust.

The inexpressible quality of the experience for which Kosinski— perhaps paradoxically—finds verbal and metaphorical equivalents, is symbolically extended to the victim, who henceforth appears as the incarnation of silence: the ordeal of immersion has deprived him of his voice and turned him into a mute. Thus his last civilizing link with human reality is severed and he is condemned—at least for the time being—to a life of gathering *im*pressions, as if the habit of seeking to *ex*press reality blurred the sensibilities and obscured one's conscious awareness of the atrocities men suffered in *l'univers concentrationnaire*. In losing the power of speech, the boy-narrator is forced to focus on what Kosinski calls "motivated action," thus reinforcing the fictional strategy adopted by the novelist himself from the beginning, that of discarding the oblique method of implying action through dialogue and drawing the reader into the physical substance of reality, the immediate act, as if the words used to describe it were illusory veils that disintegrated upon touch. Like the boy, the reader is sucked into the manure pit of experience with the explicit intention of inducing in him an imaginative access to the same nausea which literally overwhelms the boy in the novel. Such a strategy penetrates the intellectual facade of the reader as spectator and reaches the organs and nerve ends of his being, dissipating aesthetic "distance" and creating a reader *engagé*, a direct emotional participant in the experience of atrocity.

A profound sundering occurs as the boy flees from the church and plunges into the forest, as if his destiny, once symbolized by his suspension between air and earth, had finally been settled in favor of the nether region; the grotesque distortions of life are projected onto his natural environment, which not only reflects but actually embodies the partial paralysis of humanity resulting from the ruthless abuse of once-sanctified values:

> From the black earth that the sun never reached stuck out the trunks of trees cut down long ago. These stumps were now cripples unable to clothe their stunted mutilated bodies. They stood single and alone. Hunched and squat, they lacked the force to reach up toward the light and air. No power could change their condition; their sap would never rise up into limbs or foliage. Large knotholes low on their boles were like dead eyes staring eternally with unseeing pupils at the waving crests of their living brethren. They would never be torn or tossed by the winds but would rot slowly, the broken victims of the dampness and decay of the forest floor. [p. 141]

The mutilated stumps, like maimed torsos of human victims, arouse horror at the prospect of surviving—even as one of the "living brethren"—in such a world, and wonder as to the purpose—if any—of the boy's continuing such an existence. The power of cruelty which has corrupted his universe can only end by transforming him into one of its servants.

"If our life lacks brimstone," says Antonin Artaud, in a passage from *The Theatre and Its Double* quoted by Kosinski in his own commentary on *The Painted Bird*, "i.e., a constant magic, it is because we choose to observe our acts and lose ourselves in considerations of their imagined form instead of being impelled by their force." Such a statement indicts an Ivan Karamazov, the "observer" par excellence, whose absorption with the imagined forms of suffering of little children divorces him from the actual force of experience, alienates him from the roots of his own existence, and finally splits his psychological being. Artaud likened the theater to the plague, "a formidable call to the forces that impel the mind by example to the source of its conflicts." Ivan's attitudes drive him in the opposite direction; Kosinski, clearly following hints from Artaud, takes the metaphysical *Angst* whose seeds are already discernible in Ivan (though Dostoevsky intended the positions of his Zossima and Alyosha to counteract its power), and whose appeal achieves its most definitive statement in our century in Kafka, and bares the physical nausea before life implicit in it (prefigured, perhaps, by Ivan's brain fever and more so by the fate of its original victim, Joseph K, who died like a dog). Artaud's definition of his theater of cruelty, designed to shake human sensibility out of the torpor into which most prior dramatic art had encouraged it to lapse, reads like a manifesto explaining the aesthetic intentions of *The Painted Bird*:

> We want to make out of the theater a believable reality which gives the heart and the senses that kind of concrete bite which all true sensation requires. In the same way that our dreams have an effect upon us and reality has an effect upon our dreams, so we believe that the images of thought can be identified with a dream which will be efficacious to the degree that it can be projected with the necessary violence. And the public will believe in the theater's dreams on condition that it take them for true dreams and not for a servile copy of reality; on condition that they allow the public to liberate within itself the magical liberties of dreams which it can only recognize when they are imprinted with terror and cruelty.[12]

Artaud's desire to return the spectator to a "physical knowledge of images" is executed by Kosinski in his fiction, which conducts the reader, as Artaud would his spectators, "*by means of their organisms* to an apprehension of the subtlest notions." Obviously

12. Antonin Artaud, *The Theater and its Double*, trans. Mary C. Richards (New York: Grove Press, 1958), pp. 8, 30, 85–86.

Kosinski agrees with Artaud that at first this may require "crude" means—the uniformly loathsome effect of his episodes attests to this conviction—though Artaud, writing in 1938 on the verge of the Holocaust, had as inspiration only preliminary whispers of the atrocities that would roar in Kosinski's ears with unabated fury. For Artaud the theater could be a literal revelation, "the bringing forth, the exteriorization of a depth of latent cruelty by means of which all the perverse possibilities of the mind, whether of an individual or a people, are localized." [13] History confirmed Artaud's artistic intuition beyond his grimmest expectations, and although his vision of a theater of cruelty has been realized on the stage in our time, one unacknowledged consequence of his theories is a work of fiction like *The Painted Bird*, which shifts his principles to the printed page.

Artaud argues that the action and effect of a feeling in the theater—the impulse to commit a murder, for example—"appears infinitely more valid than that of a feeling fulfilled in life." If the art of atrocity that we have been discussing tests anything, it is precisely this idea, even if the action and effect of a feeling in a novel must be confined to the written word, deprived of gesture and other dramatic stratagems available to actors on the stage. The real act of atrocity discharges itself in time, "loses contact with the force that inspired it but can no longer sustain it"—and so, we might say, for the exterminations in the concentration camps, now the data and statistics of history, shrunk to a moment of experience we call the "past." But the murder of the actor, according to Artaud, and the impulse behind it, "has taken a form that negates itself to just the degree it frees itself and dissolves into universality." Perhaps the theatricality, not to say the deliberate melodrama, of the most extreme episodes in *The Painted Bird* is attributable to the fact that they solicit immediate responses from the reader without offering any opportunity for reflection, making the role of witness prior to that of interpreter. The attempts to comprehend the atrocities of our time are superfluous, Kosinski would seem to suggest, until—to follow Artaud's image—they have discharged themselves "into the sensibility of an audience with all the force of an epidemic";[14] and this once achieved—ironically—the attempt to understand may seem superfluous for another reason.

13. Ibid., pp. 80, 81, 30.
14. Ibid., pp. 25, 26.

For example, probably the greatest source of terror in *l'univers concentrationnaire,* for the victim and for those subsequently concerned with his fate, was not the fact of death but the act of dying, the manner, the circumstances, the sheer process of extinction and the fears it generates—what Camus sensed in the passage quoted earlier but worth repeating:

> No, what man experiences at such times is beyond all morality. Not virtue, nor courage, nor intelligence, nor even innocence has anything to do with it. Society is suddenly reduced to a state of primitive terrors where nothing can be judged. All equity and all dignity have disappeared.[15]

Camus was speaking of *any* execution, and his indignation is expressed through the language of protest, not evocation; yet even the agonizing and "unjust" death of M. Othon's son in *The Plague* results from natural causes, a symbolic if vivid extension of the death penalty that punishes us all. Most authors in the tradition of atrocity draw on the *prospect* of dying under unimaginable conditions as one source of tension in their work; Kosinski has been one of the few who has not flinched before the ultimate cruelty of the age of the Holocaust—dying in a situation of literally unutterable horror.

Here if anywhere art demonstrates its superiority to reality in its ability to convey some of the essential—and most barbaric—experiences of our time. Wolfgang Borchert claimed that the ultimate could not be put into words; what could be more "ultimate" in *l'univers concentrationnaire* than death in the gas chamber? Some scattered, brief eye-witness accounts exist (naturally from persecutors, not victims); but they lack immediacy for the reason specified by Kosinski in his interview: "When you describe the atrocity of the concentration camp you are immediately reminding the reader that this is not his reality. It happened, you say, it happened in such and such a time."[16] But when Kosinski presents a universalized metaphor for this specific atrocity, it "has not happened," it *is* happening, and we are confronted with a spectacle too awful to paraphrase, pure torture to read.

The context is this: the boy-narrator had run away from the

15. Camus, *Resistance, Rebellion, and Death,* p. 155.
16. Transcribed interview with the author, 4 July 1968.

carpenter with whom he had been living, but after wandering through the forest had inadvertently stumbled back into the same village he had fled; he is returned to his furious master, who resolves to drown him in a sack like a superfluous cat. In order to save himself, the boy promises to show the greedy carpenter an old, abandoned pillbox full of boots, uniforms, and military belts which he had discovered during his escape—actually, the pillbox is swarming with starving rats. The two arrive at the site, their wrists bound by a cord, and the boy quickly becomes the unconscious agent of one of the least palatable and most passionately suppressed principles of *l'univers concentrationnaire,* a stern necessity that permitted one life to be preserved at the price of another man's death. As the boy's complicity in death is suggested—paradoxically—by the bond he severs in order to salvage his life, so our involvement in the carpenter's fate is a reflection of art's ability to assault the senses, and finally the consciousness, with a universal metaphor for that moment when, as Camus suggests, all equity and all dignity disappear: the annihilation and nullification of a man. The passage is long, but one dare not trespass on the unity of its images:

> Horror-stricken, I tugged suddenly at the string, so hard that it cut my wrist to the bone. My abrupt leap pulled the carpenter forward. He tried to rise, yelled, waved his hand, and dropped into the maw of the pillbox with a dull thud. I pressed my feet against the uneven concrete flange over which the slab had rested. The string grew tauter, scraped against the rough edge of the opening, and then snapped. At the same time I heard from below the scream and the broken, babbling cry of a man. A fine shudder shook the concrete walls of the bunker. I crept, terrified, toward the opening, directing into the interior a beam of daylight reflected from a piece of tin sheet.
>
> The massive body of the carpenter was only partly visible. His face and half of his arms were lost under the surface of the sea of rats, and wave after wave of rats was scrambling over his belly and legs. The man completely disappeared, and the sea of rats churned even more violently. The moving rumps of the rats became stained with brownish red blood. The animals now fought for access to the body—panting, twitching their tails, their teeth gleaming under their half-open snouts, their eyes reflecting the daylight as if they were the beads of a rosary.
>
> I observed this spectacle as if paralyzed, unable to tear myself away

from the edge of the opening, lacking sufficient will power to cover it with the tin panel. Suddenly the shifting sea of rats parted and slowly, unhurrying, with the stroke of a swimmer, a bony hand with bony spread-eagled fingers rose, followed by the man's entire arm. For a moment it stood immobile above the rats scuttling about below; but suddenly the momentum of the surging animals thrust to the surface the entire bluish-white skeleton of the carpenter, partly defleshed and partly covered with shreds of reddish skin and gray clothing. In between the ribs, under the armpits, and in the place where the belly was, gaunt rodents fiercely struggled for the remaining scraps of dangling muscle and intestine. Mad with greed, they tore from one another scraps of clothing, skin, and formless chunks of the trunk. They dived into the center of the man's body only to jump out through another chewed hole. The corpse sank under renewed thrusts. When it next came to the surface of the bloody writhing sludge, it was a completely bare skeleton.[17]

If men can inure themselves to the most gruesome event through a feeling of relief that they share no complicity in it, art such as this purges them of complacency and—where it is not simply repudiated—introduces a quality of horror into the modern imagination which must radically alter our perception of reality.

And this is what finally happens to the boy in *The Painted Bird*, whose life henceforth radiates not from an "old" beginning symbolized by the creation of the world, but a "new" departure based on the destruction of man. Throughout his ordeal he has sampled a number of philosophies and moralities in an attempt to organize his chaotic, unprecedented experiences, ranging from the witchcraft and superstition of the peasants to the ritualistic prayers for indulgence of their primitive Christian religion, and from an unreflective innocence that could ask, "Wouldn't it be easier to change people's eyes and hair than to build big furnaces and then catch Jews and Gypsies to burn them in?" (p. 100), to a grim (and logical) demonism—given the context of his experience—that identifies survival and "salvation" with the conscious promotion of evil, and equates human effort and progress with developing man's potential for hatred. Kosinski speaks of his novel as an attempt to "peel the gloss off the world, to view life without the comfortable conceits with which we embellish perceptible reality" (*Notes*, p. 19);

17. Kosinski, *The Painted Bird*, pp. 63–64.

but he goes even further than Shakespeare in *King Lear* in reducing the human creature to no more than a poor, bare, forked animal of flesh and rags.

For in his role of unwilling executioner, the boy at another point is forced to strip the skin from a giant rabbit, which he thinks he has killed when he has only stunned it, so that the partially skinned carcass squirms away and races around the yard—following the animal analogies consistently developed by Kosinski throughout the work—resembling the flayed corpses of a Leonard Baskin woodcut, whose ebony nerves and muscles expose a peeled humanity deprived of the elementary cloak of epidermal dignity that still protects poor Edgar. Compassion finally—if temporarily—restores a semblance of order to Lear's disordered sensibilities; but the wild gyrations of the frantic creature in *The Painted Bird*—"She lost all sense of direction, blinded by flaps of skin falling over her eyes. . . . Her piercing shrieks caused pandemonium in the yard" (p. 149)—its death throes a compound of trembling tissue and bone and spurting gore, revives Lear's question in a universe that admits—that recalls—no gentle Cordelias, however grim their eventual fate: Is man no more than this? In Kosinski, he is less, forced to this conclusion by his own expendability in the climax of primitive violence, a conclusion visibly supported by the events of modern history but in *The Painted Bird* inspired by a complex interweaving of reality with universal myth, as boxcars carrying helpless victims to concentration camps and gas chambers surge through forests where legendary peasants display their instinctive affinity for beasts.

As marauding Kalmuks finally descend on the peasants near the war's end, and then the Soviet forces on the Kalmuks, the Russians avenging through a violent justice the even more brutal lusts of their turncoat victims, history dispels legend, we return from myth to time, and the boy is liberated from his nightmare ordeal. The rest might well have been silence, and in fact is anticlimactic, as if Kosinski himself recognized that survival was superfluous in a world where man had to contend with memories that dehumanize him and only confirm his legacy of hate. The major impact of the novel is to require a redefinition of "human" and "inhuman," and to exact finally—from the boy and the reader—a concession that they *must* be revised: for the so-called inhuman behavior recorded in *The Painted Bird*, whether of the primitive peasants or the "civilized" forces responsible for the death-camp trains, is so pervasive as to seem "normal," however unpleasant the implications of this admission. And conduct once considered normal—love, compassion, and forgiveness supported by intelligence and reason—appear not inhuman but simply irrelevant, as if the orgy of cruelty had been ingrained in reality and renewed itself automatically in the imagination of all survivors.

Although the Soviet soldiers who rescue and befriend the boy seek to rehabilitate him by preaching their political doctrine, their rhetoric does not impress him as permanently as the teachings of a single marksman, a so-called Hero of the Soviet Union, who slaughters at long range several peasants from a village where a number of his comrades had been beaten or killed in a drunken brawl. In a further deliberate parody of the picaresque tale and the *Bildungsroman* that educates a youthful protagonist in the ways of society so that he may enter into some kind of productive or creative alliance with it, Kosinksi indoctrinates his negative hero with a "philosophy" that promises only a bleak, hostile, and solitary future:

> A person [concludes the boy] should take revenge for every wrong or humiliation. There were far too many injustices in the world to have them all weighed and judged. A man should consider every wrong he had suffered and decide on the appropriate revenge. Only the conviction that one was as strong as the enemy and that one could pay him back double, enabled people to survive. [p. 214]

Whether this represents a perversion of the "knowledge gained through suffering" that traditionally is supposed to have liberated man's tragic potential—and his dignity—or sounds the death knell of that potential and dignity, it is difficult to estimate; certainly the boy's conviction is not a consequence of his encounter with the mere cold abstraction of death. Whereas a troubled Hamlet wrestles with the responsibility of paying the blood-debt of revenge which his father's spirit demands of him, the boy accepts it as a necessary premise of his being. Indeed, the total absence of conflict in his personality after his ordeal may offer the best testimony to the effect of the Holocaust on the possibility of literary tragedy in our time. For the contradictory impulses in human nature that once sanctioned this form have succumbed to the ruthless oversimplifications and classifications of such nature burned deep into the modern imagination by the events of *l'univers concentrationnaire;* after surviving the world of the peasants (and the world of the concentration camps which circumscribed them all), the option of "To be or not to be" seems like an exercise in philosophical rhetoric, and the boy has no one—or perhaps we should say "too many"—to avenge, and no King Claudius to personify the persecutor.

The boy in *The Painted Bird,* says Kosinski, "embodies the drama of our culture: the tragedy of the crime always remains with the living" (*Notes,* p. 28). But if the crime of annihilation was truly tragic—and Kosinski uses the term loosely here—its very enactment undermined the possibility of a sequel, in which the victim might regain his stature as a hero by confronting his antagonist. The only legitimate enemy is all of life, against which the boy henceforth directs his hatred as the sole expression of his mutilated self. No insight to mitigate the poison of his suffering is available, given the nature and extent of that suffering; the only justification for his continued existence—and this is the most awful paradox of his heritage—is to reproduce in himself an image of his former oppressors, to employ hostility as a source of self-fulfillment, to make their cruelty the basis of his strength.

Thus the boy's restoration to his parents at the end of his adventures does not mark a return to civilization any more than the concentration camp survivor's liberation assured his restoration to the world of prewar values from which the mechanisms of destruction had immured him. In the end he recovers the gift of tongue, speech, but its significance is qualified by the ominous image that accompanies its reinstatement: "Blood flooded my brain and my eyeballs swelled for a moment, as though trying to pop out onto the floor." [18] Neither the power of speech nor reunion with his family cancels his conviction, the fruit of his wretched childhood, that it "mattered little if one was mute; people did not understand one another anyway" (p. 233). So that even though he momentarily rejoices in the sound of his voice, it is an ironic and perhaps useless gift, contending as it must with the boy's pervasive pessimism. The barrier it must surmount—as with the narrator of *Night*—is the

18. Although this image appears in all prior editions of *The Painted Bird,* Kosinski omits it from the 1970 Modern Library text. See *The Painted Bird* (New York: Pocket Books, 1966), p. 213.

obstacle of memory; and given the quality of this remembered life, it may well be insurmountable.

If in *The Painted Bird* the conception of man (in the context of the Holocaust) seems degraded by reducing him to the level of beasts, in Pierre Gascar's *Beasts and Men* (in the original French more appropriately entitled simply *Les Bêtes*) the human characters are no longer the source of primary interest but appear as agents or supporting actors in a drama starring the animals—as if men and the values they once represented cease to function as the focus of civilization, and the creatures whose masters (and executioners) they once were, inherit the vitality (and occasionally the dignity) that formerly belonged to men. Just as in Picasso's *Guernica* the eye is first distracted by the central terror of the screaming horse and the stolid strength of the mysterious bull gazing hypnotically at the spectator (as if these animals held the key to the human horror), then gradually wanders across the faces of the terrified women (especially one at the edge of the canvas with a dead infant in her arms), and finally confronts the dismembered limbs of the statue-warrior in the foreground, so in the stories in Gascar's volume the reader enters an animal kingdom that seems closer to the elemental core of existence than the human-inhabited one we are familiar with. Slowly our fascination shifts to the animal creatures who behave as animals, whereas the men who behave as animals, or submit to impulses associated with them, lose the name of men, their natures turned awry. Like the hunger artist in Kafka's tale, man withers away into a diminished thing, while the spectators, oblivious of their own waning humanity, gather around the cage of the noble young panther who has displaced him and willingly sacrifice a portion of their human freedom in their admiration for the imprisoned vigor of the beast.

Again like Kafka, Gascar in his initial story ("The Horses") introduces a landscape that rouses emotions "almost detached from earthly reality," but the cause is less obscure and the imagery more responsive to interpretation. To condition the emotions of the reader, he creates his "atmosphere of damnation" at first out of familiar stuff, as his initiate, an army recruit named Peer ("war had been declared two days earlier"), wanders through a dark wood which emits odd mournful sounds that explicitly remind one of the

"damned souls in the Inferno, as Dante and his guide went by,"
though the source of this sudden assault on his senses and his
sensibilities is not a vision of men already condemned to eternal
torment for sins committed, but of beasts who represent a
convulsion in time about to be unleashed on an apprehensive,
unprepared world:

> The gusts of wind, which had just begun to grow more frequent and
> made a sigh run through the black foliage, kept stirring up this vague
> mass, this sea of animal life which otherwise might have settled down,
> if not into stillness, at least into a reassuringly peaceful rhythm. And
> then fresh and more violent sounds arose, sounds of huge invisible
> bodies in collision, the creaking of countless chains like cables in a
> storm-swept harbor; desperate neighings rang out, and the smell, for a
> while, was dissipated and lost. And it seemed then as though some
> force mightier and more mysterious than the presence of a hundred
> horses were pent up under the trees, thudding against the trunks and
> rattling the pebbles in its inexplicable anguish.[19]

Delegated to the horse detachment, Peer searches for the men's
living quarters, but ends up sleeping on a floor strewn with straw,
and awakens to find himself among soldiers reclining "with their
tunics buttoned at the waist and rumpled up under their arms so
that they looked puffed out, like corpses," while others, squatting
and eating in silence, were "staring in front of them as they
munched their hard bread as though weighed down by their animal
function and, perhaps, by some secret despair" (p. 11). Assigned to
stable duties, he has difficulty understanding the dialect of his
fellow recruits ("who are reputed to be brutal," p. 12), but is fond of
animals, and tries to imagine a course of conduct that would enable
him to achieve a peaceful mastery over men and beasts.

But Gascar's description of the men leading the horses deliberately confuses the two, so that at times "they seemed to be
physically united as in some old myth" (p. 12); yet when Peer
attempts to apply to the equine sensibility feelings that once made
this mythical harmony possible, at least in the imagination, he
discovers at the back of his mind uncomfortable sensations that
affirm the irrelevance of "old traditions of man's mastery and of
great journeys" (p. 13), of the ancient (and not so ancient) legends

that dictated a hidden but basic unity between creature and man, between Jove and the bull or swan he became to undertake his divine amours:

> a sense that, despite misleading appearances, despite manifold similarities, the race of animals that lived here was one with which he had no connection, as though the war had actually brought into being an unfamiliar animal and human kingdom, a state of visible, permanent damnation, the implacable invasion of a set of forms that had hitherto been lying in wait up above. [p. 13]

Gascar's beast fables shed light less on human behavior (in the manner of Aesop) than on the human condition, and even more explicitly, on a kind of reality "invaded" by a set of forms that fit no prior molds, that appear to come from a reservoir of uncanny dreams "up above," but which nevertheless exert an inescapable force on the affairs of men. Thus, Peer's existence becomes a desperate effort to survive amidst a seething mass of horses, an unconscious struggle to combat their primal energy with an utterly hopeless savagery of his own, until the lineaments of *l'univers concentrationnaire* emerge from the contest like the materials of a new creation and adapt themselves to the new forms of "permanent damnation" that frame the modern version of Dante's grim vision:

> [Peer] only knew that each of his blows plunged him a little deeper into a hideously grimacing universe where the horses were all ferocity, the men all hate. He was forging his own demons. [p. 18]

Yet incoherence remains a part of the uniquely terrifying world that begins to take shape in his daily labors and then to afflict his dreams, as if its final contours defy the capacity of the human imagination, like a mighty, unfinished sculpture of Michelangelo, still half-embedded in its marble stone, resisting all efforts to pry it from its primal source. In the beginning may have been the Holocaust—but in the end? "You lashed out," concludes Gascar's Peer, "and creatures died at the very moment when these lunatic gestures, this state of damnation were about to reveal the truth about this desolate world. He would come back again, unsatisfied" (p. 22).

Such exasperation seeks its aesthetic equivalent repeatedly, as we have already noticed, in the literature of atrocity, which substitutes for the usual resolution of art, a tentative, indefinite tension between history and the imagination, a tension rooted in a specific event in time that imposed on man the necessity of reorienting himself to his surroundings and redefining his own nature. Gascar even evokes the destructive imagery of deluge, but introduces no dove to announce a pure dawn and a cleansed reality; for although Peer escapes in *dreams* to a "sensation of airy flight that was terrifying at first and then brought total release," he *awakens* to the scenes of his inescapable torment, "shut up with the animals as in an ark obstinately surviving on the calm extent of waters, . . . moaning, profoundly bewildered" (pp. 22–23). As his world grows more desolate, his bewilderment increases; and his inability to comprehend this new universe begotten of atrocity is reflected by the behavior of the men in his detachment, who retreat in fear from the sound of attacking aircraft to the protection of the stables and "their uneventful past," dreading the challenge of an uncertain future where they would run "carrying their own fate, exposed to their own unpredictable swerves and conflicting instincts—and where they would be utterly, nakedly alone" (pp. 25–26).

They shrink, in other words, from the self-knowledge that once made tragic destiny possible and meaningful, as if the force unleashed on the world by this war had eclipsed man in favor of a power that only the beasts can symbolize. For the horses, liberated from their halters and stalls because of the impending air attack, and driven by instincts uncomplicated by human reason and memory, accept the challenge that timorous men must refuse; and with an instinct for unity and freedom unknown even to Kafka's caged panther, they rush forth with a confidence and vitality that seems to create a hopeful fate in the very surge of their energy—a fate from which man, deprived of both confidence and vitality by the events of history, is sorrowfully excluded:

> All individuality, all precision of form had vanished; there were no longer any thin horses, lame or blind horses, dying horses; there was only a great rushing stream of equine life, at first seeming lightly furrowed, from a close view, by the myriad folds of skin at groin and neck, but soon becoming wholly smooth and flowing with a noise of subterranean thunder toward the untroubled prospect where storms were past and miracles accomplished. [p. 27]

The deluge of battle seems to have brought to the horses a vision of a promised land, a New Jerusalem, an animal paradise that once had human equivalents, and we almost envy them their ability to transcend what has defeated man. For the beasts now appear superior to their former masters; the only human consequence of their escape is the disappearance of Peer, who a week later is listed as a deserter—though the status he abandons remains obscure, and the goal he pursues is never mentioned. Deep in his breast, we are told, he bore a secret, though in his semimadness he never disclosed it: perhaps he was reduced to silence by the spectacle of a reality in which man was spurred to covet rather than fear the condition of beasts.

This theme is replayed with variations in the other stories of *Beasts and Men*. In "The House of Blood," in which an independent butcher finds his existence threatened by the inauguration of a municipal slaughterhouse requiring him to shift the locality of his trade from his barn to its more "sanitary" premises, the poetic intensity of the language possesses reverberations beyond the immediate context of the narrative (related by a young apprentice), so that the image of the butcher and the creatures he slaughters for a living, ostensibly not associated with the world of the Holocaust, is transformed into a metaphor of the experience of humanity in that unredeemable universe, beyond reason and retribution:

> No, nothing would ever be atoned for. Here, no reckoning was made of evil and suffering, and there was no reason on earth why the butcher, with his hook fastened to his belt, should ever stop walking along those endless rows where animals—always the same animals— were lined up with their removable heads and the sentence of suffering from which they would never be reprieved. Animals are well aware of it.[20]

And men? one is compelled to ask. For if some men are just animals with removable heads—universal victims, as it were—and others, like the butcher, are universal executioners, with weapons far more deadly than a meat-hook, then we are no better off than beasts brought to the slaughter, and perhaps less so, since animal slaughter has as its end the nourishment of man.

The human extermination which gradually displaces Gascar's bloody imagery in the mind of the reader finally penetrates to the

20. Gascar, "The House of Blood," in *Beasts and Men*, p. 43.

consciousness of the boy-narrator, who discovers to his horror that his master, like the officer in Kafka's *Penal Colony, "never had been concerned with the animals"* (p. 49) who were his victims, but "with that superior order of things over which—taking into account all the revisions which it had undergone before our time—he thought it our mission to keep guard. In his piteous confusion," the boy continues:

> the butcher now called everything into question. With endless jokes and falsely playful sallies he individualized the victim, gave our deed a name, personified the knife, and, christening the poleax 'little brother,' involved us all in a sort of family party where there was no alternative but to drink deep of the wine of abomination. [p. 49]

In a curious reversal of the attitude of Kafka's officer (who rejoiced in the public executions of an earlier era), Gascar's butcher compulsively seeks to carry on his profession privately under the vault of night in the forest, until his apprentice realizes the "surreptitious bonds of complicity" (p. 53) which the necessary precautions wove between executioner and victim, and the work became so complicated that the mental strain was unbearable. The appalling conflict between municipal slaughterhouse and secret butchery finally exposes the fundamental horror of dying and the loathsome nature of the impulse to murder, and the plaintive, futile cry of the boy that concludes the story—"O God, O God, don't let them kill any more sheep!" (p. 56) echoes the pain of annihilation more than a hope that any power can terminate or diminish it.

The conviction that the events of history have annihilated not only man but a way of life, a conception of reality, a tradition of the individual and his relation to the future, finds expression in another brief tale, called simply "The Animals," whose theme is more properly identifiable with what we have come to know as *l'univers concentrationnaire*. For here a group of Russian prisoners are confined by their German captors in a barn, which is surrounded by a circus menagerie—lions, bears, a tiger and a hyena—which has been driven from its regular quarters by the Soviet offensive. The daily feeding of raw meat to the roaring, predatory beasts proves an insupportable torment to the men, who are starving on a diet of watery soup; yet paradoxically the men depend on this ritual, especially when the keeper teases the beasts before he tosses their meat into the cage: "The sight of the beasts' frustrated desire gave the prisoners a strange feeling of relief." [21]

For the hunger of the beasts is not satisfied by the few chunks of flesh they are awarded, and life becomes a contest between men and beasts for survival, both driven by primitive instincts that force us to interpret the behavior of the men in the barn in accordance with "rules" embodied by the beasts in their cages. The very designation of the guard as "keeper"—another echo from Kafka—helps to obliterate the distinction between his two types of charges, as if the impulses in human nature, commonly regarded as "civilized," suddenly vanish when life is stripped down to the primary desire of keeping the body alive. Once more we may detect murmurs of the Darwinism that finally helped to breed literary naturalism, but the social or religious protest in much of the writing of Zola, Norris, or Dreiser finds no equivalent in Gascar's bleak vision, which portrays creatures involuntarily deprived of their humanity and transformed by events terrible enough to prevent them from ever regaining their original condition of dignity.

Gascar ruthlessly destroys the illusion that this is possible, though his characters are too paralyzed by their experience to acknowledge defeat. When one of their number is assigned odd jobs outside the barn, their contact with another reality "beyond the barrier of wild beasts" seems temporarily reestablished, especially when their comrade returns one evening with the news that he has discovered a place where potatoes are stored. Every evening two men creep beneath a hole in the barbed wire surrounding their prison to steal some of these potatoes, and abruptly it appears as if the "universe was taking shape once more" (p. 64). In a world in which "normal" causality prevails, the discovery of food should restore some of the lost humanity to the men; but against their delusion that this is so, Gascar introduces some ominous hints suggesting the contrary.

Not only does the appearance of the terrain assume a portentous, Melvillian significance—a partial thaw creates "a thin milky whiteness" where the ice begins to melt, adding an "ambiguous pallor . . . to the gloom of the landscape" (p. 65); but the behavior of the beasts exposes the fallacy in the men's hope that they can escape from the consequences of such an imprisonment. For the

21. Gascar, "The Animals," in *Beasts and Men*, p. 62.

men begin to bribe the keeper with tobacco some new inmates have
managed to hide, so that each day they are given a portion of the
meat intended for the beasts; and the result convincingly demonstrates that the so-called world beyond the barrier of the beasts,
the hidden source of nourishment for the men, cannot alter
the relationship between these two dependent orders of reality.
They may change their disguises, but their roles have been
permanently established, and human effort seems powerless to
change them:

> As their own hell died down, another hell started up on the other side
> of the barn. It was the same hell: a wild frenzy that could never be
> allayed everywhere at once. The fury of the beasts condemned to
> hunger burst forth in a concert of growls and moans that left no peace
> to the inhabitants of the barn. [p. 66]

The anguish of the starving animals, tearing the floorboards of their
cages "with the spasmodic violence of creatures buried alive,"
evokes a frightful image of human victims in the last gasp before
extermination; and the men indeed see their own fate mirrored in
the suffering of the menagerie: "Like primitive creatures, they
sensed an obscure menace in the very plenitude of their revenge.
. . . they began to realize what torments they might experience
when deprived once more of their clandestine stores" (p. 67).

Yet when these sinister portents are realized, even the prisoners
find themselves unprepared to contend with them—nothing in their
prior experience has been commensurate with the implications of
such atrocities. For the Gestapo discovers the nightly depredations
of the men, seizes the two most recent foragers, executes them, and
unceremoniously dumps their frozen, contorted corpses by the door
of the barn. Then their comrades must face the "obscure menace"
they could not have anticipated, the final threat to the feelings that
define them as men. When the feeding of the beasts resumes the
next morning—the prisoners having been sentenced to nothing to
eat for three days—the two bodies of the executed men are nearly
covered by snow, only the curves of their chests still visible,
ominously suggestive "of the hollow framework of skeletons"; and
the keeper, as he flings huge chunks of black meat into the animal
cages, dares not look at any of his human charges, "living or dead"
(p. 70). Everyone shares the same impulse, but at first no one is

willing to admit it, because the men realize that a portion of their humanity hangs in the balance. For if their destiny is simply to be caged like animals, shot like dogs, and fed to beasts, then civilization totters on the precipice of utter chaos, and a devastating cloud of unreason hovers over its future.

The men's hesitant efforts to bargain for survival—"Tell them we'll exchange the two bodies for tomorrow's meat" (p. 71)—is interrupted by the sound of Russian guns heralding the end of conflict—the German front has been broken. But their desperate offer, their tentative acquiescence to a kind of animal cannibalism, looms through the rumble of victory as they contemplate in stunned silence a memory never to be clarified—how had they been used? To what had they been willing to assent? Military triumph brings hollow satisfaction as they face the dismal prospect of surviving in a provisional universe incapable of assuring them that they are human. The victim turned beast of prey in captivity, and finally prey itself, cannot recover the image of his lost humanity through the mere gesture of release; like the narrator at the end of *Night*, he must carry through life the uncertainty about his own nature, and about all of human nature, that *l'univers concentrationnaire* bequeathes to him.

When Kafka's explorer arrives on an island where an extraordinary contrivance executes an unfathomable justice in an atmosphere that cannot be explained by the laws of logic or jurisprudence, we are horrified by the uncanny system but gain some emotional relief (as does the explorer) from the circumstance that the island is an abnormal reef in a sea of supposed normality, an eccentric deviation from reality that we can sail away from, as one awakens from a nightmare, back into the "other" world of sense and reason. But in Pierre Gascar's imaginative universe the principles of Kafka's penal colony have extended their sway over all of reality, so that victims and persecutors unaccountably merge and men behave in accordance with motives that no experience with the past will satisfactorily explain. In a story like "The Dogs," set in a French-occupied military base in Germany following the war, the scene has shifted and the site of the action is historically identifiable, but the atmosphere and attitudes that prevail reflect an explicit marriage of Kafka with the Holocaust, the ambiguity of the penal colony with the concrete terrors of the world of the concentration camp. The characters in this tale continue to apply human intelligence to the crises of modern existence, but almost with a foreknowledge that success is doomed by the inexplicable serum of pain and evil with which reality was inoculated during the conflict.

Describing his relation to this reality as a "blood-stained bondage," the protagonist of "The Dogs"—a D. P. who continues to enact the role of the "hunted" in a camp for training "man-pursuing" dogs for some obscure future military purpose (though the symbolic connections are clear enough)—tries to explain his unwillingness to escape, and thus illustrates Gascar's own attempt to generalize some of the specific legacies of *l'univers concentrationnaire*:

> War is only a frightful and, after all, occasional word, but behind it lies all the stealthy horror of our time, the nameless struggles, the anonymous sufferings, the everyday oppression, and, already widespread through the world, the "state of being an enemy." I'm in that state in relation to the dogs; for them I am, unequivocally, *the* enemy.[22]

He is the Victim personified, bearing in his recollections of the vague hell he has endured a prophecy even more ominous than the explicit hate inherited by the boy in *The Painted Bird*—a prophecy that gains fulfillment even as it is uttered:

> A moment of truth in the midst of that general torpor that prevents people from realizing—I won't say the shape of things to come, but of things that are already there, looming through the fog of dawn! Every day I experience the horror of our time, a bloodless horror as yet, while millions of human beings live in drowsy indifference, with their trivial worries and their petty psychoses, waiting for some general mobilization or even for some great flare-up, and make their own mental picture to their own scale—a terrifying profile no doubt, but one that bears no relation to the face of the Great Horror, that night of the world—I see it looming through the morning fog, like another sun, when the dogs are tearing at me and I'm running to escape them, and they catch hold of me again, and I fall down, on the edge of that prophetic wood! [p. 157]

Against the narrator's perhaps too self-protective charge that the D. P. (whose name is Franz) is nurturing a personal martyrdom, and

22. Gascar, "The Dogs," in *Beasts and Men*, pp. 156–57.

in fact is creating a situation that may require another Messiah, the Eternal Victim replies, "somebody has *got* to know . . . because only thus, when the hour strikes and darkness falls on our world, it won't have been quite complete, and at least it won't all have happened without our knowledge."

The dialogue between Franz and the narrator (like Kafka's explorer, a temporary visitor to this strange encampment where dogs hunt men though, unlike him, ultimately destined to share its bizarre reality permanently, because there is no other) continues for a time at cross purposes. The narrator accuses Franz of egocentrism, of a certain complacency about his own sufferings—"although it's an inspiring thing to have knowledge, ought one for that reason to cut oneself off from the community?" (p. 158)—while Franz defends himself by rehearsing the dilemma of the anonymous victims he represents, knowing in advance that his interlocutor— like the reader?—is not yet prepared to comprehend his allusive evocation of the wasted fate of millions:

> I could talk to you for a long time about those people who have no name in history, whose life depends on a negative principle over which they have no control, who are neither one thing nor another, despite the multiplicity of foreseen or foreseeable cases, and who are quietly moving into that sort of limbo where, beyond the bounds of your Manichean universe, they will endlessly macerate in the guise of the homeless, the classless, the outcast, in a dreary and unlimited freedom. [p. 160]

"The Dogs" chronicles the efforts of the narrator to penetrate the meaning of the "negative principle" that governs the universe of the "survivor," where right and wrong no longer struggle for the soul of man but are buried beneath the avalanche of atrocities from which Franz seeks to rescue the memory of those less fortunate than himself, as an example for a mankind not sufficiently touched by the implications of their suffering. The narrator has his first glimpse of these implications when he enters the enclosure where the dogs for this odd hunt are kept: "The notion that the relations between man and beast were irremediably warped, that the dogs, under cover of perfect obedience, had secretly thrown off man's sway, that the whole place was in fact a 'kennels for men' possessed my mind" (p. 136); and in spite of his past training to the contrary, he must gradually acknowledge a fundamental disturbance in the order of things which has radically transformed the hierarchy of utilitarian relations that time and creation had established between dogs and men.

He reaches this conclusion or, more exactly, arrives at a perception of this revision in the nature of reality, only by becoming a participant in a demonstration "chase" himself, pursuing hunted men and hunter dogs into a dreary wood where no voice of reason awaits him: "The darkness had suddenly grown dense again and, with a sense of fulfillment such as one only finds in dreams, I felt myself one of a significant trio, with Franz and the Commandant [of the 'dog' battalion, organizer of the chase and utterly contemptuous of man as victim] for sole companions, in the heart of a midnight forest where our secret accounts were perhaps to be settled" (p. 170).

Tripping over a root and embracing the unfruitful earth "among the dead leaves," the narrator finally discovers in the darkness Franz treed by the dogs; but instead of submitting to the creatures in accordance with the commandant's "rules" (and thereby acknowledging his inferiority in this oddly oriented world), Franz assumes the posture of his tormentors by hurling stones at the raging animals—not in a gesture of bestiality but as a desperate assertion of the existence, if not the meaning, of the remnants of his obsessed being, an assertion born of a knowledge of a kind of hell virtually impossible to communicate in language. But the spectacle of this defiant survivor beset by baying hounds inspires the narrator to conceive of an image of a new Adam whose origins lay, not in dust and the unformed matter of chaos touched by the divine breath, but in the "Great Horror" whose birth was heralded by Elie Wiesel in a proclamation we have already encountered, "In the beginning there was the Holocaust":

> Franz disappeared into the forest, treading heavily, not like a man who is weighed down and crushed but rather like some primitive being of unusual stature and bulk, burdened with mankind's first responsibilities, who passes through an immense forest on the further edge of which he will see one of the first dawns of the world. [p. 174]

Mankind's journey through a dark wood in the twentieth century has little to do with the legendary expulsion from Eden, even less

with Dante's poetic rehabilitation of his lost pilgrim; the way back is
at once more simple, and more complex. Gascar is content to name
without describing, a new dawn of the world, whose vista is still
darkened by the night that preceded it; his emphasis, rather, is on
the need to recognize the quality of its "newness," features which
the old forms and language are inadequate to represent. A clue to
his purpose is offered in the conclusion to "The Dogs," in which the
narrator several months later receives a brief, banal note from
Franz, still at his post as official "victim," in which he twice
misspells the word *hounds* as *huonds* (French *chiens—cheins*). The
now reflective narrator cannot believe that through "carelessness or
a slip of the pen . . . the key word of this story had become
dangerously transfigured into a sort of outlandish syllable, a strange
unpolished pebble rolling along in the bed of words more slowly
than the rest. Fate, which had watched over its metamorphosis (the
most economical possible, consisting merely of the inversion of two
letters), was still present in this confrontation of man and beast"
(p. 174). But he knows that the contours of this "fate" are unfamiliar, and unresponsive to the clarifying terms of classical traditions.

Hence the transfiguration of post-Holocaust reality necessitates
first of all a revision, an inversion, a deliberate reconstitution of the
language employed to portray it. The symbolic substitution of *chein*
for *chien* can compel men to see that there are dogs and dogs, that
no conception is any longer stable, that such a metamorphosis of
words, gradually encroaching on traditional visions of human
nature, can ultimately give us "a glimpse into an animal hell . . . in
which we recognize, with an astonished sense of kinship, our own
tortured likeness, as in a scratched mirror" (p. 174). The contorted
image we view there may be the limit of the comprehension and
insight that an art of atrocity can offer us, the transformation of
chien into *chein* the initial shock required to awaken us to the larger
metamorphosis implicit in it. (Gregor Samsa's melodramatic transformation into an enormous insect anticipates this change.)

Earlier, Franz had notified the narrator that he originally came
from a town whose nationality had frequently altered during the
course of recent history, a town "situated at the intersection of
precarious frontiers . . . ready for the ravens that haunt our plains"
(p. 148). Later the narrator thinks of Franz hidden in the forest
during the chase, "crucified there, while around him lay sleeping

Europe and he tried desperately to gather it close to him—but in the end the hounds of darkness would set their teeth in its heart" (p. 168). Gascar's new man—a tortured sensibility incarnating the victim as survivor and the survivor as continuing victim—stands at the intersection of precarious frontiers, not as an Adam who has named the beasts, but "like some primitive being" (p. 174) who has recognized the hounds of darkness in himself and felt their teeth, and whose uncertain future rests on the fragile, ominous support tendered by this tentative knowledge.

6: BLESSED ARE THE LUNATICS

*The plague eats away my pale
face, a silent voice speaks
silent signs which only madmen
interpret and bear with them
unsaid and unforgotten, but at
night . . .*

Jakov Lind

*Jeder Tag war fast ein Fest.
Und was ist jetzt?
Die Pest, die Pest.*

Viennese Folk-tune

The most gruesome details of the Holocaust have caused more than
one incredulous witness to doubt his sanity and to wonder finally
whether the source of derangement lay in his own inadequate vision
or the nature of the details he was examining. As a Jew who left
Vienna while still a child and then managed to survive the war in
occupied Holland and later in Germany itself, Jakov Lind must have
been in a unique position to appreciate the macabre ambiguities of
this tension, as his facade of equanimity was constantly threatened
by the fear of discovery and deportation. Existence askew is thus
the hallmark of his fiction; his art is dedicated to a deliberate
distortion of reality, as if the fun-house mirrors that warp the human
figure in their illusory world of glass had somehow escaped the
confines of the amusement park to reflect an authentic universe of
grotesque shapes that insist on being accepted as "normal" images
of our time, in the absence of anything else to compare them with.
His theme is a world gone so mad that insanity, now the only
measure of experience, somehow seems sane; yet behind the
imaginative lunacy of his novels and tales—and he never permits
us to forget this—looms the historical deracination that inspired
it.

Revelations of the enormity of the atrocities committed in behalf
of a "higher" principle of national aspiration left the world stunned

and cowering in the shadows of an avalanche of dreadful implication; Lind simply shoved the world into its value-shattering path,
and from the ruins reconstructed a carnival of absurd horrors that
jar the sensibilities like chalk screeching across dry slate, even as it
sketches caricatures of the inmates who escaped this asylum-uni-
verse before it was driven into the abyss. Set loose in reality, these
creatures gradually dominate it, until (as in Peter Weiss's *Marat/
Sade*) their apparent madness displays a lurking, grim sanity that at
first compels the reader to doubt his own; then to question the
premises that traditionally distinguish madness from reason; then to
acknowledge uneasily that, in *l'univers concentrationnaire* as Lind
evokes it, the two have been hopelessly confused; and finally to
grope for some new conception of reality that will permit him to
apprehend the hallucinations liberated when man awakens from his
dream of reason into the mutilated world of the Holocaust. He can
no longer "reassure" himself, like the narrator in Thomas Mann's
prophetic tale of *Mario and the Magician*, that his involvement in
the nightmare of unreason is only temporary, or that in the end a
mere exertion of will can rescue him from its hypnotic spell.

These illusions lie buried in the rubble of the world beneath our
imaginary avalanche, and Lind has no intention of resurrecting
them. Rather, he invents characters and situations for which the
past appears to offer only a dim precedent, though he usually
introduces just enough allusion to historical fact to prevent his
narratives from floating off into the insubstantial realm of surrealism. For example, in a brief tale called "Journey through the
Night," which employs the train journey as metaphor central to the
experience of the Holocaust (one is reminded of Heinrich Böll's
description of contemporary man as "a traveler who climbs into a
train at his home station and sets out in the night for a destination
whose distance is unknown"), Lind recreates a bizarre version of
such a journey; though the traveler is joined in his compartment by
an amiable companion who carries a little black bag with tools and
announces with uncanny earnestness that he intends to kill his
fellow passenger, saw him in pieces, and eat him.

Time and space seem to have dissolved. The story begins: "What
do you see when you look back? Not a thing. And when you look
ahead? Even less," and the lights glimmering in the countryside
through which they are passing are equally indefinite—"You

couldn't be sure if they were windows or stars";[1] but in the midst of this incertitude the potential victim takes the perfectly reasonable attitude of doubting both the sanity and the intentions of his dapper antagonist. After all, sane men don't make such proposals, and intelligence has always been a match for such madness. But the persistence of the tranquil, modern cannibal gradually exerts a remarkable influence on the reasonable passenger: his initial resistance—"I don't believe a word of it. You can't saw me up."—turns into curiosity in which fear mingles with his fascination ("What do you do with the eyes?" Answer: "Suck 'em," p. 84), and though the threatened traveler tries to pass off his inquiries as an attempt to humor a madman, he ends up questioning the point of his own refusal to satisfy the appetite of his persecutor.

Human behavior, Lind suggests, seems outrageous or gruesome only when it is approached from a perspective of order that has grown habitual to men; behind the ludicrous logic of the narrator-victim lies a lucidity which—in the context of Lind's imaginative universe, where the mind seeks in vain to adjust to a dehumanized world that makes extermination a principle of civilized conduct—appeals to an unfamiliar but perhaps more relevant order of reality:

Death comes to every man. Does it really matter how you die? You can get run over, you can get shot by accident, at a certain age your heart is likely to give out, or you can die of lung cancer, which is very common nowadays. One way or another you kick the bucket. Why not be eaten by a madman in the Nice-Paris express? [p. 86]

The self-confidence implicit in the "cannibal" view of existence makes psychological and intellectual inroads on the complacency and assurance of the previously unintimidated traveler until he develops a mild contempt for himself and a grudging admiration for his "mad" persecutor, not so far distant from the alleged identification of the concentration-camp inmate with his SS guard—an illustration of what we might call the "victim syndrome," which Lind translates into literary (if exaggerated) terms:

A feeling of warmth and well-being came over me. Here is a madman, he wants to eat me. But at least he wants something. What do I want? Not to eat anybody. Is that so noble? What's left when you don't want to do what you certainly ought to do? [p. 86]

---

1. Jakov Lind, "Journey Through the Night," in *Soul of Wood and Other Stories*, trans. Ralph Manheim (New York: Fawcett Crest Book, 1966), p. 83.

The voice of reason is reduced to a pathetic whisper, if not total silence, in its own defense, and the confusion of values grows even more pronounced when its opponent, the voice of aberration, speaks not with the words of a raving maniac but with a compelling deliberation that apparently undermines still further the weak objections of the victim:

> I've got to eat you. In the first place I'm hungry, and in the second place I like you. I told you right off that I liked you and you thought, the guy is a queer. But now you know. I'm a simple cannibal. It's not a profession, it's a need. Good Lord, man, try to understand: now you've got an aim in life. Your life has purpose, thanks to me. [p. 87]

If such a confrontation in the end convinces neither victim nor reader, it does accomplish the more important task of requiring a reexamination—and perhaps ultimately a redefinition—of commonly accepted abstractions like "life" and "purpose." Instinct for survival goads the prospective victim to pull the emergency cord and stop the train, whereupon the little man with the black bag disappears out the compartment door into the night with the contemptuous parting thrust: "you've made an ass of yourself for life. Look who wants to live" (p. 88). But as the story ends, the dilemma of interpretation only begins, for with the arrival of the conductor and a policeman (representatives of "reasonable" authority and order), the passenger is left in the dubious position of having to explain an unbelievable and virtually inconceivable experience, with nothing to support his testimony but the feeble evidence that he, like they, is a man of rational convictions and stable character. He is poised at the border of two worlds whose premises differ, whose vocabularies do not intersect, each unprepared to acknowledge the existence of the other; and only the reader, who through the mediation of art has been able to inhabit both, can decide which of these realities should be adjudged fantasy. But how? Episodes more macabre than cannibalism have occurred on journeys through the night in sealed boxcars in our time, as Lind well knows—and maybe even cannibalism too. The event is perhaps less significant than the inability to report it, or the human incapacity to contain it and its implications in the imagination, without dismissing it as the invention of an apparent madman who vanishes into silence before his sanity can be genuinely tested.

Lind's special talent is for reconstructing the boundaries separating pre- from post-Holocaust reality, and shifting voices from one to the other in a sustained, empirical-metaphysical dialogue (like the one abruptly interrupted at the end of "Journey through the Night" by the disappearance of one participant), until the contours defining each reality dissolve and the two slowly merge, spreading out over the imaginative landscape like a swollen river flooding its banks. The river sweeps away all objects previously fixed in the landscape and redeposits them in such unpredictable patterns that when the rampaging waters recede, one wanders over the disordered terrain seized by occasional flashes of recognition or discernment, but discomfitted by an inability to establish any meaningful sense of orientation to its new topography. Our feet are still on the ground, which seems less stable (though indubitably *there*), but the mind must undertake anew the human task of seeking order amidst chaos, with even less assurance than before that such efforts can be rewarded with success. "Order" has joined "life" and "purpose" as an abstraction inherited from an exhausted humanistic vocabulary. The shapes looming out of the landscape once more resemble the grotesque creatures of a Bosch painting, but our initial response of amused disbelief—civilized cannibals, indeed!—is mitigated by a tense, disconcerting fear that a new kind of imaginative vision has vanquished the familiar forms and left the spectator gasping helplessly in its backwash.

This rather extravagant excursion into metaphor is no more exaggerated than the situations and characters which Lind introduces into the literature of atrocity, and is perhaps symptomatic of the challenge facing the critic who seeks to interpret in comprehensible terms the extraordinary non-sense of his fiction. In fact, one of Lind's favorite aesthetic predilections is the search, not for the *mot juste*, but as it were the "metaphor *juste*," a grotesque and absurd imaginative conception commensurate with the historical excesses he identifies with our time. For example, in a brief but wildly Rabelaisian tale that continues the theme of cannibalism, a young medical student from Vienna traveling in Sweden is picked up by a motorist of enormous bulk (who turns out to be a Lithuanian refugee), and is taken home by him to meet his family, who offer the hitchhiker a meal and bed for the night. Systematically, Lind develops the improbable conditions of their existence: they are nudists, so the mother and two sisters of the host greet the guest fully unclad; they have torn down the inner walls of their dwelling to make more room, and the decaying corpse of a horse hangs from the rafters; the kvas they drink tastes peculiar, until they cheerfully reveal that fresh hog's blood is a major ingredient; the pickled meat they serve, "covered with onions and swimming in oil and vinegar," tastes like human flesh, but the members of the family down huge chunks of it with eager gusto, and cannot understand their guest's aversion when he learns that they are indeed cannibals, and in fact are devouring their own children one by one, begotten of illicit unions between the host and his mother and sisters. The young Viennese, the visitor from normal civilization, as it were, restrains his nausea because as "a medical student he mustn't let anything upset him, it was a matter of professional dignity," but as he departs in fear and disgust, his mind dwells momentarily on the possibility that other systems of political reality may be little better: "True, they were naked, they ate their children, and the whole house stank. But in the paradise of workers and peasants, as his newspaper said, the people were still worse off." But Lind is not really concerned with political analogies; rather, he dwells on the isolating nature of the experience, the impossibility of communicating it despite its overwhelming impression on the student's sensibilities: "That's what insanity is like," he concludes, with laconic irony, "but none of my friends will believe a word of it. All medical men." [2]

One is left wondering how Kafka's explorer would have explained—and how convincingly—the workings of the penal colony to his associates upon his return. For the young student from the former center of culture in western Europe, the only anticipated response, as with the traveler in "Journey through the Night," is a frustrating silence; and for the reader, nudity, incest, and infanticide seem to join cannibalism as expressions of normal impulses, as Lind invests his peculiar refugee family with a vitality that makes the hesitant self-control of the medical student seem pale in comparison. As Lind delineates them, their excesses—or crimes— seem bizarre only because we are unaccustomed to them, as if "reality" were nothing more than our habitual way of seeing; if modern history has taught us anything, he suggests, it is the urgent need to modify this perspective.

2. Lind, "Hurrah for Freedom," in *Soul of Wood*, pp. 130, 133.

To accomplish this, Lind exploits the familiar, if (in this context) unexpected, literary device of satire, though we have already noticed how thinly its hilarity conceals the sinister inhumanity looming behind its facade. David Rousset, whose *L'Univers Concentrationnaire* christened a period of modern history, notes one result of his own experience in a camp: "the fascinating discovery of humor, not so much as a projection of the personality, but as an objective pattern of the universe." Under such circumstances, he observes, Ubu (of Alfred Jarry's *Ubu Roi*) and Kafka "cease to be literary fantasies and become component elements of the living world. The discovery of this humor," he adds, "enabled many of us to survive. It is clear that it will command new horizons in the reconstruction of the themes of life and in their interpretation."

Whether or not Lind heard this prophecy is unimportant; he has certainly helped to fulfill it. The humor of which Rousset speaks (like much of Kafka's) derives from the sense of disparity between our preconceptions of the human, and the aberrations from it encountered in the concentration camps (and the historical and moral environment surrounding them), a humor dwelling on the verge of horror and never far from hysteria—the "humor," one might say, of awakening one fine morning to find yourself transformed into an enormous insect (or, in a grimmer and more literal version, to find yourself a candidate for the gas chamber for the "logical" reason that your barrack is overcrowded). It is an attitude begot by the uncanny on the real: in life, somehow stretching the realm of the possible so as to enable Rousset and his companions to accept as part of "the objective pattern of the universe" a daily scene, as he describes it, "littered with the ruins of human dignities" [3] without losing their sanity; and in literature, producing a variety of gallows humor, a technique, as practiced by Lind, for diverting the outraged imagination and thwarting its objections by detouring tragedy through the distractions of comedy until the mind feels bereft of its capacity to respond seriously to the unspeakable error of dying too soon, abased and anonymous—the human imagination is actually assaulted by art with the improbabilities it shrank from in life.

With an indignation born half of pity, half of scorn, Lind exposes

3. Rousset, *The Other Kingdom*, pp. 172, 169.

the inability or refusal of both tormentor and victim to realize the enormity of what they did and suffered, as if the Holocaust had somehow reached beyond the impulses of human nature and possessed it merely as a vehicle to express a reality fundamentally alien from the mortals who enacted it. (Anyone who has ever attended or seen films of a Nazi war-crimes trial will recognize this sensation—the feeling that neither witnesses nor accused could have participated in the events being recounted, that somehow their ordinary appearance is incommensurate with the extraordinary scenes traced in the testimony.) Lind introduces a kind of prismatic perception into his narratives, separating speaker from incident, man from his fate, words from the lips that utter them; and though in his most explicit stories extermination is never a laughing matter, he leaves us wondering with a painful frustration how human creatures so ludicrously insufficient as men could have wrought such havoc upon themselves and others. The language of his characters reflects a partly deliberate, partly unconscious self-deception, as if they had donned blinders to prevent themselves from seeing a destiny they could not understand anyway; and the gruesome comedy that ensues is reminiscent of those episodes in the works of Samuel Beckett and Günter Grass where characters struggle hopelessly to comprehend their past and the very human context of their lives that—now obscurely, now insistently—afflicts them.

The need to see in meaningful terms the apparent senselessness of the Holocaust is the obstacle that intervenes between Lind's reader and his art, an obstacle that he consciously seeks to circumvent by exploiting it repeatedly as the substance of his tales. Both the title and the concluding story of his initial collection, *Soul of Wood and Other Stories* (1962) are concerned with the annihilation of the Jews, and both repeatedly undermine the logic of experience, for which the reader desperately searches amongst the inconceivabili ties of extermination. The opening line of "Soul of Wood" echoes like a dissonance weakly muted by a pretended harmony, a prelude to a world whose rules of composition only *seem* to promise the order and beauty of a completed form: "Those who had no paper entitling them to live lined up to die." The idea of a universe where man must die unless he can document his right to survive is a grim jest worthy of Alice's Wonderland, not to mention Kafka's inventive fantasies; but Lind offers it totally without preparation as a supposedly reasonable *premise* of his narrative, as if to taunt the reader with a dark truth of *l'univers concentrationnaire* that in its retrospective matter-of-factness *sounds* mad, but is supported by the evidence of millions of corpses, and to subvert the charge that the distortions of his own fiction violate the probabilities of history and human psychology. The shocking one-line preamble is followed by three brief paragraphs that announce the deportation and death of the parents of the young Jewish paralytic whose fate plays such a prominent role in "Soul of Wood," and lest the reader forget, during his encounter with Lind's own fabrications, the inspiration for his fictional lunacies, the introductory section concludes with the solemn reminder of man's fate during the Holocaust: "In the little Polish town of Oswiecim [Auschwitz] they were taken off the train by men in uniform and cremated the same day." [4]

Given the icy logic encompassed by these two lines, with their simultaneously incredible and incontrovertible implications, Lind creates a fictional counterlogic of his own, whose implausible excesses are "mitigated" only by the excesses in fact on which he founds his vision. The phenomenon of Anton Barth, the young Jew born with only a head, who gradually develops other limbs over the next twelve years until he is finally "complete" (though paralyzed and mute), belongs to the same satirical family as the stunted Oskar of Grass's *Tin Drum*, whom Barth in some respect recalls. Lind, however, adroitly translates the obsession with the Jew during the Third Reich into a combination of fairy tale, myth, and psychoanalytical nightmare.

The servant of the Barth family, a one-legged World War I veteran named Wohlbrecht, promises the boy's deported parents that he will care for him in exchange for the title to the apartment where they live. With a ruthless if comic sense of honor, faithful retainer Wohlbrecht replays with variations the drama of the infant Oedipus, perhaps the archetypal "threat" to the well-being of a dynasty, by abandoning the immobile Barth on a mountainside, ironically enough, warmly dressed and with adequate nourishment for a brief period (though Barth, of course, cannot move to feed himself). Miraculously—and here animal fable mingles with myth—

4. Lind, "Soul of Wood," in *Soul of Wood*, pp. 9, 10.

a stag breaks into the hut where Barth has been left, and "cures" his paralysis by pounding his body with its antlers. The boy spends the war years growing up among the mountain creatures, though Wohlbrecht has long since thought of him as his skeleton Jew.

Wohlbrecht himself spends the war years in the St. Veith Insane Asylum, sent there by a Gestapo officer who wanted the Barth apartment for himself. His own derangements must be measured against the activity of the institution, where a daily quota of sixty-two "incurables" are given injections—known as "special treatment," just as they were during the war—to ease them (permanently) of their supposed misery. But the purpose of this treatment, as explained by the director of the asylum to his chief subordinate, raises the question of whether the officials can really be distinguished from the inmates; or, since the victims are themselves, of course, perfectly sane, whether the atmosphere of insanity one expects from such a setting has not provided Lind with the perfect metaphor for evoking an experience which in a more literal rendering drives the imagination to the brink of disbelief. Here is the doctor's explanation:

> "You mustn't forget, my friend, the purpose of my tests is not to provide you with patients for your treatments. I would do that in any case; the purpose is to register a real change in the patient prior to treatment, thus substantiating our theory concerning sub-human enemies of the people, because otherwise, my good friend, our work would be based on a mere hypothesis, and your patient [who had denounced his impending execution as 'criminal'] would actually be right. It would be a downright crime against science if a German neurologist were unable to cure a patient's political hallucinations before subjecting him to the final treatment." [pp. 51–52]

Such reasoning, where it can be followed, reveals how success-fully language, when combined with a certain kind of bureaucratic mentality, can obscure the true nature of the reality being discussed. By suppressing the emotion of terror from an episode like this, Lind leaves a gaping vacuum in the moral and aesthetic sensibilities of the reader, who is confronted with a universe of freaks unable to imagine or meditate on the harm that they do. Lind thus manages to eliminate from the story the same dimension of tragedy which history had eliminated from life, at least during the period of the Holocaust, when an atmosphere of fantasy had corrupted the moral clarity that breeds tragedy.

Wohlbrecht had already predicted the new order of reality as he and his epileptic brother-in-law (Alois) were carrying the helpless Barth up to his mountain "refuge":

> The fewer limbs a man has, the less blood he has and the less he gets out of war. You and me and Alois, we'll always belong together. We're a blood brotherhood. The brotherhood of the sick, the crippled and paralyzed. Some day we'll run the world. Health is a menace, what does it lead to? Lunacy and crime. But we shall inherit the earth. [p. 30]

The prophecy reads like an epigraph to Lind's fiction, which proclaims (and implicitly laments) the triumph of the misfits, who gain by default (the result of "special treatment"?) a realm purged of the reasonable aims of reasonable men.

At the end of "Soul of Wood," in a kind of modern Walpurgisnacht by daylight, Wohlbrecht, his former overseers at the asylum, and a fleeing SS soldier (to whom Wohlbrecht has confided the secret of Barth) gather on the mountain top, all in search of the skeleton of the Jew and guided by the bizarre notion that it will somehow enable them to reclaim a portion of their discarded virtue and certify their good intentions. "One Jew can help a great deal," argues the director of the asylum; "To have saved even one individual would be proof positive that we were not guided by feelings of hatred in the performance of our work" (p. 61). And Wohlbrecht offers to share the skeleton with the Waffen-SS man if he gives him a lift up the mountain. But the macabre intermingling of history with fairy tale is further compounded when Wohlbrecht, turned away by his companions (who hope to benefit from his hidden "treasure" without having to share it), learns from an old crone, the proverbial witch of the mountain, that a creature resembling Barth is still alive in the region; and like a knight in quest of some kind of redeeming token, he secures from her a rope to bind his quarry in return for a night of love.

In a perverse parody of the myths of enchantment and disenchantment—the crone does not turn into a beautiful princess, for example—Wohlbrecht hopes to use the Jew to liberate him from the bond of evil he has forged by his collaboration with the officials of the asylum in their extermination of the patients. But such curses, Lind suggests, are not so easily undone, as the helpless Wohlbrecht is forced to sign a statement that his "associates" had given him "every possible help in saving Anton Barth, a victim of racial persecution, from the clutches of the Gestapo"; then is deprived of his wooden leg ("Have mercy . . . I'm human too," he cries with the arch simplicity but in direct parody of Beckett's Gogo or Didi); and finally, in response to his appeal, is dispatched by a few bursts from a machine gun. The illogic of history (and the brutality of men), not moral justice, have consigned him to the kind of fate he had "solicitously" prepared for Barth—a one-legged skeleton on the mountain, perhaps an inspiration for future legends in the minds of ancient crones. His testament to the world is his "surviving" limb, the wooden leg, which leans mutely (and soullessly) against a tree, "waiting patiently for the resurrection of its master, which will surely happen some day. Any day" (pp. 81, 82).

The dry sarcasm of Lind's tone is a hallmark of his style and attitude, an insulation against tears, like laughing at the painful antics of a mournful clown to keep from weeping. One of Wohlbrecht's charitable murderers speaks an epitaph which evokes this universe, comic in appearance, though behind the scenes numerous human creatures don masks and costumes that will capitalize on their deformities and separate their performances from their lives, deceiving and confusing a public—like the sad clown, like Mann's Cipolla (in *Mario*)—already eager to abandon its grasp on reality:

> Too bad, he said. He probably would have made a good circus impresario in time. Wasn't he wild about midgets! It was almost pathological. Well, let's not speak ill of the dead. [p. 82]

But neither the circus allusion nor the deliberately truncated analogies with myth and legend dispel the fundamental realities from which these various metaphors for experience radiate—the victimization of Barth as Jew, and the death of his parents in Auschwitz. As Barth's captors, like inmates escaped from Charenton, swarm down the mountainside bearing his bound body with them as surety against their crimes and evidence of their good will toward Jews, the fate of the Jew as victim-scapegoat has not changed, and the restoration of his humanity and dignity in a world still governed by those whose vision extends no farther than saving their own skins, is as improbable as the resurrection of the wretched Wohlbrecht. Man's fate is to learn that only wood endures.

But Lind refuses to transform this gloomy insight into tragic knowledge, preferring to put horror to ludicrous uses, as if to suggest—together with writers like Beckett and Günter Grass and Ionesco—that only a grisly form of comedy remains to open the eyes of humanity to what it has become and endured in the recent past, and the heritage such experiences have bequeathed to the present.

Lind concludes his volume with a story called "Resurrection," whose opening line introduces with frank hilarity an illogic and paradox complementary to the more somber preamble of "Soul of Wood." If the fate of the Jew in a supposedly Christian world was epitomized in that story in the epigrammatic inhumanity of "Those who had no papers entitling them to live lined up to die," such a destiny, still born of contradiction, is succinctly if humorously elaborated in the first words of "Resurrection": "Deum Jesum Christum in gloriam eternam est. Nu." [5] The prayer, uttered by a Polish Jew named Goldschmied turned Protestant and living—or hiding—in occupied Holland for the past half-year in an enclosure with the ominous dimensions of a grave, sounds like the beginning of a Jewish joke at the expense of Christians (or vice versa); and in fact, the events of the story, the dialogue and habits of thought of the characters, abound in references and intonations that one commonly associates with Jewish humor. For Goldschmied, who prays in Dutch and Church Latin with a Yiddish accent, is joined in his tiny hiding place by another refugee from Nazi persecution, a tubercular Jew named Weintraub, and the ensuing religio-philo-sophical discussions, while Weintraub literally coughs them to discovery, deportation, and death, is vaguely reminiscent of the serio-comic dialectical arguments of Naphta and Settembrini atop Thomas Mann's Magic Mountain, as civilization careens in the lowlands toward the catastrophe of war.

Neither Weintraub, who simply wants to know whether Gold-schmied is hiding as a Christian or a Jew, nor Goldschmied, who justifies his transference to the faith of the "goyim" (his own word)

5. Lind, "Resurrection," in *Soul of Wood*, p. 134.

by quoting the Rabbis and the Talmud, recognizes clearly the irrelevance of their disputation to the fate that threatens them— though Lind never suggests that cringing in fear would have been a satisfactory alternative. According to the logic of the fiction, the baptized Jew, who is also unmarried (and childless), could have saved himself and been permitted to live in freedom by consenting to sterilization, but the very word throws Goldschmied into utter confusion, as Lind probes, in a mood more sardonic than compassionate, his failure to confront his situation. "The possibility of saving his life was more than his nerves could stand," he says of his convert; and while Weintraub is infuriated by the Talmudic complications with which Goldschmied tries to defend himself, the reader is baffled by the question of finding *any* human stance adequate to the prospect of extermination under the terms of *l'univers concentrationnaire.* "The essential difference," explains the "Christian" Goldschmied, "is between killing and being killed. Murderers after their deed need human mercy—but the murdered need divine mercy in advance" (p. 152).

But even he is not convinced by this religious solace, a rhetoric designed to allay the suffering of public martyrdom, but ineffectual before the anonymous terrors of extinction in the gas chamber, which neither Talmud nor New Testament could have anticipated. Goldschmied's apparent obsession with the prospect of sterilization only confirms his desperate need to divert his attention from the real threat; and his attempt to distinguish between himself and the acknowledged Jew Weintraub on this basis introduces a macabre humor into their story, though Weintraub has more than a glimpse of the dehumanizing implications of his companion's hair-splitting distinctions. "On one rotten condition they let me live," exclaims the baptized Goldschmied; "—as a Jew, no conditions, they just kill me. They let me choose something I wouldn't wish on a dog. You have no choice. You don't have to turn into a dog; you can die like a normal, healthy human being." One consequence of this grisly and tactless comfort is to rouse the indignation of Weintraub (whose tubercular condition is rapidly degenerating in his airless confinement), who denounces Goldschmied's guiltily dishonest confession —"I didn't hide because I'm a Jew, I hid to avoid choosing"—with an outburst that illuminates the difficulty of characterizing *any* human motive, as far as Lind is concerned, in the literature of atrocity:

> How can anybody know where he stands if the victims take the guilt for themselves? No wonder they all climb into the trains of their own free will; they think it serves them right, and not that they're wronged. [pp. 153–54]

Weintraub's exaggeration explains no more adequately than the dozens of journalists and historians who have struggled with this problem an attitude that Lind attributes to a combination of fear and a failure of imagination; even as the two hidden victims argue their positions, Lind employs their dialogue as evidence of language's inability to contend with, to capture the tone and quality of the events.

A second consequence of Goldschmied's indelicate observation that Weintraub (who does not face the choice between sterilization and incineration) has the "advantage" of dying like a normal, healthy human being, is to awaken a longing that had been just the opposite aim of Goldschmied's unconsciously ironic remark. All the frustrations afflicting the human condition in *l'univers concentrationnaire* are summed up in the tubercular Jew's passionate plea for existence, a voice that strips the gloss from the essence of this atrocity and with an aching simplicity affirms what no tragic vision of suffering's transforming power could express:

> Frankly, Mr. Goldschmied, I have no sympathy for you. I'd rather be a live onlooker than a dead victim. You talk and talk. Religion, holiness, the Jews' mission. All a lot of phrases, slogans. Choice, dog, guilt. I don't give a shit about all that. In a few days they'll strangle me and burn me like a leper, and that's the end of Sholom Weintraub. They'll give me a number on a mass grave, colored with gold dust, and I'll never, never be alive again. Resurrection is nothing but Talmudic hair-splitting, mystery, smoke and sulphur, hocus-pocus, theological speculation. There is no second time, not before and not after the Messiah, and He doesn't exist anyway. I want to live, Mr. Goldschmied, I want to live and breathe and I don't care how—like a dog or a frog or a bedbug, it's all the same to me. I want to live and breathe, to live. [p. 154]

But carefully skirting sentimentalism and melodrama, Lind refuses to permit such eloquence to breed the heroic defiance of a

Stephen Dedalus, whose words become tools in his conquest of reality; Weintraub's assertion of self induces a coughing fit so loud and prolonged that it is overheard "on the outside," and in a short time he and his fellow inmate are discovered, arrested, and eventually deported. Weintraub may have won his argument against Goldschmied, but their doom has triumphed over both, and from the broader perspective beyond their hiding place, neither appears to possess the human intensity highlighted by its narrower dimensions. The darker glory of a potential tragic heroism vanishes in the light of day, and even Weintraub is unable to sustain the mood of existential urgency that had briefly crowned him with a halo of dignity. On the way to Gestapo headquarters, surrounded by trivial conversation among the arresting officers about food—"normal things"—life suddenly "seemed to him reasonable and simple again, and he was ashamed of having acted like a madman" (p. 157). All their notes from underground are forgotten, and as they meet again in the transit camp just before their final journey to Poland, their point-of-no-return, a cheerful and healthy Weintraub, buoyed by fresh air, comforts a vaguely skeptical Goldschmied: "do you really believe those stories about Poland? Now that I'm feeling better, I don't believe them any more. Sick people get such crazy fears" (p. 158).

Oedipus was confronted with a truth in some ways as dreadful as the fate Weintraub evades, yet he found the moral strength to accept his tragic destiny and pursue its implications. Lind's essentially comic vision repudiates both the premises about human nature that permitted Sophocles to create his archetypal hero, and the conception of reality—and particularly, the principles of logic and causality which in part characterized it—that made it possible for Oedipus to be an agent in his own downfall and, through his discovery of this fact, to avoid the designation of "helpless victim" of fate which a superficial reading of the play occasionally attributes to him. Hiding is a motif common in Lind's work, and its natural cause is fear (not too dissimilar from the terror of Jocasta as she urges Oedipus to retreat from his awful future into the safety of the palace); but when Weintraub and Goldschmied are detected by the Gestapo, they are powerless to establish any connection between their past actions and what they are about to suffer (Weintraub's coughing is the ludicrous link that connects the two), nor would physical or moral courage ("Goldschmied was unobserved for a moment: running isn't in my line, he decided," p. 155) avail to salvage some human dignity or insight from their situation.

Lind is determined to expose the futility of literary precedents about tragedy as well as historical premises about human nature in representing the essence of *l'univers concentrationnaire;* circumstances and that nature conspired during the Holocaust to arouse humanity's least flattering responses, until man as Victim became a creature who had lost the capacity to see himself as a complex moral being, or a monument to martyrdom. At least this is the substance of Lind's vision here; Goldschmied's reply to Weintraub's mocking comment on sick people with crazy fears—virtually the last words exchanged between the living friends—is: "You're right, Weintraub, we've got to keep our health, with all this fear we might as well be dead" (p. 158).

Lind's irony is tempered by our knowledge of what his characters, eschewing the fear in a handful of dust that lies before them, are about to suffer; but it also wrenches into permanent distortion values like sickness and health, or fear and courage, since the unspoken but meaningless horror of their fate simply negates the significance of all their conversations about alternatives. The terms of their dialectic somehow seem *external to what actually happens to them,* which Lind himself never mentions, perhaps—and this would be the most sardonic aesthetic twist of all—in an attempt to make the reader the final victim of the morbid "comedy" of life during the Holocaust (in David Rousset's sense of the "humorous" illogic culminating in death which he discovered as "an objective pattern of the universe" in the microcosm of the concentration camp).

For in the concluding lines of "Resurrection" the two companions do meet again: "Weintraub was climbing the steep stairs to his holy Jerusalem and Goldschmied to his Jesus on the Cross. For to tell the truth, the city of Jerusalem is not so very big" (p. 158), and struggling with this ambiguity, the reader's imagination is diverted from the inexpressible catastrophe that can no longer be dramatized as a tragedy. The consolations of a resurrection generous enough to embrace all faiths, including converts, anaesthetize the fears of those who prefer tales of a New Jerusalem to stories about Poland. Art, like life, can serve the delusions of men who choose—who *need*—to be deluded. But only one blind to the intolerable events of history that nourish Lind's vision could succumb to the ironic blandishments with which he tempts further prospective victims.

The ease with which men succumb to views (and then to actions) that contradict conventional notions of their moral complexity (thus raising the question of the validity of these notions for our time) is, in fact, an important theme of Lind's first novel, *Landscape in Concrete* (1963). The very title of this and his earlier volume, *Soul of Wood*, indicate a dehumanization of vital values (spirit and nature) into inanimate stuff, symbolic of the moral aridity of the creatures of his imagination. The epigraph to the novel stands in bleak but eloquent testimony to an attitude which grows increasingly evident in Lind's works: "There is a plague called man." Whereas a plague was the impetus that drove Oedipus to strive beyond his mortal limitations to achieve self-knowledge and heroic stature, Lind's protagonist seems to have been permanently infected by the bacillus and is unable to purge himself of its spiritually crippling effects. This figure, Gauthier Bachmann, a German soldier who has been found temporarily mentally unfit for further military service but who refuses to accept the implications of this judgment, is a physical giant of a man whose brain appears inadequate to his efforts to understand himself and his role as a human creature during the war. In an attempt to define his type, another character speculates on his nature in a passage that may become a *locus classicus* for interpreting Lind's view of modern experience:

> It's safe to assume that the fear of God has never touched him, he's an antediluvian monster, beyond good and evil, zoologically a new continent, *Homo bachmannus*. . . . What is *Homo bachmannus?* He has the body of a horse, the intelligence of a chimpanzee, and the soul of a dove. . . . Naturally this species survived the deluge, it will never be extinct. The whole world is crawling with them, he must have been some freak in the ark.[6]

Naturally the testimony of a single character, who has his own reasons for being contemptuous of Bachmann, is not sufficient to establish all the habits and qualities of the species, which, if it has always existed, is only beginning to be acknowledged and seriously

6. Jakov Lind, *Landscape in Concrete*, trans. Ralph Manheim (New York: Grove Press, 1966), p. 110.

examined as an enduring member of the race. Bachmann's own wanderings across Europe in quest of his regiment (which has already been decimated at Voroshenko on the Russian front) add to the outlines of his portrait, though the war reduces him to a level of nonhumanity which alienates him from the descendants of Noah we are more familiar with. One is faced with the choice of discarding the portrait from the human gallery or unbalancing the collection by admitting its grotesque dimensions.

Lind is all for unbalancing. Sergeant Bachmann begins his journey toward incomplete self-definition lost, like a famous literary ancestor, in a wood (the Ardennes)—but there the resemblance to the more pious pilgrim ends. In fact, Lind systematically denudes the landscape surrounding Bachmann of all spiritual and human values, of all symbolic possibilities:

> A landscape without faces is like air nobody breathes. A landscape in itself is nothing. The country through which German Sergeant Gauthier Bachmann was making his way on the second Monday before Easter was green but lifeless. [p. 13]

The obvious Christian allusion tempts the imagination to search for a redeeming grail; but Bachmann himself is driven by more primitive instincts, as a very un-Virgilian creature resembling a mole pops from a fox burrow into his path, a deserter who insists that he is a German. A German? cries Bachmann, himself nearly delirious with hunger: "How can it be a German? Must be some cross between a man and a beast, like those mongrels that sometimes get born in out-of-the-way places" (p. 14). Man as hybrid, neither one thing nor the other, as Gogol's Chichikov was fond of saying, is thus ambiguously introduced in the opening phase of Bachmann's adventures, and this creature, Schnotz, is the first measure we encounter for determining the sergeant's own humanity. For as Schnotz directs Bachmann to the unit he (Schnotz) has recently abandoned, the sergeant admits: "I'd like to feel human again, that's what I'm really after, I'm sick of being an outcast, see what I mean?" (p. 20). And for a moment this seems like an honest longing, especially when Schnotz ruthlessly slaughters a goose that Bachmann discovers in a grove the next morning but is unwilling to kill himself. Only gradually, as he confuses the execution of the goose with the crucifixion of the Savior, do his reflections betray an illogic that reveals a more basic instability of mind:

Men can defend themselves, but what can animals do in this world without steel and dynamite? We can riddle any animal with holes and cut it up. With people it's different, I don't know why, but it's not the same. Men are men, they have reason and weapons. [p. 33]

Men are men, Schnotz apes Bachmann, but you're not one of them: and a variety of challenges suddenly appear. Is Schnotz correct? Given the context of Lind's imaginative universe, what *is* a man? And if "reason" and "weapons" are his twin attributes or possessions (rather accurate designations, in fact), how do they affect his nature, to say nothing of each other? Blood-spattered and covered with feathers from plucking and carving the goose, Schnotz, with his scrawny neck and protruding cheekbones, resembles a vulture; so that Bachmann by contrast still seems justified in defending himself against Schnotz's charge that he is a "donkey" and a "yellow swine"—though with an admittedly dubious logic:

Me a creature? Me a donkey? Can a donkey suffer when a poor goose's throat is cut? A donkey has no pity. I'm not a donkey, but he's raving mad. [p. 33]

But the animal imagery drowns the human voice, and the allegation of madness only complicates the endeavor to disentangle the sane from the irrational: gradually one is overwhelmed by the uncomfortable feeling that the behavior of the characters can be explained only if they are not entirely in their right mind. Yet nothing confirms this suspicion, which as the atrocities unfold becomes a necessary hope more than a proven fact, with the composure of the reader hanging in the balance.

As the two sit at a table devouring the goose but unable to decide who gets the liver, they are like primitive cavemen back from the hunt, contending for the choicest morsel; but Lind is less concerned with a retrogressive naturalism than he is with the metamorphosis in human nature that resulted from the experience of the Holocaust, or at least the fresh perspective with which an interpreter is obliged to view it. In fact, Lind deliberately inverts the usual development from primitive to civilized by using the meal as a parody of various Christian rituals, from first communion to last supper, which now seem insufficient and antiquated as mythical expressions of man's spiritual heritage; for afterward, Bachmann's mind is crowded with images from his remote religious childhood, from church bells and incense to the "taste of the wafer on his palate, candy-sweet and yet a trifle bitter, like a liver," and the consequence is that he sentimentally abandons his plan to turn in Schnotz on the following day, filled with pleasure at having "sacrificed his own plan and practiced charity like a good Christian" (p. 40).

Subsequent events, however, verify Lind's ironic intentions here, though they are already anticipated by the rapid dwindling of Bachmann's joy, which ebbs and drains "like bath water" until it turns to "a bestial melancholy from which there was no escape" (p. 41). When he arrives the next day voluntarily accompanied by Schnotz, at Schnotz's former battalion, where he is to undergo the first test of his "humanity" and "manhood," Bachmann overlooks the detail that the troops are occupying a former theological seminary; but the transfiguration of *spirit* into *violence* implicit in this fact is central to Lind's *Weltanschauung*, which never misses an opportunity to mock the civilizing pretensions of institutions like the church, whose aspirations for *Homo bachmannus* suffered a fatal blow in *l'univers concentrationnaire*.

Bachmann, however, who was not present at their interment, fails to recognize the contradictions in his own life that ensue from this tension, and this in turn makes him vulnerable to the assault on his personality that undermines whatever semblance of moral character he once possessed. Lind refuses to divide the world into villains and innocents, but insists that victims and persecutors partake of each others' vices and virtues. Or rather, if history did introduce some few instruments of extraordinary evil, Lind does not regard them as grist for his literary mill. *Homo bachmannus* is both a tool of others and an agent of destruction, and the devastating effect of this circumstance on conventional ideas of human nature seems considerably more important than the question of personal responsibility or the issue of moral alternatives. Lind as an artist confronted a fait accompli that no theory of psychological guilt or aberration could organize—retrospectively, to be sure—into meaningful patterns. Bachmann's own futile attempts to understand how he gets sucked into the whirlpool of atrocity is sufficient dramatic proof of this.

Thus, as he contemplates his experience at the seminary-turned-military-camp, where he has been duped into becoming the sole member of a firing squad to shoot (fatally) at an alleged Belgian traitor and saboteur who turns out to be Schnotz, he is scarcely aware of the change that has already begun to take place in him. Expelled from the battalion camp by the officer in charge (who no longer requires his services as an "executioner"), Bachmann finds himself in the former garden of the ex-seminary, with each flower and plant neatly marked by a Latin tag, like the ordered beauty of a cloistered Eden, and reflects there on his origins and his destiny:

> There are many different kinds of plants and flowers, each one has to have its name if they are not to be confused. The names aren't picked at random, they are part of an old tradition. Like the tradition of the Bachmanns. [His father had been a master gold- and silversmith.] Even if they fade and die in the fall, they keep their names and dignity. Just like us. We're an old family too, but this phlox is still older. They've outlived Rome and the Romans and yet they've died each year. The eternal return, you can call it. [p. 59]

Bachmann's limited intelligence is clearly an anomalous source for philosophical meditation on continuity in nature and history or the resurrection of the human spirit, which contradict so sharply the episode in which he has just participated. But Lind is even more explicit in his suggestion that recent history has reversed man's alleged journey toward dignity and self-knowledge: for Bachmann's expulsion from the military camp *into* a garden (with all its comic overtones), is accompanied by an image that unmistakably derides the fate of this modern, maudlin Adam:

> He turned around only once, when he was already outside, and cast a last mournful glance back at his lost paradise, at the far end of which stood a monster that was doubled up with laughter and slapping its thighs. [pp. 58–59]

The angels of the Lord have been supplanted by the officer who tricked Bachmann into firing the fatal shot, and his contempt for his gulled victim displaces the stern but compassionate discipline of the Creator for his fallen creatures (though Bachmann returns to his Eve only much later in the novel). The traditions of the Bachmanns, of all mankind, have been irreversibly corrupted; as an executioner *malgré lui*, he enters a graceless world where the Schnotz, whom he killed on command, festers within, not as a punishment for his sin, nor as an inherited guilt, but like an uncontrollable virus that rages throughout his system, destroying all possibility of ever diagnosing or curing this plague called man: "the dead man's soul had gone into him and taken its place with everything that had already died inside him" (p. 59).

But the corpses who inhabit Bachmann—and Schnotz's, as we soon learn, is not the first—have a slow and ambiguous effect on his impulse toward self-definition, which veers from clarity to chaos like a drunken philosopher whose flashes of sober sense amidst raving simply throw into relief the extent of his lost stability. Thus Bachmann delivers a harangue outside the station toilet in Narvik, Norway (where he has been transferred after the firing-squad affair), that celebrates man's humanistic aspirations, even as the affirmation is subverted by its physical setting (following Lind's habit of deriding solemnities by incongruous juxtapositions):

> Speech is an expression of reason and reason is the critical faculty that separates the important from the unimportant, the chaff from the wheat. You've got to think things out carefully and not open your mouth until you've drawn correct inferences. [p. 66]

On the lips of this unlikely heir of Schiller and Goethe, who later quotes Nietzsche on the nature of man, such unimpeachable platitudes make one wonder which antiquated pre-Holocaust age took seriously such Socratic "wisdom." Lind has lost interest in whether reason ever was such a distinguished faculty, or what its powers may have been; its perversions have cost it its earlier prestige, and his major goal is to portray the abortions that have survived its demise.

If Bachmann's plan for reason represents a nostalgic tribute to an ancient but discredited value, his subsequent defense of his sanity, before the lieutenant to whom he was ordered to report, and who refuses to assign him to a unit because he is "mentally ill," comprises a sly but deft revelation of the abortion just mentioned:

> I'm not sick any more than millions of my comrades who are fighting for their country right now. If I'm sick, so is all Germany, all Europe, the whole world. Today the whole civilized world is fighting Bolshevism (he began to shout in his agitation), and I, I'm ready to die, to die, yes, to make the supreme sacrifice! IS THAT MADNESS? Admitted I may have my idiosyncrasies. Admitted I'm inclined to melancholy and perhaps to thoroughness. But who isn't? Is that

abnormal? Is that being sick? What's sick about me? Every German is
like me, they all do what they can. Willingly or not. Duty is duty.
[pp. 70–71]

The reply of the lieutenant reflects the critical faculty of reason at
work, discriminating, as Bachmann himself had suggested, between
the chaff and the wheat; but his conclusions, grounded in a
complacent sense of inevitability, justify the act of atrocity with a
vocabulary of morality in such a way that one is left defenseless
against Bachmann's unbalanced diatribe *and* the lieutenant's
"calm" analysis:

A war can only be fought with sound men. The highest demands are
made on every individual, it takes nerves of steel. We have to do
things that may not be to our liking. Yes, sometimes we have to do
violence to our own nature. Most of the duties a war imposes on us,
Sergeant Bachmann, are revolting, let's face it, insane, and yet the
soldier who performs them has to be fully responsible. That's the way
it is, it can't be helped. [p. 71]

This apparently impeccable logic explains a necessity without
considering the consequences, to say nothing of examining motives;
language and the imagination feel impotent against a lucidity that
invents the concept of a fully responsible insanity, one that does
violence to the nature of sound men without any apparent damage
to their individuality. Bachmann, determined to gain entry to the
ranks of these privileged heroes (" 'the idea is to get rid of normal
men like me,' he thinks. 'First humiliate us, then push us aside, and
in the end wipe us out altogether. A diabolical plan.' "—p. 72),
decides that the refusal to use his talents results from the absence of
significant "personal achievement" in his military career, and
desperately runs through his recent exploits ("Nothing outstanding.
Burned a few villages, knifed a few Russians in close combat, but
that was all routine, nothing unusual," p. 74) until he recalls one of
the "corpses" inside him, buried beneath Schnotz:

Herr Leutnant, I've just remembered. Kirov. One Sunday morning
in Kirov we mowed down two thousand Russian prisoners, I repeat,
two thousand, with machine guns. But I've got to admit it was more
boring than horrible. There were six of us, we began at seven A.M., it
was four in the afternoon before we were through. It took them all
morning to dig their graves. You can't imagine the way they dawdle.
[p. 74]

Part of Lind's literary strategy is the literal de-moralization of reality, the reduction or deflation of atrocity to a point of emotional indifference until a human being is capable of facing the most unutterable horrors with an equanimity born of—precisely *what* it is born of is one of the unknown equations in his work, a heritage to be presented with mordant irony and contemplated with speechless despair: perhaps the excess of horrors are themselves responsible for such detachment. The lieutenant responds to Bachmann's recitation by filing his nails, until Bachmann, frustrated and angry, resolves to make his own battle, to involve himself in a situation that will somehow awaken interest in his own singularity: "Then they'll understand that I belong, *they'll* wise up. *I* belong, that's settled, a Bachmann belongs" (p. 75). Yet one wonders, given the fact that he finds the slaughter of two thousand prisoners more boring than horrible, how he plans to accomplish this.

Bachmann behaves throughout as if he lives on two planes of existence: on the one hand, he suffers a genuine crisis of identity, seeking to define his own nature and establish his fundamental humanity in the midst of characteristic modern anguish; and on the other, he stumbles through concrete situations that erode his humanity (like the murder of the Russian prisoners) without recognizing their effect on his resolution to affirm and defend his individuality. His next adventure exposes the fallacy of man's hope that philosophy and action may yet intersect, so that the wish and the act will coincide in a riper civilization, and in the process unfolds a parable of atrocity which Lind uses to mock the respect still paid to the humanistic impulse in the modern world.

A Norwegian traitor recruits Bachmann to help him avenge himself on a family that threatens to expose him to the underground, the same man who scornfully defines the qualities of *Homo bachmannus*, and though Bachmann protests that he himself is a religious man and can not do wrong(!), he submits to the other's more forceful personality: "You will do what I command, because what I command is necessary. Carry out a monstrous order and despite it all remain a man—that's today's task. Are you ready?" Bachmann repeats the question, acknowledging, in a parody of previous tragic insights, that readiness and ripeness are all: "live, breathe, take risks. To be a man despite it all, that's the crux" (p. 88), but his determination to live existentially is undermined and even ridiculed by the kind of challenge that time and history create for him. Bachmann is content to carry on the verbal contest for his own manhood provided someone else originates the malice in the world about him; a built-in insurance against self-contempt—the last outpost of civilization—is assured as long as he acts only as an instrument—or can convince himself that he has done so. When this insulation breaks down—and Lind wants to accelerate the process —man will be faced with an image of himself that is more shattering than the picture of Dorian Gray—and less allegorical.

Thus, the parable of atrocity just mentioned, which Lind devises to illuminate the psychology of all participants in the deed of terror—the agent (Halftan, the Norwegian traitor), Bachmann (the "innocent" instrument), and the victims (the family Elshoved)— tests a central question of *l'univers concentrationnaire*, by extending Halftan's original inquiry to read: can one *live* in an age when monstrous orders are carried out, and despite it all remain a man? The effect on Bachmann, Halftan, and their victims, we shall see; the effect on those who share the experience imaginatively—all those who survived the excesses Lind capitalizes on in his fiction—is more problematic, and Lind self-consciously employs his art as a catalyst to the consciousness of the survivors.

His attitude toward the victims, for example—who are brutally murdered by a yawning but obedient Bachmann—dilutes compassion for their suffering with strong reservations about their unnecessary vulnerability (a delicate issue that astonished and outraged so many sensibilities after the Eichmann trial). For the Elshoved family (like Anne Frank's, like Goldschmied and Weintraub in "Resurrection") hide from reality without comprehending the plague called man with its virus, atrocity, that rages outside their refuge. Behind their "wall of innocence and clear conscience, they lived in a sanctuary of illusion":

> Good works, piety, and decency were expected to save the Elshoveds from the disaster. They wore their virtues like amulets. In 1944 they lived as in 1844, they had simply forgotten a hundred years. When the Germans came, they did not escape to England. There was no time to make the necessary preparations. They were staunch patriots and a little old-fashioned. Their fear for their private welfare was greater than their hatred of the occupants. [p. 90]

Thus tradition, respectability, and a catalogue of familiar virtues insure their death; and Lind creates a rare epiphany for our time when old Mr. Elshoved, just before he expires, screams "Halftan . . . you're mad," and the Norwegian calmly replies: "Wrong . . . you are. You're defenseless" (p. 99).

The circumstances of the slaughter of the family destroy the possibility of martyrdom, which might at least have salvaged virtue as armor for heaven if not for earth. When Bachmann slits the body of the old man's son with his bayonet from throat to abdomen, Lind's graphic imagery excludes the possibility of metaphysical prospects, perhaps even adding a sly dig at the original resurrection: "the blood gushed like a spring when the stone is taken away. A man is full of blood, the way a balloon is full of air. It was always fun to burst balloons, it made a bang, it was exciting. A man doesn't make any bang" (p. 100). Nor a whimper. Man's overestimation of himself may be one cause, during the Holocaust, of his habitual underestimation of the forces, culminating in death, which threatened him, as well as of his failure to recognize the fragility of the moral armaments that were supposed to protect him against the passionless wrath of a Halftan and the dutiful violence of a Bachmann. The Elshoveds' kind of defenselessness *is* mad, since it invites destruction without offering any compensation; thus Lind's new definition of insanity conceals a serious theme, and provides a wry commentary on the fate of virtue in mid-century Europe.

Indeed, Lind's goal seems not only to redress the imbalance of values, but to reverse it, to invent a vision of civilization founded on the brutal truths emerging from the experience of the Holocaust, and to hold up a mirror to human nature whose reflection men were still unable to see clearly because their eyes were glazed by the moral cataracts inherited from the past. Even Bachmann is divided by a schizophrenic tension between his convictions and his conduct: the dialectic is momentarily externalized when Halftan frankly admits that he used Bachmann as an alibi (since no one would believe a common soldier capable of such SS tactics as the ruthless murder) and Bachmann, in an access of conscience, groans that the victims were innocent. Halftan denounces innocence as an obsolete concept ("In a war nobody's innocent. Or everybody."), and follows this with a combination of Machiavelli and Realpolitik that mushrooms into a philosophical statement which—given the events nourishing Lind's imagination—cannot be dismissed simply as the cynical view of a disgruntled opportunist:

> There are lots of pious people in this country, they talk all kinds of nonsense, anybody who listens to them is sunk. They say for instance: The spirit is stronger than the flesh. God's justice will conquer. Brute force will melt away like snow in the spring. That's mental derangement, pure Nordic hogwash. The spirit is made of armor plate and gunpowder, spirit is brute force, and without brute force there's no spirit. A democracy that can't defend itself is a figment of the brain. [pp. 112–13]

The mere possibility of a grain of verity in Halftan's argument would send a civilization founded on the opposite principle of spirit as tenderness and charity spinning crazily from its moral orbit; whether Lind subscribes to it in part or in whole is difficult to say, and probably irrelevant here, but clearly neither the Elshoveds nor Bachmann are a match for it. Bachmann gapes as though seeing ghosts when he hears it, and his immediate response seems a degrading physical equivalent to a mystical experience, a kind of epileptic fit without the accompanying spiritual insight which Dostoevsky and others often ascribe to it. In an obscene vision that might be a vicious parody of Alyosha Karamazov embracing the earth with grief-stricken affection after the death of his beloved Elder, bathing the ground with his compassionate tears, Bachmann appears, jabbing his member into the mud with furious futility, screaming "whore" while his mind is flooded with memories of Voroshenko where his unit was destroyed, and fragments from the conversation of the lieutenant who told him of the necessity of doing violence to one's own nature. But unlike Alyosha, who rises with a clear insight into the threads that bind him to the created universe, Bachmann emerges only with a dim sense of his betrayal by earth and man, and *his* insight comprises the conviction that his brutality was misdirected, as he shouts at Halftan: "I should have killed you!" (p. 114).

But Halftan shortly accommodates Bachmann by tossing away the money he had taken from the Elshoved household, racing into a snow-covered field, and with outstretched arms and clenched fists and an appeal to his "great radiant God" (p. 110), shooting himself. It is a thoroughly unmotivated and unexpected act, and when

Bachmann concludes that Halftan must be mad, we incline to sympathize with him and are suddenly thrust once again into a totally disoriented world, just when we have begun to untangle the senseless from the meaningful. At this point Bachmann himself undergoes a reversal, consistent with the inconsistent intellectual pattern of the narrative: he decides to withdraw his appeal to the medical board against their ruling that he is mentally unfit to serve; and as evidence of his insanity, he intends to tell them the details of the episode with the Elshoveds and Halftan that has just transpired: "If they don't doubt my sanity then, they've got a screw loose themselves" (p. 120). Offering the facts of reality as evidence of insanity is a subtle variation on Lind's own fictional strategy, a way of maneuvering the reader into a fresh perspective on the contours of "normal life." Bachmann's decision to withdraw his appeal and return to civilian existence and his girlfriend Helga, the Eve we have not yet encountered, thus furnishes Lind with an opportunity to examine *Homo bachmannus* in a new context and to develop the satirical possibilities inherent in Bachmann's resolve, as he sets out for home, not to think about the events that have made him the executioner of four human beings.

Just as Hamlet's character unfolds in a series of soliloquies which wrestle with the personal problems that burden his moral sensibility—his mother's rapid remarriage, his father's untimely death, his own inaction, the appeal of suicide—so Bachmann reveals an increasing obsession with those details of his life which distort his conception of himself and divide his sense of a unified sensibility (*moral* sensibility in his case seems an echo from a vanished world)—namely, the loss of his unit in the mud at Voroshenko and the deaths he has been responsible for. But whereas Hamlet's genuine distress coincides with a high intelligence that adopts presumed madness to insulate itself from a treacherous society, Bachmann's concern is couched in a language that alternates between reason and raving in such a way that one can never be sure how sincere it is. The steady growth toward recognition that characterizes most tragic literature appears to be parodied by the intellectual meanderings of Lind's "hero," as Bachmann first expresses the authentic dilemma at the heart of his obsessions— "Murdering four people for no reason at all—how can a normal human being do such a thing? I can't understand it. It's a

mystery."—then declares his own inability to solve the mystery or
even to accept responsibility for it: "I REALIZE THAT I'M SICK. I've
got to undergo treatment. I've got to. The way I am they can't
punish me, nobody'll take me seriously" (p. 153).

But even more fundamental is whether *we* can take Bachmann
seriously, and if so, *how?* His split personality, his contradictory
impulses, resist all attempts to unify him or understand the springs
of his behavior; yet it is less a matter of seeing him as a complex
human being, than of granting him any humanity at all. Hamlet's
profound disillusionment at the rottenness in Denmark still rouses
our sympathy but seems naïvely lucid next to the wild denuncia-
tions of Bachmann, who is testifying at a police inquiry into a brawl
among foreign slave laborers in a bar, where Bachmann and his
girlfriend Helga were present when someone shouted "Lousy
Germany": "Germany's full of chestnuts," cries Bachmann at the
hearing, "and we live on rotten meat. The consequence: we're all
full to the brim with corpses, only animals so far, but it won't be
long before we start on human corpses" (p. 154). Perhaps the
deepest source of his malaise is that the morass of contamination
into which events have plunged him affords him no *action* that will
permit him to be cleansed of its stain. The odor of corruption,
whether the corpses be animal or human, stifles the possibility of
purification, as if the only gambit left him were his persistent,
frantic, unpalatable attempts to define his own nature:

> Schnotz was right, as a horse I could amount to something—as a man,
> I may as well face it, he's, that is I am, a manure pile that breathes.
> I've never learned the high art of self-deception. I have no illusions.
> . . . I'm a sick animal by the name of Gauthier Bachmann, absolutely
> unfit. [p. 155]

What a noble piece of work is a man—a manure pile that breathes.
If the Renaissance imagination could still conceive of the human
creature—even if only in an idealized form—in Hamlet's splendid
rhetoric, the modern mind, with Lind as its spokesman, can find
nothing better than ordure as its symbol for this representative
figure of *l'univers concentrationnaire*.

But Hamlet offers a single tribute, against which human achievement in the play may be measured; Bachmann keeps shifting his
ground, as if aware of the completely provisional basis of his own

judgments, which hardly merit the stable designation of "convictions." For example, a moment after his confession of his unfitness, he suddenly sinks to his knees, whispers with clasped hands, "Forgive me please, forgive me," and just as abruptly stands up and sits down "as if nothing had happened" (p. 155). His admission that he is a "sick animal" recalls even more clearly Lear's *post*-lunacy recognitions: "I am a very foolish fond old man, / Fourscore and upwards, not an hour more nor less; / And, to deal plainly, / I fear I am not in my perfect mind"; but Lear's insight leads to a tragic identification with his suffering in a world where disorder may indeed be the rule rather than the exception, causing the temporary derangement of a man like Lear. Shakespeare's landscape of reality retains a vestige of humanity which Lind abandons entirely, perhaps realizing thereby the most terrifying unarticulated implications of a play like *Lear*, where the animal imagery threatens to overwhelm civilization and its values.

For the presence, the very existence, of a faithful Kent and charitable Cordelia (her horrible fate notwithstanding) introduces premises about affirmative possibilities inherent in human nature which Lind simply excludes from his fictional portrait. Between Goneril and Cordelia, Kent and Edmund, the human distinctions are clear, if not morally consequential in terms of their suffering and their fate; but Bachmann's reflections are exemplary of an attitude that has reached more somber dimensions: human suffering finally seems less important than the nature of the reality, the landscape in concrete, that breeds creatures like himself.

Whether his explorations of this subject represent reason in madness or the reverse, Lind deliberately refuses to say. Bachmann identifies his own mental condition with a universal brotherhood, argues that it doesn't matter where a man comes from any more, and concludes that universal humanity is a huge pile of stones. But simultaneously he recognizes that his metaphor is only suggestive, not definitive, and in an effort to explain more concretely the metamorphosis of man during the Holocaust into *Homo bachmannus*, he contradicts himself:

> But men aren't stones. That is, we're not what we are. In other words, they're all sick like me. Gold has turned to dirt, man to animal, animal to stone, and from stone gunpowder and dust are made. [p. 160]

The sequence of images is not without its significance, but the essential paradox concealed in this passage is possibly the supreme challenge facing the artist working with the raw materials of *l'univers concentrationnaire:* to find "other words" for developing the idea that "we're not what we are."

As Helga and Bachmann emerge from the inquiry, where language has produced a confusing stream of relevant irrelevance, into the silence of the ominously named Alfred-Rosenberg-Platz, Lind invokes a simile that confirms the difficulty of the task just outlined: they resemble "a dinosaur couple emerging from the water to hunt for living prey in a landscape peopled exclusively by stone plants" (p. 163). Later, alone with Helga, in a riotous "formal" love scene that maintains the pitch of comedy even in the midst of these questions of deadly earnest, Bachmann returns to the perplexing dilemma of his life, which rotates on the axis of the fact that he has killed four people for the sole reason that he was ordered to. There's something wrong, he concludes, if "a man like me lets himself be hypnotized," but this incipient self-searching, which in the case of an Oedipus might lead to tragic knowledge, here leads to further labyrinths. Bachmann (and the reality which nurtures him) has no moral context for pursuing the inquiry. "What I lack is words," he concedes, in the midst of his verbal torrent; "if you don't talk, you die!" (p. 167).

The need to "call things by their names," to give "accurate descriptions" (p. 168), gnaws at Bachmann, who is imprisoned by his deeds (or misdeeds) and cherishes the illusion that language will liberate him; but Lind, who knows well that volumes of testimony have done little to uncover the moral enigmas at the heart of the Holocaust, exploits the misgivings of his character as a technique for conquering the silences of atrocity that Bachmann himself cannot contend with. If in his schizophrenic anguish Bachmann is unable to pin down his own nature, the reader's more complex perspective, which requires constant attention to the question of when he is feigning, when sincere—*if one can ever tell*—immerses us all in the baffling endeavor to unravel the human psychology that made possible *l'univers concentrationnaire.* If you don't talk, you die, Bachmann had said; and Lind, the artist as supreme talker, seems resolved to keep himself and his audience alive by addressing the ears and the eyes of the mind until it perceives the reality beyond

the appearances of history and achieves the *vision* that was essential
to Lear and Oedipus, even if the modern world denies us the dignity
of tragedy that was available to them.

As if in response to the questions posed at the end of *King
Lear*—Is this the promised end? Or image of that horror?—Lind
conjures up a vision of post-Holocaust reality at the conclusion of
Landscape in Concrete that makes the blue-tinged apocalyptic
terrors of Michelangelo's Judgment Day in the Sistine Chapel seem
cheerful in comparison. But first he reduces Bachmann to utter
frustration by having the medical board that had originally recom-
mended his dismissal declare him healthy and sane, fully recovered
and fit for active service. His behavior is not the exception but the
norm for measuring humanity; all his responses, including his
uncertainty of motive and moral perplexity about his "crimes," are
symptomatic of the "new" reality he has unwittingly helped to
create. *Homo bachmannus*, the "freak in the ark," has somehow
established his mutation as the dominant form of the species; and as
the doctors admire the features of this emergent specimen and
speculate with self-conscious irony on its prospects for the future—
"He lives in wartime and when peace comes, he doesn't die. He can
be used for anything, there's nothing he's not capable of"
(p. 182)—the narrative raises for the final time the issue of whether
civilization itself, as we have known it, can survive the survival of its
Bachmanns. Bachmann, in lame defense of himself as a man more
sinned against than sinning, offers an epitaph to his life and perhaps
the life of his time: "How are you going to get through . . . that's all
I want to know. You do it or it's done to you" (p. 181). Whether this
represents a diluted version of the Golden Rule whose moral vitality
has been exhausted by the events of modern history, an ethic of
unreflective impulse rooted in fear rather than conviction, one can
only guess; but as Bachmann, a comatose Hans Castorp, marches
back to war, his arms to his sides and his fingers flabby and lifeless,
he embodies no principle of being familiar to our philosophies, and
is marked as a creature among the living only by his motion.

Then Lind grants us his vision, as an air-raid interrupts Bachmann's return to battle by demolishing the city and razing the
physical reality that had caused him so much uneasiness about his
status as a man. As if in a dream—or a nightmare—the earth stirs
beneath its blanket of corpses and disgorges (from the air-raid

shelter) two creatures, apparently the sole survivors of this local holocaust, Helga and Bachmann. In a gruesome parody of rebirth, that mocks the human capacity to endure affliction, they survey the desolate terrain:

> They rose from the grave to the surface of the earth and looked around. As far as the eye could see a desert of ashes under a lead-gray sky. The stillness was palpable, as colorless and bare as the walls of a monk's cell. Nothing moved in the deathly silence, nothing crawled, rustled, or murmured. [p. 188]

This "gray ocean of an extinguished landscape," which they mistake for Paradise, differs from the more familiar Eden not only in its sepulchral imagery, but also in the conception of the creatures who inhabit it. For as Helga and Bachmann retire for this first night in a shattered world, although "they were afraid like helpless little children," they have neither divine guidance nor nostalgia nor hope to console them. Memory fades and fails; the night-sound of stones falling into water "might just as well have been the old illusions bursting with a slight pop." Neither rational words nor reasonable action can convey the rupture between past and present reality, so when Helga exclaims with apparent incoherence that all things "have changed their face, the seed is ripe, the eyes are falling from the trees" (pp. 189–90), Bachmann charges her with delirium—now the only remaining defense of a reality that the imagination can no longer contain.

The last image of all in *Landscape in Concrete* spews up the refuse that the Holocaust has made of man, and as Bachmann wonders with disgust why he has allied himself with Helga, Lind momentarily merges with his character and, in an agonizing access of creative nausea, questions the motive and value of his art even as he forges its graphic power with his language:

> Why had he pulled the dying beast out of the ocean? To let it rot in the heat. Everything about it was contaminated. And he had tasted of it. His stomach tightened like a clam, fought off a deadly spasm. The sweetish taste of pestilence was painful to his palate. The plague had fought its way into his brain cells. He felt millions of tiny crabs clinging to an abscess. Too late for help, nothing that can be done, remedy is nothing but a word, stale medicine, nothing can revive dead cells. [p. 190)

Side by side, Bachmann and Helga resemble two enormous blobs of flesh more than a resurrected Adam and Eve, two gigantic behemoths cast up to fester in the heat, a modern Moby Dick and his mate void of symbolic status and reduced to a physical mass that is less animal than sheer, decaying matter, the plague called man, the plague *become* man which was the solemn epigraph to Lind's novel.

The mystery which drives the artist to create in such an atmosphere of nihilistic despair is almost more fascinating than the dilemma of Bachmann's nature; the loathing implicit in this culminating vision resembles a submerged feeling that sporadically floats to the surface of Swift's prose, and frequently appears in the late writings of Mark Twain. But their satiric scorn was often modified by a contrary impulse to celebrate certain affirmative potentialities buried in human nature, while Lind, poisoned (and this is the crucial difference) by the cynical revelations of *l'univers concentrationnaire*, has not yet found an antidote to the disease. The irreversible damage done to the human brain cells by this pestilence has brought about a progressive degeneration of the human figure (and the reality surrounding it) as substance for fiction, and Lind has resolved to employ the grotesque mutations resulting as emblems of this decay. Bachmann's penultimate gesture, following his discovery that "remedy is only a word," is to plunge his long yellow teeth into Helga's throat, sundering love, human community, or even the possibility of shared pain; and he ends the narrative, where he began, marching off "toward the East" (p. 190), searching for his regiment once more.

But Lind is convinced that the plague bacillus has already infected the vast, unexplored territory eastward of his perverse Eden, the future of human civilization. The Holocaust has created its own mushroom cloud, and it hovers over his artistic horizon as permanent witness to the metamorphosis history has wrought on the materials of imaginative fiction. The dimensions and obsessions of *Homo bachmannus* may shift from work to work, but the fantasy, madness, violence, and unassimilated guilt that converge in his nature, and which eliminate any hope of ever untangling cause and effect among these attributes, persist in Lind's characters; and these, in turn, exact from those readers willing to accept his premises, a painstaking effort to interpret a world increasingly dissimilar in its outlines to anything we might vaguely call normal reality, while in its depths it stubbornly adheres to the conflicts which *l'univers concentrationnaire* has bequeathed to the modern mind.

The paradox of meaningless meaning, of an indecipherable present teetering precariously on the unshored fragments of a crumbled past that flings intermittent echoes of familiar names, places, and events to readers desperately straining to salvage their own sanity—such unreassuring tensions distinguish Lind's second and more exasperating novel, *Ergo*, whose original German title (*Eine Bessere Welt—A Better World*) reflects with greater accuracy and irony his lapse into satirical despair about the prospects for human nature in the post-Holocaust era. The "philosophy" implicit in *Ergo* is perhaps best expressed by one of its characters, all of whom, like the speaker, are more or less demented: "In this world . . . , you're in luck if you lose your reason, because if you don't you go plumb crazy. Isn't that a healthy attitude?" [7]

What are the features of "this world?" Another character, a quasi philosopher who ranks among his intellectual ancestors Kierkegaard and Nietzsche, to say nothing of Spinoza and Kant, develops in a kind of metaphysical occupational therapy a "Placental Theory of Existence," among whose axioms is the central principle that "the afterbirth is the origin of existence." Although the philosophy itself is manifestly absurd—"the work was so nonsensical he had every reason to assume that only the writing of nonsense is worthwhile, since, as everyone knows, sense can have no sense" (p. 58)—it offers a clue to Lind's own satiric purposes, since just as afterbirth is a consequence of birth, so the reality of the novel proceeds from historical episodes which lurk behind the nonsense of its events. Chance remarks, glimpses into the obsessions of the Austrian lunatics who inhabit Lind's native Vienna, concrete allusions to the past—to the supposed "sense" preceding the nonsense—provide the reader with a tentative orientation to the novel's imaginative world. Any subsequent difficulties—and there are many—though not clarified by these allusions, at least console one with the certainty that they occur in time: the novel itself is an afterbirth of the Holocaust.

7. Jakov Lind, *Ergo*, trans. Ralph Manheim (London: Methuen, 1967), p. 66. This should not be confused with Lind's dramatized version of the novel, also published under the title of *Ergo*.

Numerous hints confirm this, though the reader is left to sift the
mocking connotations from the grave ones. For example, the author
of the Placental Theory is celebrated as follows:

> He's got the power of spirit, you've never seen the like of it. He's all
> spirit. Austrian spirit. German spirit too, if you like. In his opinion,
> violence is an absurdity. Nothing can be done by force, he says. Not
> any more. [p. 64]

This neoenlightenment of the Teutonic *Geist,* with its repudiation
of force, carefully circumvents the details of atrocity that marked
the culmination of a hundred years of nonempirical German
philosophy; elsewhere, another unbalanced member of Lind's
human menagerie offers a complementary and more explicit
commentary on this supposed dedication of spirit: "I said it then
and I say it now: people who deserve a Hitler get a Hitler, and
people who don't deserve a Hitler don't get a Hitler. Hitler can't
help it" (p. 9). The time sequence is confused but not destroyed in a
further juxtaposition, a kind of historical collage in which the chief
items of Austrian tradition, legend, and history are superimposed on
each other (insofar as sequential prose can suggest this). The result
is a "placental aesthetic" which permits man to wallow in his own
afterbirth and enjoy his own madness, a confirmation of Lind's
conviction (and a premise of his art) that in our era at least, "sense
can have no sense"—and perhaps must not:

> In the municipal hospital [in Vienna, the city Lind refers to in this
> passage] where the Saviour was born into the world, the Saviour of
> the Kahlenberg who went upstream to Kriau to free Richard
> Loewenherz from Mauthausen, but now he too is dead and buried at
> the central cemetery, to sleep forever side by side with Lueger and
> Seitz, Kaltenbrunner and Mozart. There he lies with Dollfuss and Fey
> and Robert Stricker of the Zionist League and Prince Eugene who
> freed Vienna from the Turks and the heroes of Karl-Marxhof and the
> heroes of the Heimwehr and nobody knows how there can conceiva-
> bly be such a city.
>
> Which calls itself the teat of the occident and has suckled nothing
> but madness. [pp. 9–10]

Anyone familiar with Austrian history will recognize the names in
the list, identified with the shame and the glory of a civilization; but
when the lines of history lead from the Saviour and the Crusades to

a Mauthausen (the most notorious of the Austrian concentration camps), or from Mozart to a Kaltenbrunner (Austrian-born Nazi head of SS security police, executed at Nüremberg), who is to blame Lind for inventing a society where all roads lead to insanity?

The placental aesthetic also includes a "loincloth" theory of language, which encourages the representation of a disoriented reality:

> The more tattered and transparent the garment the more ragged language is, the more clearly it reveals what is hidden. The disclosure of thought is the true function of language. Consequently, where the skin is concerned, not only ragged language but wrong thinking as well is in order. [p. 60]

Conscious of the baffling course of civilization from the Crucifixion to the gas chamber, Lind acknowledges the futility of creating a coherent imaginative form out of these contradictions, making this very circumstance part of the substance of his novel. If all Western philosophy is a skin disease, as Lind's pseudo-thinker asserts, then neither lucid words nor a clear narrative pattern will illuminate its symptoms; hence the unorthodoxy of Lind's technique, which mingles grotesque distortions of reality with just enough reference to place and period to raise the uncomfortable suspicion that his fantasy is something more than fancy.

The protagonists of this fictional asylum, once close friends, are now archenemies whose rivalry is rooted in obscure causes. Roman Wacholder has "a thing or two on his conscience" (p. 17), though we are never told what; yet at one point he insists that he had been a dangerous Nazi, because he "wanted what happened to happen" (p. 53). He spends most of his time in bed in a cellar of an old, abandoned Customs House, beneath mounds of confiscated papers, contemplating his eighteen-inch sex organ (where his guilt-feelings are concentrated) and plotting to annihilate (through verbal threat, not action) his foe, Ossias Würz. Würz, whose past is also veiled (though we know he was once a gasman(!) by profession), passes his hours composing defensive replies to the intimidating letters he receives from Wacholder, while maintaining with an obsessive devotion the antiseptic purity of his house—he fears germs. One of his main problems is how to protect himself from the smoke from his stove; he first decides, rather ominously, that after "every incineration we take a hot bath," then concludes that "dirt is our misfortune, the misfortune of us all" (pp. 23–24), and makes his struggle against it the purpose of his life. But Wacholder's insinuating letters (written in fact by his adoptive son, Leo the philosopher) prove a more potent weapon than the dust in disrupting Würz's equanimity; they make him dream of P.O.W. camps and committing mass murders.

The content of this weird correspondence confirms the lunacy of both participants, while its "ragged language," if it does not exactly reveal more clearly "what is hidden," serves as a nonfigurative metaphor for language's inability (and therefore the human intelligence's?) to define clearly the difference between the human and the inhuman. Man as afterbirth suffers from incoherence, an affliction which Lind elsewhere equates with his favorite image of the plague, an "ineradicable feeble-mindedness" spread by the contagious knowledge that "everything is senseless. Writing books too" (p. 61). One excerpt from this correspondence will have to serve as an example of the breakdown of reasoning power, as if man had lost the key to the jigsaw puzzle of experience but forced pieces with similar shapes together anyway, even though the pictured fragments did not correspond to one another:

> I know what I want [Würz writes to Wacholder]. I want man in the negativized area of his present constitution with the feelings of a human human in the esoteric salon of intellectual conversations on the childbed of the immutable nonman inclining it is to be hoped to a fate and to the power of the inhuman nonhuman, the morality, culture and artistic interest of the religion of the citizen who confronted by the military constitutional state only the dashing of hopes and sustaining a regime of blood and violence developing a humanity of his own into the thwarted object lesson of such failure and dissolving his impotence into the striving for a better world and a more human future. That is what I want. I think I have made myself clear? [p. 70]

The passage recalls the breathless avalanche of words that tumbles from Lucky's lips in *Waiting for Godot*, when prodded by Gogo and Didi to exhibit his humanity by "talking." Interspersed through Lucky's apparent rantings are fragments of meaning, evoking man's desolate condition in the midst of a rhetoric that seeks to drown him.

It is more difficult to mine coherence from the lode of Lind's language, and perhaps we must be content with the significant antitheses that serve as a poor substitute for particles of gold, antitheses like "human human" and "inhuman nonhuman," or "regime of blood" and "a more human future," which include the poles of modern experience whose ions will not go into solution, but swirl in ceaseless rebellion through the turbid medium Lind calls life. Interpreting Würz's letter duplicates the mockery of making sense out of that area of history which obviously torments Lind's own artistic consciousness; the reader seizes with intuitive faith on the phrase "striving for a better world," then finds himself at a total loss to explain how it represents a sensible conclusion to the "reasoning" that has preceded it. Thus Lind succeeds in displacing hope with confusion and intellectual despair, repeating the pattern of Beckett's dramas and leaving one wondering whether this bewildering atmosphere of post-Holocaust reality is a practical joke or an earnest reflection of the desperate human condition.

Ergo suspends judgment; its appeal is its elusiveness. Aslan, Wacholder's other adoptive son, like Lind himself, is writing a book called "The Better World," but he can get no further than the first five pages, dealing with his childhood, as if after that period in time reality stopped for him and subsequent events ceased to have meaning. For Aslan, "The Better World" is a title in search of a book, and though Lind makes of this futile quest much of the substance of his own novel, he seems uncertain of the nature or value of his personal achievement. Aslan first foils a plan of Wacholder and his philosopher son to "annihilate" Würz by voting his nonexistence at an assemblage that resembles a scene from *Alice in Wonderland*—Aslan simply refuses to vote in favor, thus undermining the necessary condition of unanimity, then retires to his bed at home to meditate on the dialectic of his own existence, to justify his own being, as it were, now that he has opposed the nonbeing of a Würz.

In a dialogue with himself, more intelligible than most in the novel (though possessing its share of nonsequiturs), Aslan outlines the arguments for and against not only his own derangements, but for the artist's (and hence Lind's) obsession with them. The "voices" are those of God and the author of "A/The Better World" (again, Aslan *and* Lind), and the two places about which they dispute,

Greenland and Austria, apparently represent (Greenland) the realm
of the writer's imagination, where he can freely invent characters
based on universal human motives, and (Austria), a land inhabited
by "unwashed, lice-ridden people who are kind of mad" (p. 106)
and represent the afterbirth of a specific historical occasion, the
Third Reich. God chides the writer for his fascination with lunacy,
his pessimism, his low estimate of human nature—"why not come
right out and say people are evil period and the crummiest of the lot
are the austrians" (p. 107)—his indifference to other imaginative
possibilities implicit in experience, his unwillingness to stop beating
an obviously dead horse, his inability to "look into the future and
forget guilt and the guilty" (p. 108), and finally introduces an
insidious charge to explain the writer's immersion in a single theme:
"you can't forgive them for not calling you in to help with the
robbing or murdering" (p. 109). Neither Lind nor Aslan pursues this
avenue of cynicism, but its mere mention is a startling revelation of
the unexplored corridors of guilt that still exist in the labyrinths of
the literature of atrocity. No Theseus has yet dared to unwind his
thread through this one.

Encouraged by the silence ensuing from this low blow, the voice
of God grows more explicit; its parting thrust defines the nature of
reality "then" and "now" and finally accuses Aslan of incorrigible
spleen for believing that nothing has really changed:

> before hitler they were divided the intellectuals persecuted the
> intellectuals the rich the rich and the poor the poor when hitler came
> in everybody persecuted everybody at once the poor the rich and the
> rich the poor. today persecution is infrequent because tomorrow
> everybody's going to be slaughtered. . . . dear Aslan . . . you can't
> unburden yourself here in this world go to the eskimos, either/or.
> [pp. 108–09]

Kierkegaard in the asylum, the schizophrenic dialogue might be
called. The once tragic choice echoed by this dilemma ("austria or
eskimo. that is the question," p. 109) with its alternatives of life or
death, the leap to faith or the plunge to despair, a choice made
meaningful by premises about order that neither Aslan nor his
creator can any longer sustain, reduces the options themselves to
absurdity. Aslan's ramblings mix pertinence with unintelligibility,
though only the reader—sometimes—can distinguish between the

two. For Aslan is a reflection of the literary sensibility poisoned by the very nature of reality until its powers of expression are silenced; and though Lind has not lost control of his own language, part of the poison has obviously seeped into his pen.

In his reply to God, that other part of his tormented self, whom Aslan (like a good Austrian) addresses as "herr doktor," he explains—or tries to—that he needs reality to feed his sense of unreality, just as he depends on guilt (his own and others') to furnish material for his novel "The Better World." Gide's Edouard, at the end of *The Counterfeiters*, had protested that certain episodes in reality (like Boris's suicide) were too unexpected and illogical to furnish inspiration for his art; Aslan seems to revel in just the reverse of this principle (and Lind *certainly* does)—namely, that the disordered events of *l'univers concentrationnaire* have so embedded themselves in the imagination that they wither all other nutritive possibilities that might have fed the imagination in more "normal" times.

Aslan thus retreats from the notion of a "greenlandic aesthetics," cryptically insisting that "our austria is in greenland packed once more in pack ice. in the smooth ice of art. that is a world apart"—perhaps an elusive defense by Lind of the uniquely unreal reality of his own art—then, in a moment of lucidity, offers a glimpse into the minds of writers like Lind who are simultaneously imprisoned and inspired by the Holocaust: "we'll never be rid of austria even if we write in greenlandic like some of my fellow writers. that only makes the problem more unintelligible. aestheticism won't rid us of guilt" (p. 109). For Lind, the aestheticism which separates history from literature, fact from imagined event, which employs fantasy to exclude rather than to absorb the most sordid implications of the Hitler era and uses language and form to transcend these implications, simply ignores the circumstance that gross and cruel times require a gross and cruel aesthetics.

Aslan closes his *apologia pro vita sua* by stating frankly a principle of the aesthetics of atrocity that represents a fair version of Lind's own literary (and perhaps philosophical) attitude: "you can't make a better world by spiriting away the shit that's lying around the country with high-sounding words" (p. 110). Normally, manure fertilizes the ground it touches; but the ordure Lind refers to has insinuated itself into the minds of his characters and has perma-

nently corrupted the faculty that organizes experience and inter-
prets its application to their lives. And by a kind of literary osmosis,
it infects the readers' view of their lives too: the brains of Aslan,
Wacholder, Würz, and the others go on functioning, but because
they all seem mad, paradoxically—measuring sanity by their own
behavior—they all seem sane too. In their hermetic world (in
Würz's case, this is literally so), normality as we know it has ceased
to exist, and we are forced to adjust allusions to Hitler and the
Austrian past to the standards of lunacy established in *Ergo*.

Thus, when Aslan, after the elaborate defense of his creative
efforts, determines *not* to finish writing his book, his decision seems
to support the perverse logic of the novel which Lind himself does
somehow bring to a precarious end—namely, that any effort by
either reason or art to achieve a finished form for the events of the
Holocaust must result in failure, the defeat of man by the reality
that has consumed him and crippled his emotional and intellectual
unity. The hulk left behind continues to gesture, as Lind obsessively
continues to record the obsessions of his half-creatures: and the
spectacle might be hilarious, were these creatures not so clearly and
lamentably the offspring of a portion of our history that neither
convenience nor forgetfulness can eclipse.

The only posture available, Lind suggests, for individuals searching through this morass for their humanity, is transference or
abandonment of their human identity. Neither Würz nor Wacholder can reason his way through to regeneration, since time—their
own past—has debased and contaminated the words and thoughts
that are the only instruments to lead them to this goal. Lind
parodies both moral terminology and mind's ability to conceptualize
moral distinctions—traditionally man's noblest capacity—in one of
Würz's last meditations, and in so doing exposes their utter
irrelevance to the kind of reality he is concerned with, the afterbirth
that succeeded the "motherbirth" to which Würz refers:

> man is good . . . yes indeed. good. and so are we all. good. we dear
> good people. You dear good world. and so on. . . . the world is better.
> the new age is motherbirth. what comes of a mother is good. . . .
> everybody is human. even the wicked are good, as good as the good if
> not better. everything is good or becoming good. evil is inhuman like
> the good. man is inhuman, therefore he is good. the truth proves the
> opposite. and so on. [p. 115]

This ethics of et cetera, which equates evil with good and thus negates both, is virtually Würz's farewell to speech; screaming "dissect my würz," he abandons his humanity, begins to bark and howl like a dog, buzzes through his nose, and starts to smell his hands. Beyond lunacy now, odor is the only assurance of his existence: man is a creature who sniffs.

Wacholder rejects Würz's alternative—"i'm not an animal," he whispers desperately into the void, "not i. no, i'm not an animal, but i'm not anything else either" (p. 123)—but finds no other. His "lower-case" personality, alienated from the human community by its earlier behavior, can find no basis to rejoin it, because he has lost respect for it and himself. "That's my country," he mourns bitterly. "The country of men without character. In this country a man's ashamed to have character. . . . A country that shipped off its own citizens as if they were rabbits for Christmas and has the gall to complain about it now is no country at all. I can't stand it here any more" (p. 119). But this moment of moral clarity, revealing, perhaps, a glimpse of Lind's own baffled and dejected eyes through the mask of Wacholder, only intensifies the madness to which Wacholder returns: the mind's arrested vision is conquered once again by an orphaned reality that can find no home in either history or art.

Wacholder's last gesture—a comic requiem to the novel—has nothing to do with the logic of existence, even less with the sequence of Lind's narrative: his theme frustrates the tragedy of insight, or any other profoundly meaningful conclusion. In conversation with his adoptive sons, Wacholder digs his own grave, even as their exchange undermines the dignity of dying and translates man's final ritual into a farce:

> father, i've got to laugh.
> aslan, i'm not a joke.
> who says you're not, wacholder? [p. 126]

And with an injured sensibility that nevertheless leaves this vital question unanswered—"all right, aslan, go right on laughing in the meantime i'll die"—he piles dirt over himself and expires, "just to give the others something to laugh about, but the others didn't laugh" (p. 126). Man is a creature who dies without knowing why, but the farce of his death is not funny.

If physical extermination seems less loathsome here than in a novel like Kosinski's *The Painted Bird*, it is because Lind has systematically destroyed our confidence in the power of human intelligence to formulate attitudes toward concepts like loathsomeness, a power that itself assumes a hierarchy of values denied to Lind's poisoned brains. An important discovery resulting from the Holocaust, or emphasized by it—one that has done much to thwart the possibility of literary tragedy in our time—was the almost totally random nature of death, to the point of extinguishing the significance of the individual, not only in the eyes of the public, but in his own estimation too. Martyrdom, as Anthony Hecht suggests in the poem quoted at the beginning of this study, is a powerful stimulant to human dignity: the tragic figure is always a martyr to his mortality, and is graced by the self-knowledge that accompanies it. Self-knowledge, in turn, celebrates the human intelligence, the ability to impose sense on an experience which seems to contradict reason, and indeed, in Lear's case, drives him temporarily mad.

Lind's characters, one might argue, never recover from Lear's temporary mental aberration; in fact, Lear's outbursts, crowded with allusions to the events that have battered and destroyed his mind, appear lucid when compared to the ranting of Lind's creatures, whose reflections on cause and effect are more random than Wacholder's death. Like Didi singing his circular refrain about the fate of dogs in *Waiting for Godot*, they are incapable of the intense act of recognition that would permit them to see their own fate clearly as a link in a continuous chain of history and human experience. The Holocaust has snapped this chain, and into the ensuing space surges the awful ludicrousness of their lives. Unable to define the nature of their suffering, with truncated sensibilities and a permanently distorted perspective, their antics may indeed seem comical. But above Lind's mockery, his exaggerations, and his unbalanced creatures, hovers the origin in time of all this deranged and deranging woe; and the desolate spectacle of its paralyzing effect on the once glorious figure of reasoning man stifles laughter as well as dissent.

L'univers concentrationnaire
shrivels away within itself.
It still lives on in the world
like a dead planet laden with
corpses.

David Rousset

. . . the Holocaust was the beginning
of an era, not its end—an era of
turmoil and upheaval, of irrationality
and madness, an era of Auschwitz.
We are now [1970] in the 29th year
of that era.

Alexander Donat

Although the writers considered in this study seem united in their conviction that the events of the Holocaust have radically altered our conception of reality and created an urgent need to find unique ways of transmitting this view, their literary strategies and philosophical emphases are as varied as the abundant windows in Henry James's spacious house of fiction. Each devised his own technique for surmounting the common barrier erected by atrocity between language and expression, and staked out a particular acre for his literary domain. If the neat categories dividing man's physical and psychological nature were demolished by the experiences they confronted, one can nevertheless distinguish the rape of childhood emotions in Ilse Aichinger's *Herod's Children* from the visceral visions of Kosinski's *The Painted Bird*, and differentiate the cerebral corrosions of Jakov Lind from both. The abuse of the feelings, the body, and the mind in *l'univers concentrationnaire* maimed these qualities beyond recognition, and we have examined the attempts of writers to portray men's permanently scarred sensibilities in a world that frustrates any effort to discover a meaningful context for the abuses themselves. An implacable past encroaches on all attempts to restore imaginative (if not actual) tranquillity to the literary landscape, a circumstance which other authors recognized as a theme worthy of special attention: the Holocaust assaulted the very notion of temporal sequence, and led to some vital experiments with the manipulation of time (as concept *and* principle of structure) in fiction, experiments which undoubtedly owe an ancillary debt to Faulkner but gain a special force, as in other instances of this literature, from their foundation in an inexorable past that refuses to submit, like Faulkner's South, to the less intransigent rhythms of historical memory.

For characters like Quentin Compson and Ike McCaslin in Faulkner are obsessed with a past that represents a living tradition, explainable by the logic of historical development despite its injustices, and part of a continuing force in time even though it may drive Quentin and Ike to suicide and renunciation. The "South" implies values and actions which have shaped the attitudes, the psychology of entire communities, a whole geographical region, and the problem in Faulkner is less to deplore the presentness of the past, than to sift the still fruitful ideas from the barren ones without succumbing to personal or social decay. The death of Quentin and the despair of Ike testify to the complex task of understanding this heritage—Jack Burden in Robert Penn Warren's *All the King's Men* faces a similar challenge, but Jack's destiny proves that such confrontations with the past do not necessarily exclude the possibility of surviving into a future still fluid with aspirations, though its boundaries may be considerably diminished.

The Holocaust, on the other hand, bequeathed a historical legacy whose most dismal implications elude the contours of the Faulknerian formulation, the "presentness of the past." Whereas in Faulkner the elaboration of genealogy or the sorting out of chronologies comprises a vital moral activity, an initiation or act of discovery—it constitutes a major part of young Ike's education in *The Bear*—the kind of atrocity at issue here assaulted the very coherence of time and led to the breakdown of "chronology" as a meaningful conception. The reader, whose perspective is naturally broader than Quentin's or Ike's, can transcend their paralysis and frustration and extract from the concatenation of past and present some significant interpretation concerning their influence on each other, and thus impose an intellectual order on apparent literary disorder. Faulkner himself never repudiated the heroic energy and impulses of men like Sartoris and Sutpen, even though events muddied the channels

through which they coursed. But the literature of atrocity introduces ancestral voices which echo through time despite the survivor's desire for silence, and the result is a temporal dissonance
which no modern harmonics—neither reader's nor character's—can
resolve into a satisfactory pattern of sound.

Such elaborate metaphor is itself inadequate to describe the
inability of the individual to master time implicit in the experiences
of *l'univers concentrationnaire*. The three novels discussed in this
chapter are all concerned with this failure, which is embedded in
the *fact* of atrocity rather than in the mind of those who seek to
understand it. André Schwarz-Bart in *The Last of the Just*
deliberately adopts the chronological method, as if he would pit the
full weight of generations of Jewish suffering against that single
culminating instant of Jewish extinction in the gas chambers of
Auschwitz; Heinrich Böll, employing in *Billiards at Half-Past Nine*
an antichronological technique reminiscent of Faulkner, departs
from Faulkner to use the intersection of past and present to destroy
the conventional meaning of both, leaving an ironic vacuum of
despair in their wake; and Jorge Semprun in *The Long Voyage*
embraces what we might call a *non*chronological method by using a
narrative sequence that draws at random on past, present, and
future in such a way that the boxcar journey to Buchenwald which
is the central "event" of his novel finally seems to occur in a fourth
and independent dimension of time, displacing or fusing the other
three and asserting itself with a primacy that dramatizes its
uniqueness within the familiar contexts of temporal reality.

The Last of the Just begins in chronicle, those ancient accounts of
heroes and crises that mingle legend with truth, and moves swiftly
through brief narratives of earlier Jewish persecution to the present
time of the Holocaust. The dispute over whether this represents a
singular atrocity unparalleled in previous history or "merely" an
extreme and more thorough example of the periodic assaults and
pogroms which the Jewish people have suffered throughout time
will probably never be settled: Schwarz-Bart offers it as a crucial
dramatic issue of his novel. For in tracing the annals of the Levy
family, and the legend that in each generation one Just Man exists
as an emblem of the suffering which is the lot of his fellow Jews,
Schwarz-Bart introduces the only possible "logic" that might
explain (if not justify) the most egregious excesses in *l'univers*

concentrationnaire: precedents in time. If he can somehow make imaginatively acceptable the notion of a tragic destiny among these people that establishes extraordinary suffering as their human fate, enhancing their dignity even as it ignobly deprives them of their lives, then what they endure appears less shocking to our civilized instincts, less a betrayal of the faith in human continuity that protects each man against a random and anonymous death.

A subsidiary but essential question is the role of God in this supreme oppression of his people, a question never before explored in fiction so thoroughly except perhaps by Elie Wiesel; for sub specie aeternitatis the shield of divinity seems to offer a patina of logic, similar to the temporal one, that permits the mind at least to conceive of extinction in such proportions within a familiar context—namely, faith, mercy, and the profound mystery of being. Schwarz-Bart plunges the reader into a narrative illuminated along the way by these well-known lamps of the mind and soul, and as he extinguishes them one by one, in his tale's relentless march toward the darkness of Auschwitz, he leaves the reader groping for a taper but dubious as to whether the values that once ignited them have retained sufficient potency to kindle a light ever again.

Thus Ernie Levy, the last of the Just Men until his annihilation in the gas chamber, incarnates in his own career the fruits of a tradition that has sustained his family and his people for generations, a tradition that has insured continuity in time despite the sporadic acts of violence that have decimated their ranks. When a pogrom destroyed the East European village of his grandparents, they managed to escape; and the only surviving son (later Ernie's father), makes a fateful decision when he chooses—quite at random—to emigrate to Germany. The "future" is still a meaningful possibility to Ernie's father, even though a young Galician Jew he meets in Berlin, the sole survivor of another pogrom, anticipates in a self-protective tone of mockery the incursions on time and transcendence that his auditor's son Ernie will later experience with even greater perplexity:

Yes—every morning when I open my eyes it seems to me that the pogrom came last night. Is it the same with you, *dear brother?* Strange, really strange, the way time stops like that. Myself, you see, I'm always down in the well where I'd hidden. I have the same water right up to my mouth, and I still see the same circle of blue sky—that hasn't changed either. And then I hear the silence. No shouts—silence. Because in my town, when I came up out of the well, there wasn't a soul alive in the whole village. There was no more synagogue; there was nothing. Only me, of course. . . .[1]

It is *not* the same with Ernie's father, who cannot understand the feeling of the Galician prophet that one instant of annihilation may exclude all other moments of time; the victim here anticipates a response that Ernie himself, heir to the persecutions of the Third Reich, will rediscover and transform into a principle of being for all men.

But although his father weeps and murmurs that he "knows," he is really perplexed by the Galician's fevered confession that at a "certain moment the sky shattered" like a mirror, revealing an apocalyptic vision devoid of spiritual truth: "as closely as I could look I couldn't see anything but blood, and more blood, and blood again. But meaning?—none. So what place does Jewish blood have in the universe?" (p. 101). Ironically, however, the Galician's anticipation of the Holocaust has come too "soon"; his companion still has "one foot in the old days. In the . . . dream . . ." (p. 103) —in the belief in the possibility of rebirth out of suffering, the tradition that has sustained his ancestors through generations and centuries of oppression and now supports his reluctance to accept the prospect of a reality in which blood is spilled without meaning and death spreads across a desert of values until it saturates man's moral landscape, leaving only bitterness, cynicism, and a baffled despair in its wake. The father of Ernie Levy is unable to imagine a kind of terror appalling enough to nullify this tradition.

This discovery is reserved for the child Ernie himself, who, in a now familiar reversal of the *Bildungsroman* formula, commences a ceremony of initiation that destroys his innocence and replaces it with a blank futility fitting no previous pattern of the entrance into maturity that had characterized his predecessors in this literary legacy. But first Ernie passes through the rite of knowledge and intuition to which earlier heirs to the rank of Just Men had been exposed, creating a momentum in favor of temporal continuity that

1. André Schwarz-Bart, *The Last of the Just*, trans. Stephen Becker (New York: Bantam Books, 1960), pp. 100–01.

is only gradually eroded by the daily events of his life. Schwarz-Bart thus establishes a tension not only within Ernie but in the expectations of the reader as well, whose imagination is consoled by the indefatigable faith of the Levy ancestors even as Ernie's humiliation and degradation at the hands of his Nazi teacher and classmates reverberate with a contrapuntal theme. The solace and strength of the Just Man—"He senses all the evil rampant on earth, and he takes it into his heart!" (p. 195)—dissolves into rhetoric, leaving Ernie morally speechless and destitute of other resources.

When his classmates surround him one day after school, beat him, expose his nakedness before the eyes of his little blond Aryan girl-friend (who has maliciously led him into the trap), Ernie *feels* that "all these things were without precedent," that such ruthless behavior from children introduces a challenge to his capacity for suffering totally alien to anything his imagination might conceive. His reflections represent perhaps the most explicit statement in the literature of atrocity of the "unreal reality," the fusion of the fantastic with the factual that makes Ernie's attempt to interpret his experience a locus classicus in the genre:

> The little boy did not budge, staring at the spinning disc of the sun. These events concerned someone else. Nothing like them had ever happened to anyone. There was not the slightest allusion to any such phantasmagoria in the Legend of the Just Men. Desperately tense, Ernie searched his memories, hoping to find a clear path, a road to help him through that forest of strange circumstances, which did not seem entirely real though they bore a certain appearance of reality. . . . He found no road. [p. 262]

In Faulkner, such efforts flood the mind with a torrent of recollections—often, to be sure, with paralyzing and disastrous effect; but here, an abyss springs up between the jungle of "phantasmagoria" that terrifies the child now, and all the legends and true stories he has heard from his elders that might offer reassurance at his moment of incomprehension. Unlike the young hero of earlier novels of education, who despite a sense of alienation can fall back on their lonely determination to conquer the future through personal intellectual and creative powers, through love or some equally individualized hard-won achievement, Ernie faces a situation which reduces all these resources to impotence. The prowess that unique men have drawn on throughout history (including the history of literature) suddenly meets a challenge that the human imagination cannot recognize—as if a strange force had without warning deposited Ernie in the midst of creatures from an unknown planet, whose hostility humorlessly mocks the irrelevance of all his attempts to resist it.

But this dead end of the imagination cannot negate the reality that frustrates it: Ernie must find an attitude, or cease to exist as a human being. The experience wakens hatred in his heart, but in the absence of any avenue of escape it remains marooned there, until it finally turns inward and begins to gnaw at his own vitality. The "beast in his heart," as Schwarz-Bart calls it, roars in pain and hunger but is deprived of prey to quench his rage; and this dammed-up poison spreads through his own personality, rousing intuitions of emptiness that finally drive Ernie to a contempt for the living shell he has become. Wandering through a field, dismembering and crushing insects in a gesture of disgust with created things, Ernie experiences a nullification of self reminiscent of the appalled horror of the young Elie Wiesel upon arriving in Auschwitz, an exact reversal of young Alyosha Karamazov weeping tears of pain and love and embracing the earth following the death of his beloved Elder Zossima:

> As he thought, "I was nothing," the little boy buried his face against the earth and intoned his first cries. At the same instant he felt astonishment that his eyes should be empty of tears. For half an hour he cried out, his mouth against the earth. He seemed to be hailing someone far off, a being buried deep in the earth from whom he wanted only an echo. But his cries only exaggerated the silence. . . . Finally he knew that nothing would answer his call, for that call was born of nothing: God could not hear it. [p. 272]

Man suspended in time, a flaccid vessel of flesh from which all air of the spirit has been pumped, seeking instinctively to reestablish some resonance with creation though aware that the unprecedented nature of his abasement leaves him no appeal within reality—this is the figure of the boy Ernie Levy, who chooses suicide in a final vain and ironic effort to enact, in the midst of his naked despair, the last possible vestige of cause and effect in his life. But he fails even in this, as if Schwarz-Bart wished to suggest how the Holocaust could deprive the individual of the very conception of his own humanity, of all sense of control over the context of his existence—as if the melodrama of a self-inflicted death itself were powerless to lift him out of the helpless anonymity to which his Nazi tormentors have reduced him.

Thus, Ernie's failure to conquer time and rehabilitate his image in human memory (if not in eternity) assumes the significance of a symbolic ritual for his people; even though he survives the slashing of his wrists and a plunge from his bathroom window, he is henceforth referred to as "the late Ernie Levy" by Schwarz-Bart, who describes the episode as the first death of his hero. Its profoundest impact is not on the victim, however, but on the reader, who recognizes that whatever happens to Ernie henceforth will be anticlimactic, almost superfluous, certainly anomalous: time stopped for him when he no longer saw—though still a child—how he could see himself as a human being.

But paradoxically time continues, dragging in its wake that part of him which has survived his own "death," and he must listen to disputes between members of his family about whether their suffering makes them a sacrificial tribute to a God who moves in mysterious ways, or simply the prey of the wicked. The Levys postpone but do not escape these dismal alternatives by transferring their household from Germany to France; for after the outbreak of war, in which Ernie enlists to protect his family from persecution, they are nevertheless sent to a detention camp for enemy aliens, where they remain as helpless sheep conveniently penned for deportation and slaughter when the triumphant German forces overwhelm the French. The only consolation Ernie receives in a last letter from his skeptical father emphasizes their collective isolation from a tradition that once certified the meaning of their suffering: "To be a Jew is impossible" (p. 315).

In the circumstances of tragedy, no dilemma is so elusive or frustrating as to forbid all possibility of a human posture; but the condition of atrocity, which is Ernie's affliction, has eradicated all roots that nourished his civilized longings, creating that schizophrenic temperament we have encountered before, one of the chief bequests of l'univers concentrationnaire: a sensibility so shocked that it can no longer take seriously its efforts to remain alive, even while another part of its nature automatically continues with the motions of survival. "Ernie exiled from Levy is a plant without light" (p. 322), he defines his divided self, and resolves to do everything humanly possible to turn himself into a dog, as if this grotesque, imaginary metamorphosis might ease the pain of his circumscribed and futile existence.

Taken up by some local villagers in a free-French town where he has fled, Ernie astonishes the intoxicated company by "galloping around the table at a frantic, desperate rate . . . tears running down his cheeks while he barks hoarsely, as if at death—barks, barks endlessly" (p. 325). If silence is the most appropriate homage to the Holocaust, as some have argued, Schwarz-Bart (who depends on words for his art) offers a literary equivalent in the canine howls of baffled anguish that emerge from his hero-victim's throat.

But even this would be too simple an exit from the predicament threatening the humanity of Ernie Levy. For his metaphorical transmigration into the soul of a dog is only a device to protect him from further abuses *in his own eyes* against his status as a man, a temporary measure that ultimately founders on the rocks of reality, which refuses to acknowledge the alteration he wishes to effect. When the inhabitants of unoccupied France decide that his Jewishness is a liability even among them, he murmurs to the night a judgment against himself and all being—"Dirty dog"—and dismisses the role that for a time had confirmed the indignity of his existence. Casting about for a gesture to restore the balance of his self-respect, some act of human assertion, he ironically chooses the attitude of self-abasement cherished by his biblical ancestors:

> sitting down in the middle of the dark path, surrounded by shadows that seemed to be the shadows of his life itself, he hunched forward and strewed earth upon his hair, in the immemorial Jewish technique of humiliation.

But neither this nor the succeeding self-inflicted pain upon his physical person wakens his anaesthetized sensibilities: "he saw nothing there before which he could reasonably abase himself" (p. 340). Unlike Job, whose sackcloth and ashes (however unconvincing) are at least dignified by his prior recognition by the Voice from the Whirlwind (to say nothing of his earlier accusations as a man of outraged moral intelligence), Ernie Levy stares out at a universe whose blank moral visage confronts his suffering with an implacable indifference. Under such circumstances, Camus's rebel—with Sisyphean defiance—declared war on the metaphysical enemy, death, thus affirming his right to repudiate the fate he could not defeat—and this is noble. But Schwarz-Bart replaces the abstract terrors of the plague with the concrete horror of the gas chamber; and this transition from symbol to fact conditions the basis of our aesthetic response (since here, as it does not in Camus, the reality of Auschwitz hovers urgently on the edge of the imagination), and derprives Ernie Levy of a meaningful gesture. When he finally releases a long dormant flood of tears by splitting his cheek with a rock, his heart opens to a "light" that only deceitfully illuminates the darkness of his inevitable destiny, the concrete horror whose foreknowledge in our own minds corrupts every effort of Ernie Levy to rejoin the familiar stream of time.

Thus, the tender interlude of love that follows his return to Paris, a foolhardy decision growing out of his determination not to glorify himself (itself a supreme delusion, given the impetus of the novel) or separate himself "from the humble procession of the Jewish people" (p. 354), is shrouded by the certain gloom of the lovers' future. The illusion of love as a possible redeeming experience in *l'univers concentrationnaire* is painfully illuminated in a brief exchange, as Ernie and his beloved sit in a public square forbidden to Jews (having temporarily doffed their yellow stars):

> "Imagine," Ernie said, "thousands of people have sat here before us. It's funny to think about it. . . ."
>
> "Listen," Golda said, "I existed before Adam was created. I've always been one of two colors. Thousands of years have gone by and I haven't changed at all. What am I?"
>
> Ernie said, "My father had little anecdotes for every occasion. Yours has riddles."
>
> "I'm Time," Golda said dreamily, "and my colors are Day and Night."
>
> The same thought drew them together while Time hurtled by around them with cruel speed, branding their happiness with a star. [pp. 363–64]

The central paradox of *The Last of the Just,* and perhaps of the Jewish people themselves, lies locked in Golda's conundrum: does the circumstance that Time existed before the moment of creation insure the continued, meaningful existence of those created within time, and of the motions of the heart and the will to endure which give Golda the courage to play defiantly on her harmonica, in the midst of their enemies, Hatikvah, the ancient Hebrew chant of hope? The instinctive human impulse to believe in the significance of suffering, to discover evidence of a tradition to support its meaning, is pitted against Golda's simple question, why have Christians always hated and persecuted Jews?; and both her question and Ernie's reply force the dilemma into a framework of historical perspective which, given the concluding events of the novel, provides a deliberately dubious "explanation" of this culminating catastrophe of the Jewish people.

More to solace his beloved than himself, Ernie resorts to the characteristic device of inventing a legend whose tone of compassionate sadness creates the illusion of comfort by imbedding their present suffering in one of the many archetypal mosaics from the past. He imagines a conversation between Jesus ("a little old-fashioned Jew, a real Just Man") and Golda's father, in which the former's assertion that "the Jewish heart must break a thousand times for the greater good of all peoples. *That* is why we were chosen, didn't you know?" elicits from the latter the gentle rejoinder, coated with salving humor, "Oi, oi, didn't I know? Didn't I know? Oh, excellent rabbi, that's all I *do* know, alas . . ." (p. 365). This knowledge, illuminating as it does retrospectively the fate of an individual and his people, seems to preserve the possibility of tragedy for Ernie and the Jews, and even a kind of secular salvation, a visionary redemption; but against it Schwarz-Bart would have us measure the appalling certainty of Auschwitz, which no vision could anticipate and which darkens the future of the lovers with a shadow that mocks the irrelevance of Golda's riddle about time and brands their happiness with the infamous yellow star.

The shattering impact of the closing sections of the novel may be ascribed in large part to the carefully contrived quality of their apparent inconclusiveness: they attract the sensibilities of the reader with traditional literary and spiritual expectations while simultaneously confusing—and ultimately appalling—them by dramatizing situations to which these sensibilities can hardly respond. Golda and her family are abruptly arrested and sent to Drancy, notorious transit camp for deportation to the ominous East, and the desperate Ernie swiftly decides that he must join her there. One is tempted to admire the heroic impulse which drives him to tear the yellow star from his jacket and fling it in the street before the eyes of a Gestapo officer at the entrance to the camp (thus assuring his "entry"); and one associates this gesture with the courage of the lovers in removing this same star in the earlier episode. Moreover, the aura of romantic challenge surrounding the flinging down of this symbolic gauntlet, despite the unknown danger awaiting Ernie on the other side of the wall, awakens echoes of earlier instances of the forlorn individual facing with bold if uneasy determination an overwhelming fate. But literary expectations are violated by concrete instance, and Ernie himself has not the slightest illusion about the nature of his act, even though he cannot imagine its immediate consequences: "Ernie saw himself, with heart-rending clarity, as a ridiculously agitated ant at the foot of the redoubtable blocks of concrete" (p. 377).

But even the insect perspective seems noble after Ernie is reduced by systematically vicious torture to a scarcely human creature capable only of an infantile babbling. For Camus, the confrontation between Ernie's longing to rejoin Golda and the impersonally implacable cruelty of the Gestapo might result in the principle of absurdity (like Sisyphus and his rock) and a residue of dignity for the all too human victim; but the exigencies of *l'univers concentrationnaire* diminish Ernie Levy to the undefined status of a "creature," and his pain-wracked body and numbed mind can return to reality not through direct confrontation but only via the devious route of a dream-vision, an odd, vivid blending of yearning with prophecy. For in his semiconsciousness Ernie imagines his wedding with Golda, and this in turn glides into their departure in a "little train" for Poland, and culminates in a sense of the sheer physicality of his suffering, "the wind plucking at every naked fiber of his body," as he realizes that "separation from a loved one is the most painful foretaste of death" (p. 391). Schwarz-Bart does not qualify the repeated cry that issues from Ernie's lips as he wakens from his unconsoling dream, but it is clearly more akin to Lear's desolate "howl" than to the ultimate grim defiance of a doomed man.

The final chapter of *The Last of the Just*, called simply "Never Again," is a lamentation for the fate of Ernie and the Jews, crystallizing a problem which permeates the literature of atrocity,

the search on the part of victim *and* survivor for a viable attitude to
make endurable, if not comprehensible, the human and spiritual
implications of that fate. Rejecting the later suggestion of George
Steiner that some truths in reality are beyond the scope of art, and
of Kosinski that the writer must discover universal metaphorical
equivalents for the grotesque horrors of our time, Schwarz-Bart
deliberately plunges the action into the deepest heart of Holocaust
darkness, the gas chamber itself, and by this bold stroke compels the
imagination to gasp, together with Ernie Levy, for some breath of
lucidity in the very crucible of extinction.

For the crucial test in interpreting both the experience and its
representation in literature is to decide whether the perspective of
time can clarify the silence and blackness that characterize these
somber events. As Ernie is sealed into his boxcar, he utters, along
with the others, a cry of help; as if, Schwarz-Bart suggests, he
wanted one last time "to stir up a void against which the human
voice could echo—however feebly" (p. 407). Some of the great
figures of world literature during the past century, from Captain
Ahab through Ivan Karamazov to Camus's eloquent rebels, have
sought to do precisely this—to impose human significance on a
reality that threatened to abase if not extinguish man's solitary
dignity.

But Ernie's physical confinement reflects a confinement of spirit
and paralysis of will uniquely unlike theirs, while his status as Jew
and victim and the history of his misery have endowed him with a
conviction of futility that places his own efforts to "stir up a void" in
a thoroughly ambiguous light, affecting Schwarz-Bart's attitudes as
well as his own. For in order to support the terrified spirits of Golda
and the children who accompany them to Auschwitz, Ernie
indulges in incantations of consolation that he himself does not
believe, rituals of hope to banish the fear of death, though the
"gentle, happy words" of his imagination often remain frozen in
"the ice palace of his mind" (p. 413), as if invention were blocked
by the massive concrete of reality and lacked the strength—and the
conviction?—to clamber over or escape beyond its fearful confines.
Ernie's knowledge that "no heir, no memory would supervene to
prolong the silent parade of victims" (p. 419) strains in these closing
pages against a contrary momentum to find a language and a
temporal context for the unutterable truth that "the ancient

procession of stake and fagot ended in the crematorium" (p. 395).

Just as part of the nightmare of the gas chamber is the irrepressible impulse to reject its terrifying finality even at the moment of annihilation, so for the victim in time, here Ernie Levy, the last instinctive gesture is to vindicate the terror of the present by somehow uniting it with the past, hurling a desperate affirmation at life's denial of him and his fellow Jews: as the fatal gas drowns his senses and he sinks into unconsciousness, Ernie recalls the legend of an ancient Rabbi which his father had often recited to him. Martyred by the Romans for teaching the Law, wrapped in the scrolls of the Torah upon his flaming pyre, the Rabbi was asked by his disciples what he saw; "I see the parchment burning," replied the martyr, "but the letters are taking wing." "Ah, yes," echoes Ernie, in his dying gasp, *"surely the letters are taking wing"* (pp. 421–22).

But Ernie Levy is not ringed by disciples at a public martyrdom, only other anonymous victims, and the parallel and precedent which he tries to establish between his own fate and Jewish legend may only confirm the discontinuity between the two, the end and not the perpetuation of a redemptive tradition of suffering. At the moment of Ernie's expiration, the meaning of his death, and that of six million others, is transferred to the imagination of the survivors, and the letters of which he spoke in his dying breath are transformed into the words of Schwarz-Bart's novel: the only living memorial to Ernie Levy is *The Last of the Just* itself, and whether or not it "takes wing" and endures will depend on one's private response to and interpretation of the experience which it records.

The penultimate paragraph of the novel compounds the dilemma of interpretation by introducing a dreadful antiphony that polarizes two possible realities of the Holocaust even as it attempts to interweave them. This union of celebration and lament—"And praised. *Auschwitz.* Be. *Maidanek.* The Lord. *Treblinka.* And praised. *Buchenwald.* Be. *Mauthausen.* The Lord. *Belzec.* . . ." (it is longer than this, and metaphorically might be interminable)—introduces these alternatives: either the horror of the concentration camps is enveloped by a spiritual transcendence that can include even such catastrophes in its vision of human history; or the names still fearful to the ears of men muffle the paean to God with the terror-stricken echoes of unredeemable suffering. The choices diverge and confound language's attempt to join them in a paradoxical, disquieting balance, a dramatic instance of the writer's frustrating desire to translate the cacophony of fact into the antiphony—by now we must realize the futility of expecting harmony—of art.

The novel should properly have ended here, leaving the imagination of the reader-survivor with the responsibility of struggling toward a point of view; but Schwarz-Bart unaccountably—and unfortunately, I believe, for the aesthetic impact of the novel—felt compelled to add one more brief paragraph, in which he introduces the narrative voice, a projection of his own person, thinking that "Ernie Levy, dead six million times, is still alive somewhere, I don't know where . . . ," while a drop of pity falls from above and a "presence" (p. 422) seems to add a grain of consolation to his trembling despair. Such sentimentalism must be regarded as a lapse in artistic taste *unless* we explain it—and such irony *would* be consistent with the previous tone of the novel—as a last, compassionate tribute to the human imagination's need to invent an echo in a universe that has passed into the chaos of moral silence. Man would sooner choose the void as purpose, Nietzsche reminds us, than be void of purpose himself.

The primitive mind was spared these dilemmas by the presence of ritual, which allied its life in time with eternally recurring myths of creation or destruction that confirmed an unconscious continuity in the existence of the race. But the return in dream or memory—to say nothing of art—to the Holocaust experience, imprisons the survivor in an uncycled moment of time, the moment of unparalleled dread, dehumanization, and death that makes man the victim of an insulated instant and nullifies for *us* (if not entirely for him) Ernie Levy's pathetic desire to link his fate with a universal pattern, since there is no ritual precedent—certainly not the martyrdom of an individual Rabbi whose name has passed into legend—for the event that leads to his extinction. For his fate represents a unique ritual of anonymous *un*creation, whereby the individual is permanently divorced from time and thus from the opportunity for a mythical participation in the idea of recurrence.

Although the Levys begin in legend and move into time and history, they end in a dimension for which there is as yet no verbal (or conceptual) equivalent; and novels like *The Last of the Just*, together with Böll's *Billiards at Half-Past Nine* and Semprun's *The Long Voyage*, dramatize the need for a fresh examination of temporal reality that the Holocaust has imposed on the human imagination. Our natural instinct to contemplate the victims' destiny in a familiar context of values, temporal and otherwise, stumbles against our inability to translate their suffering into the exemplary or the archetypal, grisly, perhaps, like the tale of the sons devouring the father, but acceptable because it illustrates a deep-lying pattern in mythical reality, a drama of human desires that transcends the desolate mortality of the individual. The Legend of the Just Man seems simply inapplicable (and hence, retrospectively, impotent?) in the gas chambers of Auschwitz—but then, what categories *do* apply there? Ernie's consolations are surely only that—not revelations of a higher reality, a deeper truth, a spiritual meaning to redeem the horror: the awful void that sucks his vital breath, while space displaces time as the locus of his destiny, negates the very time that sanctioned his life in history and orphans him from a past and future that might justify his merging with a mythical and universalized truth.

The art of Heinrich Böll in *Billiards at Half-Past Nine* superficially seems to owe a technical debt to the dynastic fiction of William Faulkner such as *The Bear* and *Absalom! Absalom!*, but the resemblance does not extend much further; for the Civil War as a cultural episode in the life of America had a fundamentally different effect on the imagination of Faulkner than World War II had on the imagination of the younger German novelist, himself a participant in and survivor of the event. Like Faulkner in *Absalom! Absalom!*, Böll in *Billiards* employs a variety of narrative voices to recreate the events of the past which shape the quality of reality in the present; but whereas young Quentin Compson pursues the secrets gradually revealed by these "voices" through murder, fratricide, miscegenation, and incest to the final, ancient relic of his heritage, Henry Sutpen, still hiding in the family mansion, and then tries desperately to organize their implications for his life in the present, Böll's characters are imprisoned by the privacy of their own recollections and discoveries, scarcely sharing them at all, so that the narrative voices coexist but do not intersect, as if the fragmented pieces of reality each is obsessed with cannot, of their very nature, be

combined into a coherent and meaningful whole. Faulkner was
concerned with moral confusion, deviations from norms of value
that readers might use to assess the extent and consequences of the
confusion; but Böll is immersed in a situation of moral chaos, and
although it is clear that for him the familiar norms of value have
gone up in smoke together with the millions of victims, it is
questionable to the end whether his characters can succeed in
inventing new ones to enable them to restore inner order to their
lives.

In this respect Böll resembles Henry James more than Faulkner:
in *Billiards* he cares less about reporting what happened, the human
(and inhuman) facts of existence prior to and during the war, than
about the mind's effort, having survived, to achieve some moral
perspective on these events. Unlike most other authors considered
in this study, who focus on the dilemma of the actual victim in the
Holocaust, Böll turns to the problem of the civilized German—is it
legitimate to call him a different kind of victim?—who inherits its
spiritual rubble, and dramatizes the attempt to sift through the
debris of the past in search of usable attitudes toward guilt,
responsibility, and—given the grimness of their recollections—the
possibility of elucidating this heritage for future generations. The
effort, indeed, may be more significant than the results, since the
human imagination seems doomed to sift through the rubble of the
Holocaust ad infinitum without uncovering anything but further
debris. Like Thomas Mann, Böll depends on irony to sustain the
tone of his narrative; considering the raw material of the reality
he—and, in fact, all other writers committed to the art of
atrocity—has to work with, an ironic shield may be the only defense
against the necessary failure of all efforts to create order and
meaning out of this unalterable chaos.

Irony is so pervasive in *Billiards at Half-Past Nine* that one must
exercise the most extreme caution in judging even the simplest
details and episodes. Like Joyce's *Ulysses*, the chronological time of
the novel covers less than one day, September 6, 1958—the
eightieth birthday of the patriarch of the Faehmel family. The day is
to culminate in a celebration attended by three generations of
Faehmels, but when this moment arrives, it is not clear whether
they have more cause for grief or joy, as the old man's memories
gradually dominate and suppress the fact of his survival, while the

memories of the other family members further obscure the "triumph" of this dynasty's endurance. Times past, in other words, persistently intrude on and corrupt the purity of time present, and cast a tentative and by now familiar cloud of uncertainty over the prospects for the youngest generation in the future.

Like the individual members of the Faehmel family, the reader is plunged repeatedly into these "times past," forced to sort out in his own consciousness the complex of chronology and genealogy, guilt and recrimination, suffering (particularly during the Nazi era) and relief, that afflict this representative (or is it?) portion of the German mentality with an obsessive concern for deeds committed and left undone, and the need for a moral justification of both. Böll's vision probes steadily and remorselessly inward, assaulting that realm of "inner emigration" claimed as a sanctuary for their probity during the war years by so many Germans who never swallowed the "Host of the Beast" (Böll's metaphor for Nazism, itself never named in the novel)—only to discover that the notion of probity is incommensurable with the recollections that haunt his characters' chambers of memory. Thus the "birth" day is an ironic reminder of a series of atrocities which in their unexplained finality sever the "normal" cycle of death and renewal and destroy the harmony of reflections that might otherwise make of this day—which in fact happens in Joyce's *Ulysses*—a compendium of the tragedy and comedy of human existence.

Böll's genius for finding an objective correlative for this difficult circumstance is revealed by his choice of a controlling image for the novel, the architectural image—or more precisely, perhaps, one should say "statics." For all the Faehmel males, Heinrich the grandfather, Robert the son, and Joseph the grandson, are students of architecture, experts in achieving a precarious balance between stress and strain, thus mastering a potential for construction and demolition, creating or destroying beauty and form, which pierces to the heart of the essential tension in the novel. And by extension the human mind and imagination are faced with a similar problem: balancing events suggesting an inherent disorder in reality against conceptions of order that traditionally sustain our idea of civilization. Old Heinrich has been a builder: the supreme achievement of his career was the Abbey of St. Anthony, a structure he gained the right to build as a young man by winning a competition against older and more established architects; and just as his entry into the competition had been the result of a carefully organized plan, including the submission of his proposal at the virtual moment of deadline, so the abbey has come to symbolize the order of his career, his mastery of time, his conviction that life can be made to submit to human control, that the unexpected can always be anticipated.

Part of the impact of the novel is *our* discovery of his error, though to the very end his own insights are far more tentative, as his natural outward composure and restraint struggle against his inner sense of a default in commitment, a failure to challenge the antihumanistic spirit in German life which finally permitted the Host of the Beast to flourish. He himself is an unwitting symbolic source of the splintered life of his era, as one son, Otto (later killed on the Russian front) became a supporter of the Party, blackmailing his own parents, while the surviving son Robert, when still a student, was forced to flee the country before the war because of his association with friends who attempted to assassinate a gym teacher guilty of persecuting those who opposed the Host of the Beast. The division between brothers, between parents and children, oppressors and victims, dignity and humiliation, power and helplessness, all are reflected in old Heinrich's attempts to reconcile his aspirations with the destiny which time and history have imposed on himself and his family.

Robert the son suffers an even greater frustration than his father, for he feels a personal (if indirect) responsibility for the death or exile of his comrades: Schrella, forced to flee for his life (and whose sister Edith later became Robert's wife); the boy Ferdi, arrested and executed for throwing the ineffectual homemade bomb at the teacher; another anonymous boy who loses his life for transmitting messages to Robert's parents from their son, also in exile—the list is long; and though memory continues to raise these unavenged ghosts, conscience has not yet invented a form of justice to placate Robert's sense of complicity in their fate. Time as memory thus continues to assault the coherence of his being, and though like his father he invents rituals—the daily billiard-game which lends the novel its title—to give the appearance of regularity and discipline to his external existence, nothing seems to ease the confusion of sequence and absence of harmony in his consciousness.

Part of his unarticulated guilt derives from his own good fortune: through the intervention of his mother, a close friend of a high Gestapo official, Robert was permitted to return to Germany and enter the army as an officer; and near the war's end, finding himself in the vicinity of the abbey built by his father, he persuades the commanding general to let him demolish it, though his memory does not confess the reason until thirteen years later:

> He had wanted to erect a monument of dust and rubble for those who had not been historical monuments and whom no one had thought to spare. Edith, killed by a piece of shrapnel; Ferdi, would-be assassin condemned by process of law; the boy who had pushed the tiny slips of paper with his messages into the letter box; Schrella's father, who had disappeared; Schrella himself, who had to live so far away from the land where Hölderlin had lived; Groll, the waiter in The Anchor [who had been another contact between Robert and his parents]. . . .[2]

But the irony of monuments which are no monuments at all only intensifies memory's inability to memorialize deaths that nullify all attempts to explain them through cause and effect, through some connection between act and punishment that has always provided a framework for conceptions of injustice as well as justice. There *is* no meaningful niche in reality (or in consciousness) for these victims; hence they assert their "homelessness" in time and eternity, permitting those who have survived them neither act nor attitude to cleanse themselves of the stain of *having lived through* what killed the others.

Each victim thus becomes a leitmotif in the psychic life of the elder Faehmels, who though alienated from each other in actuality are united in a far profounder way by the common source of their inner purgatory; and thus Böll can suggest that the reign of the Host of the Beast through a silent osmosis has created a complex dilemma of memory and conscience which affects the national image in spite of itself, as well as the individual will. With subtle variations, the leitmotif of the act of atrocity intrudes into everyone's consciousness, until the reader recognizes it as the "organizing" principle of Böll's art, the unconscious link between the minds of his characters,

2. Heinrich Böll, *Billiards at Half-Past Nine*, trans. Leila Vennewitz (New York: Signet Books, 1965), pp. 146–47.

even as they struggle in vain to harmonize its strident echoes. In conversation with his son, old Heinrich reveals the extent of his own obsession:

> I laughed at your childish plots, but the laughter stuck in my throat when I read they had killed that boy. He might have been Edith's brother, but later on I knew it had been almost human to kill a boy who after all had thrown a bomb and scorched a gym teacher's feet—but the boy who pushed your slips of paper through our letter box, the Pole who raised his hand against the gym teacher, even an uncalled-for glance, certain kind of hair, certain shape of nose were enough, and the time came when it took even less. The father's or grandmother's birth certificate was enough. [p. 173]

All their minds are imprisoned by these specific facts from the past, even thirteen years later, as if in medias res has been translated from a literary formula to an unavoidable necessity of real life, marking the death of chronological time, except in the most superficial sense, as a controlling pattern for human experience. And the reader, who seeks orientation in this world of the memory-persecuted present, is doomed like Böll's characters to grope through these dim realms of discontinuity, perpetually feeling as if he is "in the midst of things" that history or the narrative promises to conclude, but never can. Several motifs in the novel are strictly verbal, not referring to characters, and the most prominent among them is "whywhywhy," the eternally recurrent question looming out of the past as an antidote to the narcosis which eludes the Faehmel conscience.

The extraordinary relevance of Böll's novel to Holocaust fiction and *l'univers concentrationnaire* is nowhere clearer than here: for the failure of the retrospective imagination to find meaning in history or in the consolations of tragedy dramatizes the absurd position of man as Survivor: the act of recollection, instead of forging links with the past, only widens the exasperatingly impassable gulf between the dead and the living, creating a void which makes new beginnings for the future equally impossible, until some way of reconciling the fate of those dead with the present can silence the influence they continue to exert on the living. But no rational explanation can accomplish this end, for as Robert and the others know—another recurrent verbal motif that invades the

Faehmel memory—"reason led to nothing in a world where lifting your hand to someone could cost you your life" (p. 124). The inner world, crowded with such motifs, becomes the only real one for the family members, while the daily routine of existing resembles a devitalized ritual that passes time but cannot pacify it.

For example, Robert is invited by the abbot to the reconsecration of the abbey his father built, he destroyed, and his own son Joseph is rebuilding; he agrees to come while simultaneously thinking: "I'm not reconciled, not reconciled either to myself or to the spirit of reconciliation which you in your official speech will proclaim. . . . I am not reconciled to a world in which a gesture or a word misunderstood can cost a life" (p. 209). Still, Robert agrees to come, as does his father, even though, like his son, the old man *inwardly* reflects the same spirit of dissent: "Don't be shocked, Reverend Father; I'm not reconciled with my son Otto who was my son no longer, only my son's husk, and I can't celebrate my reconciliation to a building, even if I did build it myself." Then he adds ironically—but still in the silence of his reflections, not aloud— "Strengthen your heart with hymns, Reverend Father, and consider carefully whether you are truly reconciled to the spirit which destroyed the monastery" (p. 210). But the permanent schizophrenia that afflicts the Faehmel spirit offers no means of communicating this question, so it remains buried in Heinrich's consciousness, further irritating the psychic wound that alienates him from himself and his generation.

In fact, one of the most distressing consequences of the Holocaust, as it was enacted within Germany itself (and as Böll clearly perceives) was a sundering of each generation from the other; the unique quality of the cvil rifc during this period entrenched it in the private mind, disqualifying it from the possibility of shared experience, of communal suffering, one might say, or communal grief. As a result, family feeling between Robert and his children, Ruth and Joseph, has been ruptured, and the events of the past remain a permanent obstacle to any efforts to use love to ease the harshness of memory. Ruth cannot understand the odd coolness of her father's and grandfather's attitudes in the presence of the abbot; and Böll makes dramatically clear the futility, not to say the folly, of trying to do so.

Ruth, half-orphaned by the war in more than the literal sense,

was only three when a piece of shrapnel killed her mother during an
air raid; and ever since, though she is now nineteen, she has had to
fight her own battle with time's disorientation of her consciousness,
and especially her attempts to recall her mother: "when I think of
her, I think of seventeen or of two thousand years. Twenty-four is a
figure that doesn't suit her; it should rather be something under
eighteen or over eighty" (pp. 212–13). This juggling with figures in
memory, which is part of the family obsession in its hopeless
encounter with an unreconcilable heritage, suggests even as it veils
the deeper dilemma of *why* Edith had to die at twenty-four in such
a manner, which in turn summons up the unanswerable question
looming through Böll's imaginative world: how a Germany filled
with Faehmels ever became the abject realm of the Host of the
Beast in the first place. Ruth knows that the family home is
inhabited by ghosts, and has a few of her own that rise from her
childhood recollections, such as the corpses brought up from cellars
after an air raid and thrown on trucks like sacks, while her brother
tries to convince her that they were only sick and are being taken to
a hospital. Deception has always been simpler than truth when
human communication was at stake, but when truth proves a
powerless alternative—knowing the truth in this context cannot
make one free, since its implications only harass the imagination
more—then the inner life reaches a dead end, while the outer world
remains in the grip of a protective irony, half self-deceptive, half
compassionate.

For even after Ruth learns (though not from him) that her father
had been the one who blew up the abbey, she evinces neither
surprise nor outrage, nothing to induce a greater human honesty
between them: "We'll go on playing father and daughter. Precise as
a ritual dance." Such a revelation is palatable, if a little puzzling; a
more difficult and unmanageable secret, however, lies shrouded
behind the fate of the matriarch of the family, Heinrich's wife, who
sometime during the war was declared insane and sent to a
sanatorium. "I don't want to understand Grandmother," thinks
Ruth, "I don't want to; her craziness is a lie" (p. 214). But in the
so-called madness of Grandmother lies a key to the imaginative
vision of the novel, as well as to the experience it records: for if
reason casts only dark and troubled shadows backwards in time,
then perhaps the perspective of insanity—and the spirit of Jakov

Lind stands applauding in the wings—can shed a luminous glow over events that thus far have resisted the efforts of Böll's other characters to comprehend them as part of the culture of our time.

Even before Johanna Faehmel's narrative voice is introduced, we have come to appreciate her unusual character, since she is the one Faehmel whose moral vigor does not defer to the principles of composure and restraint, but translates feeling into language and action, whatever the danger; she says openly what her husband and others only think privately, and thus creates a possible model for the way of uniting the inner and outer self that eludes the other members of her family. During World War I, at a military reception, she had frankly exclaimed before her husband's superiors "That fool of a Kaiser" (p. 81), and years later Heinrich admits to himself that instead of apologizing profusely for his wife's odd behavior, he should have said, "I agree with my wife absolutely." During both wars Johanna had refused to accept from the abbey milk and honey and additional produce while others were suffering from the food shortages; but the crucial act of her life and the one that makes her point of view essential to an understanding of the novel is suggested by a small detail almost casually introduced: in 1943, "she went down to the freight yard and tried to go along in the cars with the Jews. Screwball, they said. They locked her up in the looney bin" (p. 27). And fifteen years later she is still there, as if releasing her (and thereby confirming her moral and psychic "health") would shatter an illusion about their inaction that the Faehmels and the nation have used to insure the minimal tolerability of their own lives.

Only the "mad" Johanna has a notion of time adequate to the events of the Holocaust, one that preserves these events in cocoons of isolated horror and thus confirms their irreconcilability with any tradition of civilization: "Here we don't think of time as an indefinite continuous concept but rather as separate units which must not be related and become history" (p. 217). The discrete moments of the past that flood her memory admit no chronological distinctions: "With us," she insists in her sanatorium, "time is always *today*" (p. 219), and "today" represents the date each of her dead ceased to exist, nearly all of them victims of the attitude which culminated in the Host of the Beast. For them, she recognizes, time was "nothing but a means of bringing them closer to death"

(p. 139); hence her imagination, through a combination of insight and perversity, resists the impulse to reenter the world of regular time herself, since this would demean her dead by somehow assenting to the force or power that killed them. Her future and the German future died when they did; for Johanna, the terminus ad quem of history was 1943. This explains her unwillingness to see her grandchildren, presumably young and happy, whose joy would represent a desecration of the unatoned suffering of the victims who are enshrined in her memory.

But the mind's effort to do justice to their suffering by dividing it into separate, unrelated (and therefore individualized) units meets a counterpoint from history itself, whose momentum—we see its effect in the minds of the Faehmels other than Johanna—impels one to conceive of time as that very "indefinite continuous concept" she would reject. Johanna's view may be satisfactory within the sanctuary of the asylum, protected from any encounter with the stream of daily life, just as her conception of the Holocaust as an episode arrested in time—one shared, in fact, by many survivors— can be sustained if we accept it as an island suspended in that stream, cut off from contact with any other shores. Böll compounds the complexity of his vision by having Johanna's uniquely private world of time confront chronological time when she decides to attend her husband's birthday party: at this point, she must leave what she herself calls her "inner emigration" (an expression resonant with meaning for her countrymen), bounded by the years 1917 and 1943, and face "September 6, 1958, that's the future, the German future" (p. 141) as she once again herself admits.

Böll dramatizes the possibility and impossibility of fusing these two universes in a passage rich in symbolic irony: for in order to ease herself back into temporal reality, Johanna dials the "time" on the telephone, and as it "flowed into her face and blanched it deathly white . . . 'Six o'clock precisely, September sixth, 1958,' said the soft voice" (p. 221), all the dead flood her memory once again, momentarily silencing the recorded words of the operator in the present. As the seconds and minutes of chronological time tick by in precise and exact order over the receiver, Johanna wonders (again with acute relevance reaching far beyond her personal situation) whether there's too much lost time to be made up, lamenting that "all the time I've played truant with and denied is

still in me like a hard lie" (p. 222). Fearful of her ability to enter the
"future" (which for the other Faehmels means the present and for
the post-1958 reader the past), she prepares a motive, a gesture to
justify her decision: she secures a pistol, and determines to shoot the
gym teacher (now chief of police). The abortive attempt to
assassinate him had begun the cycle of atrocities for the Faehmel
family which culminated in Johanna's being certified insane in order
to protect, and probably preserve, her life. Thus armed, she is
"ready with death in my handbag to return to life" (p. 220),
cognizant of chronological time but simultaneously behaving as if
two decades had not intervened between the failed attempt and her
resolution to complete it successfully—the one Faehmel still hoping
to exorcise the ghosts of the past by accomplishing a deed that had
been left undone. The inability to do this has doomed the other
members of her family to a life of unreconciled moral frustration.

Johanna sees her act of violence as a kind of ransom payment, an
avenging of her own and all their passivity in the past. But Böll
himself refuses to admit such a simplified solution to the dilemmas
of the novel: the multiplicity of points of view endures to the very
end, and it will take more than Johanna's bullet to unify them into a
collective destiny, a shared fate that might restore a measure of
tranquillity to their life in time. When Edith's brother Schrella
returns to his native city after an exile of twenty-two years, he is
arrested at the German border because his name has never been
expunged from the list of wanted "criminals," where it had been
placed during the war by the Gestapo. He is quickly released
through the intervention of a former schoolmate, Nettlinger, himself
a Gestapo member earlier and now a confirmed democrat and
prominent public official; but the irony of the arrest, and of the
personality of the "savior," only confirms Schrella's suspicion that
not much of fundamental importance has changed while he has
been gone. One old waiter at the hotel where his father used to
work even whispers to him: "But be careful, Mr. Schrella, watch
out; sometimes I think: *they did win after all*" (p. 167). And
Nettlinger is a frustrating embodiment of this prospect; for although
it would seem that pure hatred were the only legitimate response to
his hypocritical time-serving—he had been responsible for the
execution of the boy Ferdi, the one who threw the homemade
bomb—Schrella also discovers for the first time that Nettlinger had

repeatedly protected his sister Edith from arrest and probable
death, and had been instrumental in securing permission for Robert
Faehmel to return from exile before the war.

Thus, like the others, Schrella is doomed to face the past, with its
injustices, without a viable moral attitude—retracing quite literally
the steps of his boyhood wanderings, he meets Ferdi's sister, but
senses the uselessness of reopening old wounds. Like his own father,
who was taken away in a car one day by the Gestapo and simply
"was not seen again," the atrocities that nag the memories and
consciences of Schrella and the Faehmels have left a moral and
emotional vacuum that no feeling, no anger, no gesture can
adequately fill. But Böll carries Schrella's symbolic role further, for
as the only untainted survivor from those days of evil—in exile
Schrella did not suffer from the proximity of the Host of the Beast,
as the Faehmels did—Schrella is in a better position than the others
to recognize the futility of paying homage to memory, even though
he is equally powerless to devise a satisfactory formula for the
future. Reunited with Robert, he joins him in a game of billiards,
that "sacred" ritual which had protected Robert's external life from
the inner turmoil of his recollections; and the hotel boy who
has regularly served Robert as a daily auditor to these recollections concludes that Schrella has broken the spell, disrupted
the rhythm of the game (and of Robert's life?), and has rein-
troduced a "perpetual present"—"six-fifty-one on September 6,
1958" (p. 245)—that shifts attention from "why" to "when" and
asks what men are doing—what they can do—in the present to
prevent the breeding of more wolves (the pastoral-Christian imagery is Schrella's) and develop the feeding and shepherding of
lambs.

Schrella is afraid of rejoining an existence where it is so easy to
"let yourself be convinced of the banal fact that life goes on and
that you get used to anything in time" (pp. 245–46); he is less
dismayed by the survival and "rehabilitation" of the Nettlingers and
their kind than by the absence of the other kind, the good men who
had refused like himself to be associated in any way with the Host
of the Beast. But Schrella's faith in the process of "becoming," of
using the lessons from the past to improve the present and remake
the future, is tempered by his disillusionment at learning that with
one exception the surviving "good" friends of his youth have
merged into the commercial-political mediocrity of contemporary

Germany. The exception has become a priest, but Böll adds his own transparent disillusionment to Schrella's in commenting on his fate: he has been transferred to an isolated village and fallen under suspicion "because he makes the Sermon on the Mount the subject of his sermons so often" (p. 248).

Schrella, like Melville's Ishmael, has thus survived only to become another orphan. Perhaps the real question of the future must be settled not by those who lived through the war but by those who were born in it, its literal offspring—and in *Billiards at Half-Past Nine* this role is filled by the youngest male Faehmel, Joseph, and his fiancée Marianne. September 6, 1958, had begun as an ordinary day for Joseph, full of anticipation of the family celebration, where he would introduce Marianne for the first time; but earlier that afternoon the foreman of the demolition company clearing away the debris of the ruined abbey that Joseph was helping to rebuild had called to his attention the remnants of a fresco beneath the rubble. Ordering it to be preserved, Joseph suddenly noticed chalked in a corner of the picture-fragment his own father's architectural symbol, the letters XYZX, and in an abrupt instant of insight he realizes that they are written at a "statically significant" point, and that Robert Faehmel must have been responsible for blowing up the abbey at the end of the war, not the Allied forces, as most had hitherto assumed.

Joseph's previously untroubled sense of security, his feeling of unity and identity with the past, growing out of the acceptable (if ironic) principle that former destruction makes future creation possible in the "natural" order of things, is rudely shattered by his discovery of his father's inexplicable betrayal of the family tradition, the monument to their greatness. Having understood the moral corruption associated with that "greatness," Robert had been driven to his act; and it is of no small consequence that the blotched fresco which had led Joseph to the revelation of his father's responsibility for the abbey's fate is a depiction of the Last Supper, with "the dark leather of Judas' purse" (p. 182) clearly visible beneath the mildew. Joseph's disillusionment, his immediate decision to abandon the job of supervising the abbey's reconstruction, his renunciation of a past he cannot possibly understand fully, accentuates the dilemma of the youngest generation who have inherited a dark legacy for which they do not feel guilty, but from whose implications and consequences they are unable, if they are sensitive, to dissociate themselves. The mere suspicion that his father must have had a profound reason for committing such an extraordinary act of repudiation is sufficient to undermine Joseph's will to renewal, and to disturb the rhythm of his life and alter the formula for the future.

Once more, probing for truth (in this instance an accidental effort), has had the reverse of the expected effect; for instead of being liberated by his knowledge, Joseph is plunged into the shadowy realm of a defaced patrimony in spite of himself, without the psychological "consolation" afforded his father and grandfather of wrestling with his memories. He suffers consequences even though the atrocities that obsess them are not part of his consciousness; but he is compelled to join the other Faehmels nonetheless, who also struggle with a knowledge that they cannot convert into fruitful feeling because of the missing link that joins cause to effect, reason to result. Hence Joseph is left in a professional limbo, determined to study statics, but uncertain whether he will use his training for construction or demolition.

Nor can he bring himself to confess his troublesome discovery to Marianne; instead, he elicits from her the story of her own childhood during the war, and though unlike Joseph her burden involves no mystery, it too is not a matter of conscience but a gratuitous act of violence unreconcilable with any sense of human reality which she or Joseph possesses. Marianne reconstructs the vivid scene from her childhood when her father, a Nazi official, lay dead at war's end as a suicide from a bullet in the mouth, while her little brother dangled by a noose from the rafter and her distracted mother murmured fanatically, *"He ordered me to."* Saved from a similar fate by the chance intervention of a neighbor, Marianne has lived with this leitmotif as her heritage, spiritually orphaned like Joseph and Schrella and in fact the older Faehmels too, but unlike them preserved from alienation and inner torment by her love for Joseph and his for her, and their hope for a life together. Marianne has somehow come to terms with her ghosts, though her path affords no pattern for the others who have survived: her father is dead, and she had rejected her apologetic mother when she sought to reclaim her some years later with the simple rejoinder: "There are some things you can't be sorry for" (p. 191). Unencumbered by recollections of her personal involvement with the Holocaust—she was only five when the war ended—and liberated from any moral connection with her family, Marianne seems less obsessed with the past than any other figure in the novel, content to confess her wretched memory to Joseph chiefly in the hope of convincing him of the value of unburdening himself of the secret that is distressing his own soul.

In a traditional narrative Marianne might thus be entrusted with the crucial role of redeemer, the victim who has retained purity and innocence despite suffering and sheds a glow of spiritual possibility over the lives of the other characters. But Böll, who has avoided simple solutions in handling the temporal structure of *Billiards at Half-Past Nine*, is equally ambiguous about the significance of Marianne's nature; he resists the impulse to choose such a conventional climax. Throughout the novel, allusions have been made to a tourist site in the town where the action occurs, the so-called "Roman Children's Graves," remnants of an ancient Roman settlement uncovered when Robert Faehmel (who after the war became the local expert on which buildings were safe enough to remain standing, which had to be destroyed) ordered an old guardhouse to be blown up, thus exposing the signs of an earlier civilization hidden beneath. While the Faehmels and those close to them have been contending with their memories of a more recently demolished past, visitors have been inquiring about the way to the Roman Children's Graves, and these two relics of time, ancient and modern, finally converge in the closing pages of the narrative, as Joseph, his sister Ruth, and Marianne, the youngest generation, pay a visit to the site before joining the rest of the family at the birthday celebration.

The literal scene is an excuse for its symbolic reverberations, since the young people have no particular reason for this excursion at this moment on this day; but even its symbolic importance is deliberately obscured, as if Böll wished to create another tension between what might traditionally be done with such an episode and the impossibility—given the effect of the Holocaust on the nature of literary reality—of doing so. For as the three journey downward in space and backward in time—passing, as the "guide" explains, the modern, medieval, and ancient layers of existence, clearly marked by white cross-lines on the concrete (reminiscent of the chalked lines Joseph had encountered in other ruins earlier in the day)—as they journey downward and backward toward the graves, are we not reminded that time moves in cycles wider and more enduring than the daily and annual chronology that has been paralyzing the Faehmel mentality on September 6, 1958, and that man has the opportunity to annul his imprisonment in history, to release himself from the shackles of contemporary time by recognizing the universal spectacle of grief, the eternal tragedy of dying young (Ferdi, the anonymous boy who passed notes from Robert, Edith, even Otto), and by identifying his own fate with that of the Roman children buried beneath the tombstones that signify humanity's common doom?

This is a tempting interpretation, parallel in certain respects to the paradox that concluded *The Last of the Just*: perhaps mankind requires perspective, temporal distance in order to placate the ghosts of the Holocaust and return them to the universal rhythms of history. For even this apparently unredeemable horror may seem less terrible sub specie aeternitatis; as Marianne stands before the tombstones and hears the guide translate their Latin inscriptions— "Hard is fate, indeed, for parents / . . . But in grief for those of tender age / . . . Eternal hope gives balm," (p. 236)—she weeps, and grief seeps into the hearts of the most hardened spectators, a cosmopolitan audience of tourist-mourners.

But Böll's bitterest irony is reserved for precisely this moment, as the response of his characters is insulated from the attitude of the readers, who share with Böll a knowledge that Marianne and the others cannot or refuse to see: the entire spectacle is a fraud! They aren't Roman children's graves at all, we are informed by a narrative voice instructing the guides not to reveal the secret, "merely tombstones which weren't even found on this particular spot" (p. 235). Thus this ceremony of purgation in the underground affords to tourists hungry for sensations an unexpected opportunity to lament man's fate with a minimum of personal anguish or complicity; while they weep below, the genuine cause for grief, the immediate German past, lacks a focal monument but remains, like the discontinuous moments in Johanna's definition of time, as fragments of a tortuous reality that gives no peace to the few sensibilities it afflicts.

But what of Marianne's tears? In the context of the episode as

Böll carefully shapes it—that is, a cheap duplicity exploiting the gullibility of the curious—her grief is merely sentimental, perhaps a private tribute to her own aborted childhood, but elicited, we cannot ignore or forget, by a monument rigged to suggest painful secrets in gloomy cellars from a time with which the spectator can scarcely connect himself except in an abstract way. Since the circumstances of the death of the children whom the alleged tombstones memorialize must remain a mystery, a victim of time, rituals of grief can have no truly regenerative effect, connecting consciousness with event and restoring to the individual a meaningful attitude toward the human cycle of eternal recurrence; thus, when the three return to the "surface" and Marianne stops sobbing, nothing has really changed in their lives, the interlude has been just that, exposing one more inadequate device for incorporating instants of unassimilated atrocity into the flow of history. The young are as powerless to control the future as the old; though Böll, by concluding the novel with the birthday party of the patriarch of the tribe, would seem to indicate that any gesture of reconciliation or judgment regarding the events that have driven the human imagination to an impasse from which it cannot extricate itself, must come from the older generation.

And gestures and judgments abound in the final pages of *Billiards at Half-Past Nine*, but they are introduced with such a combination of irony and seriousness that one is tempted to conclude that even the artist cannot reconcile the disparate tensions in his creation, as if Böll were unwilling to concede to his art the power of organizing the moral disorder of his theme. Robert adopts Hugo, the bellhop who has served him faithfully over the years in the billiard room, and this is clearly a human gesture, a breakthrough from the inner isolation of memory that has immured him from reality; but if Hugo is merely a substitute for the unnatural silence which persists between Robert and his real son (especially after Joseph's discovery of that afternoon), then he has circumvented without confronting the experience that alienated them in the first place.

Johanna does fire her shot, but at the last moment changes her target, choosing instead of the old gym teacher an official of a new right-wing political party—they are all watching a parade of military veterans—thus shifting her focus from past to future menace, since as she pulls the trigger, she thinks: "My grandson's

murderer is sitting nearby on the balcony, can you see him, in his
dark suit, respectable, oh so respectable?" (p. 233). Once again
seriousness and irony interlock, as Böll acknowledges the necessity
of the warnings and the futility of the way, without introducing any
alternatives. Just as earlier Marianne had told her real mother that
there are some things you can't be sorry for, so Johanna's bullet
reminds us that there are some things you can't forget, or accept,
without striking out in behalf of justice.

Johanna is obsessed with the indifference of the spectators to
their own history: "Respectable, respectable, without a trace of
grief. What's a human being without grief?" (p. 230)—but in a
carefully planned structural sequence, Böll follows this episode with
Joseph, Ruth, and Marianne's visit to the Roman Children's Graves,
a wry commentary on the fate of grief in the post-Holocaust world.
Johanna's act will be attributed to mental derangement, and since
the wound does not prove fatal, the consequences will soon be
forgotten. Thus her gesture, too, is reduced to a frustrated effort to
unsettle the void that has closed down on past atrocities, a
temporary shock that interrupts the routines of September 6, 1958,
without permanently altering the visage of the present—or the
future.

And when the long-awaited celebration finally arrives, Heinrich
refuses to grieve for his wife's action, consoling the other members
of his family with the innocently ominous reassurance, "Order is
half of life—I wonder what's the other half?" (p. 254). Time and the
past flood the room, the old man's office, as those present seat
themselves on neat piles of the eldest Faehmel's papers and
architectural designs, distributed according to year. Joseph sits on
1941, and when four waiters from the café where Heinrich has
taken his breakfast each morning for decades—another external
ritual that displaced the active inner moral life—enter bearing a
covered gift that resembles a corpse, they place it on trestles resting
on papers from the fateful years 1936 to 1939. The gift, a miniature,
elaborately detailed model in pastry of St. Anthony's Abbey, revives
on the last page of the novel the architectural image that was to
have consecrated the Faehmel name to God and to history,
perpetuated their identity and, indeed, justified their lives. Böll
deliberately permits image and gesture to carry the full weight of
meaning in this concluding scene, forestalling any articulated

insight that might elevate the tone to tragedy—it remains serio-comic to the end. As Heinrich slices the spire from the abbey and hands the first piece of cake to his son, the fragility of the "sugared edifice" reflects the tenuous quality of the ideal to which they had devoted their lives.

But there is insufficient evidence to determine whether their devouring of the image that has hitherto symbolized their own, Germany's, and perhaps all of Christianity's spiritual energy signifies a reversal in their relation to the events of time and recent history that have thus far been consuming them. Böll suspends judgment, as he must, because of the literal impact and temporal proximity of his subject: art itself is still too close to the reality it would transcend. At this point one can hardly resist the conjecture that *Billiards at Half-Past Nine* departs from the tradition established by Böll's great predecessors in the modern German novel, Mann, Hermann Broch, and Hermann Hesse, all of whom shared the conviction that art was an attempt, in Hesse's words, to replace the insufficiency of life, "to sublimate in the spirit the indigestible aspects of reality." [3]

One of the unique arguments of the literature of atrocity is that the insufficiencies of moral life during the Holocaust have created a kind of aesthetic dyspepsia (so beautifully consistent, by the way, with Böll's final image) that precludes the artistic and spiritual unity which represented the goal of writers like Hesse. Or to return to Faulkner as a possibly more relevant example: the multiple points of view in his greatest novels, partial, inconsistent, and often untrustworthy because of his narrators' limited perceptions, require the imagination of the attentive reader to disentangle literary truth from falsehood and complete the aesthetic order implicit in the apparent chaos of the narrated reality—the concluding image of *The Sound and the Fury* is a dramatic example.

But the various points of view in Böll's novel are not divergent or contradictory, they are if anything overlapping by design, as the same specific atrocities in the past harry the minds of all the chief narrators with a relentless insistence. Memory for the Faehmels is never unreliable; on the contrary, it is all too trustworthy,

3. Quoted in Theodore Ziolkowski, *The Novels of Hermann Hesse: A Study in Theme and Structure* (Princeton: Princeton University Press, 1965), p. 276.

confirming what we have already seen: that their dilemma (and ours) is not one of interpretation but of simple remembrance, of not forgetting and not being able to forget. Artistic form itself is trapped by this event in time, limited, arrested, determined beyond the artist's ability to redesign: the abbey without its steeple is among other things an image of *incompletion*, the perpetual fate of a present with *such* a past. Both Dilsey's tranquillity and the shape of *The Sound and the Fury* itself placate the chaos that destroys Quentin Compson in time; but nothing can pacify the implacable memories that visit the Faehmels, no unity of vision equivalent to the one that subsumes reality in Faulkner's novel.

Similarly, Hans Castorp escapes briefly from time in the snow-episode in *The Magic Mountain*, and though he must return to his routine at the sanatorium, his excursion adds a perspective of the mythical and timeless to our interpretation of his experience on the mountain and complicates our sense of human mortality as Mann develops it in his novel. Hesse projects an ideal of timeless spirituality as the goal of human endeavor in several of his novels, and no contradictions in time can destroy the validity of this ultimate vision. For Hesse and Mann, art serves traditionally as a mediator between the worlds of temporal and eternal values, while the aesthetic experience—more and more in the twentieth century —enables the reader to live in one and glimpse the other. A novel like *Billiards at Half-Past Nine*, in its theme as well as its structure, accentuates the rupture that the Holocaust has riven in this synthesis, and confesses the absence of any myth—at least for now—to reestablish the lost unity.

One of the principles governing the literature of atrocity, as we have seen, is that where the Holocaust was concerned, reality often exceeded the power of the imagination to conjure up images commensurate with the experience the artist wished to record, with the result that the writer was confronted with the dilemma of converting into literature a history too terrible to imagine. One source of the problem was that details of a concrete past intruded on the "timeless" realm of the aesthetic vision, which incorporates human experience in a fixed design that theoretically insulates it from the assaults of the temporal. For reasons I have tried to suggest, the Holocaust has resisted such transfiguration, so that most writers in the tradition have been forced to absorb this paradox or tension into the work itself. The reader's *real* memory of the Holocaust becomes part of his aesthetic experience when confronted with *literature* devoted to this theme, and at least one novelist—Jorge Semprun—seems to have recognized this sufficiently to have built it consciously into the substance of his novel—*The Long Voyage.*

Unlike his predecessors, Semprun complicates memory by making it an act of *anticipation* as well as recollection, thus adding to the familiar "remembrance of things past" a seemingly impossible "remembrance of things to come." He achieves this by constructing his narrative around a single event, a boxcar journey to Buchenwald, while his narrator, himself imprisoned in the boxcar, reaches backward in time to the period prior to his arrest and also forward in time to the period after his liberation, thus establishing a fictional pattern that deliberately violates normal sequence without substituting any definable, alternative temporal scheme to guide the floundering reader. The reader must accustom himself to and finally learn to recognize the unannounced time shifts by the allusions that identify them; but recognition does not bring clarity or a sense of unity, since one motive behind the unique structure of Semprun's novel is to suggest that the voyage to Buchenwald and the experience in the camp have severed past from future, that from Buchenwald as center (and after one has finished the novel it seems as if Buchenwald and the voyage to it must be the axis of reality, both retrospectively and prospectively, forever) the mind radiates and returns without discovering any coherent form to connect these disparate realms of time.[4]

Thus the unity of the aesthetic vision disintegrates even as it takes shape, and one has the feeling as he reads that Semprun's theme

4. Semprun's manipulation of past, present, and future differs fundamentally from the technique used occasionally by Ladislav Fuks in *Mr. Theodore Mundstock.* Semprun's narrator is concerned with actual experiences: he did fight with the Resistance, was captured by the Gestapo, endured the journey to Buchenwald, survived the camp, and afterwards can recall the details of his ordeal. His immersion in memory and time becomes a structural principle of the novel. Reality presses on his imagination, which resists all attempts to order the events in a chronological sequence. Fuks's Mr. Mundstock, on the other hand, projects the future as fantasy only. His attempts to anticipate the experience of the concentration camp, including his own execution, reflect the imagination's inability to validate such future horrors using present reality as a base. Mr. Mundstock's fantasies are powerless to alter his fate, or even to elucidate it. Semprun's narrator uses the form of the narrative itself to master time and memory and thus to impose a pattern on his fate.

makes this so *of necessity*, art negating its own purpose even as it strives to achieve it. The central experience recorded in the novel is "the reality of the nightmare" of the voyage to the concentration camp; but like Primo Levi's recurrent dream of awakening in Auschwitz, Semprun's fictional nightmare endures beyond the liberation, casting shadows across the future, as it were, before it has occurred. The paradox is suggested early in the novel, when the narrator takes us inside and outside the event as the boxcar rolls through France: "when I describe this feeling of being inside which overwhelmed me in the Moselle valley, seeing these people walking down the road, I am no longer in the Moselle valley. Sixteen years have passed. I can't confine myself now to that particular moment. Other moments have superimposed themselves on that one, forming a whole with that violent feeling of physical sadness which filled me in the Moselle valley." [5] In this instance superimposition breeds confusion as well as multiplicity of vision, since the three time senses—past, present, and future—exist simultaneously, insofar as prose is capable of recreating this sensation; and one gradually realizes that *The Long Voyage* is concerned not only with the question of whether individual memory or imagination can record actual fact, but also whether art is able to contain this reality so elusive to its grasp.

The fact of having once been inside a boxcar on the way to Buchenwald dominates the narrator's life, including his attempt to reduce it to a part rather than the whole of his experience:

> Later, a year later, it was spring again, it was April, I too walked along that road [outside the concentration camp] and went to that village. I was outside, but somehow I couldn't bring myself to enjoy being outside. It was all over, we were going to take this same voyage back in the opposite direction, but maybe you never take this voyage back in the opposite direction, maybe you can never erase this voyage. I don't know, really. For sixteen years I've tried to forget this voyage, and I did forget this voyage. No one around me thinks any more about my having made this voyage. But the fact is that I forgot this voyage while realizing full well that I would one day have to take it again. In five years, ten years, fifteen years, I would have to take this voyage all over again. It was all there, waiting for me. . . .

5. Jorge Semprun, *The Long Voyage*, trans. Richard Seaver (New York: Grove Press, 1964), pp. 22–23.

OF TIME AND ATROCITY

Perhaps one can't take this voyage back in the opposite direction.
[pp. 23–24]

Once "inside" this experience, one never entirely regains the feeling
of being "outside," even if one survives and is liberated: surely this
is the intuition which links the boy at the end of *Night* with the boy
at the end of *The Painted Bird*, and both with Gascar's prisoner-
protagonist in *Season of the Dead*. And similarly, once "outside"—a
different but more frustrating kind of doom, perhaps—one can
never recapture the exact experience of having been "inside,"
though the compulsion to try is the fate of Semprun's narrator. And
the *process* (not only the idea) of doing so is one of the submerged
themes of the novel. Trying to explain to a German girl after the
war what it was like inside the camp, the narrator recognizes the
impossibility of the task, and turning his frustration inward, he
espouses a view we have encountered before: "This evening I no
longer know whether I dreamed all that, or whether I've been
dreaming since the whole thing has ceased to exist" (p. 143).

The point is that for him alone it has not ceased to exist, a
circumstance that makes him a kind of intellectual orphan marooned in a sea of indifference, buoyed up by the persistence of a
memory that clamors for expression even though no congenial ears
yearn for the words. A combination of the events of the voyage and
later external events have engraved on the imagination of the
narrator a sense of the unreality of life "inside" *and* "outside,"
which in turn has required a steady reorientation of the individual
(as survivor) to the facts he is surviving and has survived (and of the
artist to the raw material of his fiction, the details of the Holocaust).
This "feeling of unreality I experienced during the fourth night of
this voyage," the narrator recalls,

> was not as strong as the one I experienced upon my return from this
> voyage. The months of prison had doubtless created a kind of
> familiarity. The unreal and the absurd became familiar. In order to
> survive, the organism has to adhere closely to reality, and reality was
> actually this totally *un*natural world of the prison of death. But the
> real shock occurred when I returned from this voyage. [p. 69]

The shock is dual: first, his discovery that those who have not shared
in the experience cannot possibly apprehend its horror—he learns
this by leading two neatly uniformed French girls arriving the day

after liberation through the crematorium, torture chamber, and courtyard where a twelve-foot high pile of still-unburnt corpses lies in a hideously twisted mass, and realizes that their familiarity with a natural world makes the "unnatural reality" of the skeletons unendurable and incomprehensible; and second, his discovery that whereas the only tribute remaining for the dead is a "pure fraternal look" and "to be remembered," the effort to produce this response runs aground on language's inability to depict the nature of the reality.

Shock merges with insight as Semprun searches for a way of seizing completely "the complacent horror of all the details and detours, the comings and goings of this long voyage of sixteen years ago" (p. 199) without driving his readers into boredom or madness, to say nothing of disbelief. For the "nature of the reality" must contend not only with all the preceding difficulties, but with the reality of nature itself, its quality of renewal that literally envelops the decaying symbols (earlier the decaying realities) of the camps. "Revisiting" the site of a Resistance hideout after his liberation, the narrator (himself a Resistance fighter before his arrest) discovers that "the forest is fast effacing all trace of that life now three years old," that everything is losing its human aspect, that even the fragments of metal and wood that once helped to shape and preserve the destiny of courageous men are being reintegrated "into the cycle of vegetative life and death" (p. 189). His "anticipative memory" then shifts to a reflection on nature's effect on the camp at Buchenwald, and in a remarkable passage the various levels of experiencing reality combine and dissolve, reopening the question —the novel does this continually—of what is real and what is not, and how best to convey the sensation and the idea of that reality.

For as he conjures up the image of the camp while he was a prisoner there, the narrator sees the beech forest (a literal translation of the German "Buchenwald") encroaching on the wood and cement of the barracks in an act of repossession, as if a tranquilly indifferent nature would subvert the human horror and suffering of the place, diminishing its impact on the imagination by proclaiming with a silent relentlessness nature's supremacy over man's most unnatural symbols of destruction, and leaving in its wake only a doubtful memory of what has succumbed to its onslaught—small and uncertain treasure to serve the artist in his attempt to reconstruct a memorial through art. Long after the other buildings of the camp have crumbled, thinks the narrator, one image of "truth" will remain:

> years later, remaining standing the longest, like the remembrance, or rather the evidence, the special symbol of that whole, the massive square chimney of the crematorium, till the day when the roots and brambles shall also overcome that tenacious resistance of brick and stone, that obstinate resistance of death rising among the waves of green covering over what was an extermination camp, and those shadows of dense black smoke, shot through with yellow, that perhaps still linger over this countryside, that smell of burning flesh still hovering over this countryside, when all the survivors, all of us, have long since disappeared, when there will no longer be any real memory of this, only the memory of memories related by those who will never really know (as one knows the acidity of a lemon, the feel of wool, the softness of a shoulder) what all this really was. [p. 190]

The paradox of the Holocaust *for the artist* is its exclusiveness, the total absence of any shared basis of experience that would simplify the imagination's quest for a means of converting it into universally available terms—to find, in short, in the events of the Holocaust the kind of immediacy of impression, of direct communion, that one senses in the acidity of a lemon or the feel of wool. Even as he summons up their equivalent in his Buchenwald experience, Semprun acknowledges the futility of the quest, since the startlingly vivid images of the dense black smoke shot through with yellow rising from the crematorium, or the smell of burning flesh, inevitably retain a quality of abstraction because they do not belong to a shared reality, because even for the artist they represent a unique moment recollected and never repeated, one he himself is forced to doubt sometimes, since nothing in reality can reinforce the memory of that moment.

As nature engulfs the evidence, which then vanishes, the artist-as-survivor (or assuming the *role* of one) will be forced to draw on memory alone, while *his* successors, the second generation of Holocaust writers, as it were, will have only experience once removed to appeal to (raising a specter of Plato's cave), the source of inspiration having eluded them entirely—and then both artist and audience will be faced with the perplexing question of when to stop trusting, and whom. If it was impossible to "know . . . what all this really was" while it was happening, the opportunity to do so, Semprun suggests, decreases with every moment that the event recedes into the past; and art's attempt to fix and perpetuate it so that later generations may contend with its meaning at their leisure may merely be a confession that for this experience, so incommensurate with anything men have ever known before (as incommensurate as the acidity of a lemon with the acrid odor of burning flesh), it is always *too* late to comprehend what all this really was, too late and too useless.

But this is only one tendency of Semprun's vision: *The Long Voyage* contains a countermomentum, as if the narrator's indescribable journey toward (and sojourn in) Buchenwald implies, indeed coexists with, his need to survive and return in order to tell the tale, his compulsive feeling that it can and must be done. The reader thus sometimes feels as if he is immersed in the paradoxical situation of floating in a stream with twin currents running simultaneously in opposite directions, the one drawing him toward the horror of Buchenwald itself, the heart of darkness of the Holocaust experience, the other toward the narrator's account of his life before and after that experience (bringing with it the reassurance, perhaps minimal but at least certain, of the temporal beginning and end of that horror). But as he struggles to maintain equilibrium, swimming now in one direction, now in the other, he is unable to determine which current represents the "genuine" drift in the flow of reality, and which a freakish and temporary aberration.

In a sense, to vary the image, the narrative represents a perpetual palimpsest, one where nightmare imposes itself on normality, only to find normality recurring on top of it in a process repeating itself ad infinitum; and as the reader penetrates the layers of superimposed texts he learns that the "meaning" of each layer depends on the one above and beneath, to the exclusion of none. So Semprun's "long voyage" moves "in" and "out," on toward death and back to life; and just as we retire with the narrator to survey what happened on that journey sixteen years ago, we find ourselves plunged back into its timeless anguish, echoing the refrain of the "guy from Semur," the narrator's neighbor and chief auditor in the boxcar: "This night will never end." The intimate bond that develops between these two during the course of the trip is a major impetus in the narrator's decision to tell what happened *even though* the only ones who might understand him would be those unfortunates, like his friend, who did not survive the ordeal.

Thus, the human impulse to express, the will to endure through art, vies with the deeper silences implicit in memory's gloomy recollections and the imagination's despair over its inability to organize and communicate the authentic quality of this long voyage into the dark wood of Buchenwald and the death of body and spirit which that arrival signified. If the literal reality addresses the sensibility of the reader (as well as the consciousness of the writer) more dramatically and convincingly than the imagined one, then Semprun's frustration can be better understood, and in fact this dilemma, too, he incorporates into the novel. Literal reality is not intrusive but a natural part of the narrative, whereby Semprun is able to exploit an inarticulate feeling about the theme that both he and many of his readers bring to it.

For example, Semprun transforms the conversation between the narrator and the German girl mentioned earlier into a parable of the conflict between the imagined and the real in the literature of atrocity, by contrasting the girl (named Sigrid) with another figure who belongs to the "real" experience of Buchenwald, the notorious wife of the commandant, Ilse Koch. For the narrator, Sigrid represents "the oblivion of this past which cannot be forgotten, the will to forget this past which nothing can ever erase but which Sigrid rejects" (pp. 147–48); and her beauty, her refusal to "remember," her dedication to the future and to happiness, appeal to him and to all men, rouse their desire to possess her and all she symbolizes, as if her face and body were there "only in order to make us forget the body and face of Ilse Koch," with her eyes "fixed on the naked torso . . . of the deportee she had chosen as her lover a few hours before, her gaze already cutting out that white, sickly skin" (p. 148).

Thus the narrator's wish to forget, to simply accept the laughter of Sigrid, "so young and full of promise," is opposed by the insistent "other laughter of Ilse Koch" (p. 149), and although for the narrator the two women belong to one reality in the sense that he has experienced both and is doomed to associate them with each other forever, Semprun himself creates a distinction between the imagined character of Sigrid and the recorded one of Ilse Koch; and the latter's infatuation with lampshades made from human skin sheds an inevitable glow of shallowness over the invented personality of the German girl, as if no creature of the imagination could compete for dramatic impact with the real figure of Ilse Koch. Nor can any universalized image elaborate on the concrete and essential truth of the lampshades made from human skin.

Semprun thus gradually injects a skepticism into his narrative, a skepticism about the possibility of creating an audience for his tale, about the necessity *and* the inability of that audience to validate his story, as if without them the human anguish he recounts would lapse into meaningless anonymity, but with them would sacrifice some of the sanctity with which its uniqueness endows it. The narrator (and Semprun) drifts from one position to the other, embracing both, unable to moor his vision in a fixed imaginative harbor. At one point he confesses that the purpose of the book he is writing is "to evolve some semblance of order for mysflf out of the past," since the passing years only continue to assail him with "absolutely vivid memories that arose from the wilful oblivion of this voyage" (p. 126). But at another moment—scarcely distinguishable from the previous one, since in Semprun the narrative does not provide simple chronological distinctions—he reflects:

> There's no one left to whom I can talk about this voyage. It's as though I'd made this voyage all alone. Henceforth, I'm all alone, when I remember this voyage. The solitude of this voyage is probably going to prey on me for the rest of my life. [p. 139]

This is a retrospective sentiment, but it confirms an apprehension felt "earlier," on the boxcar voyage to the camp:

> perhaps my death will not even manage to be something real, that is, something that belongs to someone else's life, at least one person's. Perhaps the idea of my death as something real, perhaps even that possibility will be denied me, and I cast about desperately to see who might miss me, whose life I might affect, might haunt by my absence and, at that precise moment, I find no one, my life hasn't any real possibility, I wouldn't even be able to die, all I can do is efface myself, quietly eliminate myself from this existence. [p. 197]

Only the survival of his former associates in the Resistance, or the guy from Semur, pressed close against him in the boxcar, can link his death to reality; but, as he knows in advance through his "anticipative memory," they are all dead, he alone has survived, and the problem of their death is now inextricably fused with the question of his life, as if only their mute ears can justify his testament to their private ordeal. In a profoundly paradoxical sense, the guilt must remain forever with the living for having survived, for having abandoned their dead comrades: the last words of the guy from Semur to the narrator are "Don't leave me pal" (p. 213), and the narrator is left supporting a corpse, "nothing but an undecipherable shadow, heavy to hold, in my clenched arms." And at precisely this instant, with "the living and dead welded together," a frozen image of human woe, the boxcar clatters to a halt and its "motionless voyagers" (p. 214) must surrender to that timeless moment which is the culmination and source of all other memories in the novel—arrival at Buchenwald.

The narrator calls it *Walpurgisnacht,* but as he recollects its macabre details, exploding "like a great shower of flashing light and furious barking" (p. 214), it seems more like a spectacle from Wagner than a scene from *Faust.* And as he releases the body of his friend before leaping out onto the platform to meet his fate, he articulates the crucial significance of this instant, though perhaps without realizing all its implications: "I lay down his body on the floor of the car, and it's as though I were laying down my own past, all the memories linking me to the world of the past" (p. 216). What he means is that throughout the voyage he has been feeding the guy from Semur a steady stream of recollections about his experience prior to his capture, almost as if this exercise in the liberty of consciousness represented a final effort to salvage a semblance of "self" in a free world before arrival at Buchenwald deprived him of all sense of freedom, physical or otherwise—so that when the guy from Semur dies, the narrator's self-conscious and reflective ego, his "I," perishes with him, including that part of the past with which his "I" is associated, and which we have slowly pieced together in the preceding pages.

But by extension it has died to be reborn in these very pages, transmitted into the consciousness of the reader until he too is a participant in that instant of all-inclusive stasis that welds together the living narrator with his dead companion. The essential reality of the voyage and of the novel is enshrined in this image which simultaneously embodies an end and a beginning irrevocably united, the death of the guy from Semur and the arrival of the narrator (and all men) at the concentration camp, bringing that terrible moment of confrontation (if not yet realization) with the truth that the physical death of others can be merely a prelude to a drama immeasurably worse for those victims who have survived its embraces on the voyage.

Paradoxically, the death of the guy from Semur, if not exactly tragic, is somehow expected, implicit in the suffering he has endured on the journey toward Buchenwald, and when it occurs, one struggles to suppress a sigh of relief at this "logical" literary conclusion to an unusual dramatic experience. But all these feelings die with him, together with the memories linking the narrator to the world of the past; and as they vanish, they are replaced by the physical and spiritaul terrors of *l'univers concentrationnaire*, a different order of existence, where the constant prospect of annihilation becomes a way of life in a setting that does not accord with any rules or rituals known to the narrator in the past from which he has just been sundered. The long opening movement of the novel ends here, less an account of "what happened" than the dual effort of the narrator's consciousness to set down his memories on the voyage *as they happened* and concurrently to *recall his recollections*, years later, after they have been dimmed by the passage of time. Past and future thus merge in a perpetual present, creating a unique experience for the reader, who is caught in the shifting perspectives of the act—or more precisely, the *process*—of recovery, which is the true significance of the narrator's life, and to which Semprun in *The Long Voyage* has dedicated his art.

He complicates this art by adding a brief coda of about a dozen pages in which the narrative point of view is abruptly altered from the first to the third person, preparing us for the move from subjective participant to objective spectator, since we are not destined to enter the camp gates with the narrator—now named Gérard and referred to as "he," in confirmation of the silence to which he is reduced by his SS guards, who forbid conversation in their initial reduction of individuals to an undifferentiated mass. As Gérard and his companions cover "the few hundred years still separating them from the monumental gate" (p. 235) of the camp—a final, vivid example of time's transformation into space and the victim's total alienation from temporal reality—the reader is unwillingly driven off by the exigencies of aesthetic distance, forbidden to cross the last obstacle which divides him from *l'univers concentrationnaire.*

In the closing pages of the novel the two worlds momentarily drift apart, raising the basic challenge inherent in *The Long Voyage* and most of the literature of atrocity we have been studying: how can the imagination span the interval that isolates the "conceivable" universe *outside* the gate from the forbidding realm within? Approaching the frontier between the two, Gérard and his friends (like the reader) "are still imbued with the prejudices, the realities of the past, which makes it impossible to imagine things which, in the final analysis, will be proved to be perfectly real" (p. 235); and as the column approaches its goal, in the closing passage of the novel, Gérard seeks desperately to absorb all the impressions of the moment, to engrave them on his memory with some as yet unformulated intuition that he may want to dredge them up again in the future.

Already, even as the real drama of his ordeal in Buchenwald begins to unfold, his imagination asserts its claim in conceiving of the event; for as Gérard marches down the monumental avenue toward the entrance to the camp flanked by stone columns surmounted by Hitlerian eagles, he laments the absence of "the noble, solemn music of some fabulous opera" which *aesthetically* might complete the inadequate real setting that destiny has furnished for this crucial moment of his life. Simultaneously, he thinks vaguely "that it is well within the realm of possibility that the impending death of all the spectators may efface forever the memory of this spectacle" (p. 236), and in so doing creates a motive for writing *The Long Voyage*, while raising the question of finding a way of translating "impending death," with all its implications, into the enduring forms of art..

Hence, it is scarcely accidental that Gérard begins to hear, or to imagine, the noble, solemn music whose absence he had just deplored, and with this a "ready-made phrase whirls dizzily in the deep recesses of his brain"; the voyage is truly at an end, and to conclude it—the ready-made phrase echoes rhythmically as the closing words of the novel, at once description and illumination of the episode that is transpiring—one has to "leave the world of the living, leave the world of the living" (p. 236). And although earlier in this nonsequential narrative we have had glimpses of existence on the other side of the gate—a focal symbolic episode of atrocity, as so often in this fiction, is the narrator's excruciatingly painful account of "the day I saw the Jewish children die" (p. 162)—at the end one has the feeling that the entire experience will be closed to us unless a voice can orchestrate the musical theme which Gérard first hears as he approaches his destiny.

The Long Voyage is undoubtedly this orchestration, Semprun the "arranger" of the score, and though he and his narrator have literally survived, one has the uncanny sensation that a part of each has also left the world of the living and never returned, as if their scarred consciousness, in reconstructing the long voyage to and through and back from *l'univers concentrationnaire*, has made of language, of the "ready-made phrases" of the novel, an act of homage to the dead, to the guy from Semur and the Jewish children and the other anonymous victims; and we are left to grope unassisted through the debris of temporal decay, the shards of memory, intellectually aware of all the barricades that exclude us from the dark heart of this universe but emotionally and aesthetically drawn to its center by the unquenchable impulse of the imagination to piece together the fragments of the mystery we call the Holocaust. And once having left the world of the living to make this vicarious long voyage through the pages of art ourselves, who among us can ever return the same?

INDEX

Absalom! Absalom! (Faulkner), 265
Adorno, T. W.: on art after Auschwitz, 1–3
Aesop, 193
Aichinger, Ilse, 168; *Herod's Children*, 118, 126, 134–64, 171, 250; Wagnerian leitmotif and, 156
Alice in Wonderland, 139, 212, 244
All the King's Men (Warren), 251
Améry, Jean: *Jenseits von Schuld und Sühne (Beyond Guilt and Atonement)*, 70–73; on Auschwitz, 71
"Animals, The" (Gascar), 196–99
Anne Frank: The Diary of a Young Girl, 140, 141; Wiesel's *Night* and, 76–77
Arendt, Hannah, 179
Aristotle, 22
Artaud, Antonin: *The Theatre and Its Double*, 182–84
Atrocity, literature of: realism and, 3, 43; fact and fiction in, 8, 91, 193–94, 284–85; sentimentalism and, 21; violence and, 21; melodrama and, 21–22; reader and, 22, 25, 72, 91–92; aesthetics and, 22, 164; fantasy and, 23, 24; surrealism and, 24; significance of, 30; dreams and, 44–59 passim; "irrealism" as technique of, 45–46, 49, 149–50; fate of Jews in, 61; death in, 65; naturalistic dialogue and, 89–91; central tension in, 102–03; tragedy and, 110–20; role of history in, 115–16, 119; the absurd and, 129; future possibility and, 147; guilt and, 245; time and, 251–97 passim
Auerbach, Erich, 74
Auschwitz, 1, 16–19 passim, 75, 170
"Auschwitz. Our Home (A Letter)" (Borowski), 89–91
Auschwitz trial (1963–65), 31–33; testimony quoted, 32, 132–33

Bacon, Francis (painter), 103, 181
Balzac, Honoré de, 16
Baskin, Leonard, 188
Bear, The (Faulkner), 251, 265
Beasts and Men (Gascar), 191–204
Beckett, Samuel, 47, 144–49 passim, 212, 216, 217, 244; *Waiting for Godot*, 243, 249
Beradt, Charlotte, 52; *The Third Reich of Dreams*, 44–49, 136–37
Bergen-Belsen, 77
Bettelheim, Bruno, 77
Bildungsroman (novel of education), 75, 123;

reversal of pattern in, 82, 84, 254–55; *The Painted Bird* as parody of, 189
"Billbrook" (Borchert), 37–40
Billiards at Half-Past Nine (Böll), 92, 265–84
Böll, Heinrich, 206; on actuality vs. reality, 92–93; *Billiards at Half-Past Nine*, 92, 265–84; Faulkner and, 265–66; Henry James and, 266; Joyce's *Ulysses* and, 266, 267
Borchert, Wolfgang, 51–64 passim, 80, 114, 147, 156, 185; *The Man Outside*, 34; "In May, in May Cried the Cuckoo," 34–36; "Billbrook," 37–40; Nelly Sachs and, 38, 39; Walt Whitman and, 39–40
Borowski, Tadeusz: "Auschwitz. Our Home (A Letter)," 89–91
Bosch, Hieronymous, 209
Broch, Hermann, 283
Brothers Karamazov, The (Dostoevsky), 56, 95, 97, 183, 232, 256; suffering of children in, 125–33 passim
Buchenwald, 3, 18, 252, 285, 289–94 passim

Camus, Albert, 30, 83, 101, 110; *The Myth of Sisyphus*, 78, 105–06, 130; the absurd and, 120–21; suffering of children and, 128–32 passim; *The Plague*, 129–35 passim, 140, 185; on art and reality, 133; "Reflections on the Guillotine," 134; on executions, 185, 186
Celan, Paul, 15, 24, 92; on language, 9–10; "Fugue of Death," 9–14, 20, 25; "Fugue of Death" quoted, 10–11
"Chorus of the Rescued" (Sachs), 27–29, 59; quoted, 28
City Beyond the River, The (Kasack), 52–54
Concentration camps: Auschwitz, 1, 16–19 passim, 75, 170; Bergen-Belsen, 77; Buchenwald, 3, 18, 252, 285, 289–94 passim
Conrad, Joseph, 171
Counterfeiters, The (Gide), 246

Dante Alighieri, 17, 20, 42, 48, 66, 84, 111; descent to the underworld and, 59; language as source of unity in, 169
Darwin, Charles, 197
Death in Venice (Mann), 71
Dehumanization of Art, The (Ortega y Gasset), 166–72 passim
Deputy, The (Hochhuth), 79
Dickens, Charles, 16, 22
"Dogs, The" (Gascar), 199–204

297